Endangered Daughters

This unique and groundbreaking book asks the controversial question of why millions of girls do not appear to be surviving to adulthood in contemporary Asia. In the first major study available of this sensitive and emotive issue, Elisabeth Croll investigates the extent of discrimination against female children in Asia and shifts the focus of attention firmly from son preference to daughter discrimination.

The book paints a vivid picture of daughter discrimination across Asia today, from excessive child mortality to the withholding of health care and education on the basis of gender. It argues that daughters still cannot substitute for sons and that the increasing availability of sex-identification technologies will serve only to supplement older forms of infanticide and neglect. Startlingly, it reveals that, in China, India and across East and South Asia, daughter discrimination is actually on the increase despite rising economic development, declining fertility and the generally improved status of women.

This compelling account of a phenomenon still hidden and unacknowledged across the world is essential reading for all those interested in gender and children in contemporary society.

Elisabeth Croll is Professor of Chinese Anthropology at the School of Oriental and African Studies, University of London. She has written widely on social development and gender issues in historical and contemporary China. For the past five years, she has worked along side UNICEF in Asia to promote awareness of girls' issues and rights in the region.

Endangered Daughters

Discrimination and development in Asia

Elisabeth Croll

London and New York

First published 2000
by Routledge
11 New Fetter Lane, London EC4P 4EE

Simultaneously published in the USA and Canada
by Routledge
29 West 35th Street, New York, NY 10001

Routledge is an imprint of the Taylor & Francis Group

Typeset in Baskerville by
Wearset, Boldon, Tyne and Wear.
Printed and bound in Great Britain by
University Press, Cambridge

British Library Cataloguing in Publication Data
A catalogue record for this book is available from the
British Library

Library of Congress Cataloging in Publication Data
Croll, Elisabeth J.
  Endangered daughters : discrimination and
  development in Asia/Elisabeth Croll.
    p. cm.
  Includes bibliographical references and index.
  1. Family size–Asia. 2. Sex of children, Parental
  preferences for–Asia. 3. Girls–Asia–Social conditions.
  4. Daughters–Asia–Social conditions. 5. Sex
  discrimination–Asia. 6. Women in development–Asia.
  I. Title.

  HQ762.A78 C76 2000
  305.23–dc21   00-055330

ISBN 0-415-24764-0 (hbk)
ISBN 0-415-24765-9 (pbk)

'Only when Development reaches the last house in the last village and the last person in the last house will Development be achieved.'

After Mahatma Ghandi

'Writing with both strength and grace, Elisabeth Croll has produced an important synthesis of scholarship on daughter discrimination in Asia. She provides the first in-depth comparison of the situations in China and India and convincingly combines solid documentation with activist critique and suggestions for change.'

Barbara D. Miller, Professor of Anthropology & International Affairs and Associate Dean, Elliott School of International Affairs, *The George Washington University*, USA

'Elisabeth Croll masterfully weaves together the meticulous demographic analyses documenting recent severe losses of young girls in Asia. She then puts meat on the bones of our stark statistics with her own and other rich ethnographic and field reports showing how attitudes within millions of Asian families can lead to tragic and often fatal discrimination against their daughters. Her book speaks to our heads and to our hearts.'

Judith Banister, Professor of Demography, Hong Kong University of Science and Technology, and former Chief, International Programs Center, *US Bureau of the Census*

'This original book by an outstanding scholar assembles a range of valuable material. It belongs as part of a single story but has not been made into one before. The book will have lasting significance and deserves a wide audience.'

Robert H. Cassen, Department of Social Policy, *London School of Economics*

Contents

Figures

Maps

Tables

Preface

This book is born of a concern, a concern which has increased during many years of anthropological research on gender, the family and most aspects of urban and rural socio-political and economic development in China. Here statistical and field-work investigations, alongside interviews, personal narratives, anecdotes and observations over the past 25 years, have all suggested that daughters not only continue to be discriminated against in a wide variety of venues but that, in certain circumstances, this discrimination has been exacerbated despite dramatic reductions in fertility and rapid economic development. This long-standing concern with the weaker destiny of young daughters in one country was magnified once others began to identify the numbers of girls 'missing' from other East and South Asian societies. It increasingly seemed that in the context of development, it was daughters who constituted Ghandi's 'last person in the last house'.

This has not been an easy book to write, largely because of the variety of societies that make up East and South Asia and the inter-disciplinary approach required to examine this rising discrimination and undertake a holistic but nuanced and non-ethnocentric study of such a sensitive subject. To make this investigation more manageable, this book largely focuses on the two largest societies of East and South Asia, China and India, and combines anthropological and demographic approaches and source materials. This study is based on my own field work as an anthropologist of China and on the ethnographic enquiries, first-hand observations and personal testimonies of others in China and elsewhere in East and South Asia. These include first-hand reports from a wide variety of sources including historical documentation, contemporary media, circulated anecdotes and, very importantly, autobiographies and other oral recorded and written personal narratives. These less formal sources are a crucial aid in countering an ethnocentric approach in the translation of cultures and in furthering an understanding of how 'others' perceive their choices and their behaviour. This approach is based on the belief that the demographic data together with ethnographic insights can be merged advantageously to provide both a broad yet detailed, and analytical yet empathetic study of the economic, political and cultural factors underlying discrimination against Asian daughters. However, in a comparative study of this kind there will be some injustice to nuance and detail, but the consequences of gendered ways of thinking about children, unfortunately all too common everywhere, have led in one set of cultures to such imbalances in sex ratios at birth and excessive female mortality during infancy and childhood that these demand both a broad research approach and wider policy attention.

In the writing of this book I am grateful to many writers, colleagues and friends who provided help and support. I am indebted to Chen Yongling and Fan Yuhua of the All-China Women's Federation and Fahid Rahman, Edwin Judd, Lakshman Wickramasinghe and Zhang Yali of the UNICEF Office in Beijing for arranging field trips and projects centring on the girl child. I am indebted to Gu Baochang of the China Population Information and Research Centre in Beijing, Mary-Ann Burriss and Joan Kaufman of the Ford Foundation, to Caroll Long and Andrea Lee Esser of the East and Southeast Asian regional office of UNICEF and to Julia Leslie, Jens Lerche and Subir Sinha of SOAS for drawing my attention to materials relevant to this book. My students Pun Ngai, Liu Xin and Ku Hok Bun at SOAS have provided case studies drawn from their very fine field work, and the work of many demographers and ethnographers of East and Southeast Asia including Judith Banister, Monica Das Gupta and Patricia and Roger Jeffrey have been important in the drafting of this book. I am grateful to UNICEF, SOAS and the Universities China Committee for providing financial resources for the field work, a sabbatical year and help in the preparation of the manuscript. Lastly I would also like to express heartfelt thanks to colleagues and friends Monique Charrette, Felicity Edholm, Harriet Evans, Richard Fardon, Waddi Hunt, Helene and Jeremy Hurles, Deniz Kandiyoti, Hilary Laurie, Maxine Molyneux, John Peel, Tony Saich, Christina Toren, Cornelia Usborne, Frances Wood and Elizabeth Wright for their support and interest. My thanks are also due to my mother Joan Sprackett, my sister Anne Skinner and to Jim, Nicolas and my own daughter Katherine Croll. This book is dedicated to the cause of daughters worldwide and to M.

Elisabeth Croll,
London, November 1999.

1   A weaker destiny

Daughter discrimination

Why does this book single out daughters in East and South Asia for investigation and analysis within a development context? There is one most important reason and that is the increasing scale of discrimination against daughters and numbers of 'missing girls' in much of East and South Asia where there has been both rising economic development and improvements in the status of women. In his path-breaking article in the *New York Review of Books* in 1990, entitled 'More than 100 Million Women are Missing', Amartya Sen suggested that world-wide and especially in Asia, women were 'missing' in their millions from the population totals of many societies. He argued that the number of missing women in any population can be estimated by calculating the numbers of extra women who would have survived in that society if it had the same ratio of women to men as obtain in other regions of the world where both sexes receive similar care. He surmised that if equal proportions of the two sexes could be expected, the low ratio of 0.94 women to men in South Asia, West Asia and China would indicate a deficit amounting to 6% of their women, but that since in countries where men and women receive similar care the ratio is about 1.05, the real shortfall is about 11%. For China alone, he estimated that, taking 1.05 as the benchmark ratio, this amounted to 50 million 'missing women'. Sen calculated that when this number is added to absent females in South Asia, West Asia and North Africa a great many more than 100 million women are 'missing'. He concluded that these numbers 'tell us, quietly a terrible story of inequality and neglect leading to excess mortality of women'.[1]

In a later refinement of Sen's argument, the demographer Ansley Coale also calculated the number of missing females in these same societies by drawing attention to unusually high sex ratios at birth and high female mortality rates relative to males, especially in the early years of life and for daughters with elder sisters.[2] He drew attention to the elevated female death rates and the low respect accorded to female infants in populations where high masculinity rates reflect discriminatory treatment offsetting the natural lower mortality of females. To give a rough approximation of the numerical impact of excessive female mortality, Coale also estimated

Table 1.1 Estimated deficits in female populations caused by excess female mortality: Selected areas, latest available data

Country or region	Ratio of males to females		Number of females (millions)	Percentage of females missing[b]	Number of missing females (millions)
	Actual ratio	Expected ratio[a]			
China 1990	1.066	1.010	548.7	5.3	29.1
India 1991	1.077	1.020	406.3	5.6	22.8
Pakistan 1981	1.105	1.025	40.0	7.8	3.1
Bangladesh 1981	1.064	1.025	42.2	3.8	1.6
Nepal 1981	1.050	1.025	7.3	2.4	0.2
West Asia 1985	1.060	1.030	55.0	3.0	1.7
Egypt 1986	1.047	1.020	23.5	2.6	0.6

[a] Based on a model stable population incorporating levels of fertility and mortality prevailing some ten years earlier and assuming 1.059 as the sex ratio at birth.
[b] Females missing as a percentage of the reported female population shown in column 3.

Original sources: United Nations (1991), except for China, where figures are from preliminary tabulations of the 1990 census, and for India, where preliminary results of the 1991 census are taken from *The Economic Times of India*, 18 April 1991, taken from Ansley Coale, 'Excess mortality and the balance of sexes in the population: an estimated number of missing females', in *Population and Development Review*, Vol. 17, No. 3, December 1991, p. 522.

the ratio of males to females in selected populations that would exist in the absence of such discrimination, and thus the total number of 'missing' females derived from this calculation. For example, for the populations of China, India, Pakistan, Bangladesh, Nepal, West Asia and Egypt, he calculated the total number of missing females to be 60 million, of which 56.8 million are in East and South Asia (see Table 1.1). He concluded that, although his lower estimates are based on alternative and more realistic calculations than Sen's 100 million 'missing women', they confirm 'the enormity of the social problem brought to wide public attention by Professor Sen'.[3]

Subsequent and extensive reading of demographic and ethnographic studies in East and South Asia suggest that Sen's 'missing women' and Coale's 'missing females' could more aptly be referred to as 'missing girls', given that it is excessive female mortality before birth, at birth and in infancy and childhood which more than any other factor accounts for the imbalance in sex ratios and the absence of many, if not millions, of Asia's daughters who do not survive to womanhood. Demographic studies show that, although in East and South Asian populations mortality rates are abnormally higher for females than for males for most age intervals, more detailed country studies suggest that the most important discrepancies reside in sex ratios at birth and high female death rates in the first 5 years of life which are due both to parental discrimination and differential familial resource allocation. Ethnographic studies too suggest that concern for the 'missing' females or women in the demographic literature should be focused on son preference which demeans and discriminates against daughters. Thus it is more appropriate to talk of 'missing girls' and to examine the many forms of discrimination which affect the survival and development of daughters in these populations.

There is a large literature on son preference, fertility transition, the family and gender in various Asian societies, but the common story of accumulative daughter discrimination in East and South Asia suggested by demographic statistics and confirmed by ethnographies and personal narratives has not been entirely or widely told for each country, let alone continent-wide. Although there have been extensive Asia-wide collections of academic papers on women, gender and the household, few of these studies have investigated girlhood or gendered children, leaving daughters an under-studied category. This book is an attempt to bring together the findings of some very fine demographic and anthropological studies of many East and South Asian societies and the personal narratives or stories of Asian daughters to write a continent-wide study for a wider audience. In so doing this study not only attempts to fill a gap in the existing literature, but it also deliberately seeks to shift the focus of attention from son preference to daughter discrimination, from population control to family planning, from women to girlhood and from the socio-economic characteristics of parents (or mothers) to children differentiated by their gendered value, their birth order and sibling configuration. In sum, these shifts aim to further awareness and understanding of the types and degrees of gendered discrimination against daughters, or more particularly against some categories of daughters, in many regions of East and South Asia.

To take much of the continent of Asia as a regional framework for analysis rather than any one of its single constituent societies challenges several cross-cultural assumptions commonly held in demography, development and gender studies. First, the coincidence of declining fertility, rising economic development and increasing son preference in East and South Asia defies historical experience elsewhere, and therefore questions previous analytic, policy and practical expectations of reproductive behaviour and cross-cultural policy responses. Fertility decline in East and South Asia has been rapid at both higher and lower levels of economic development while son preference has continued, if not increased, with rising economic development, declining fertility, smaller family size and improved status of women. This is so across the various countries and societies of East and South Asia even though they are probably as diverse in socio-economic conditions, rates of development, political systems, physical environments, and cultures and religions as are those of any of the five continents. East and South Asia as a whole embraces extreme levels and rates of economic development from rapidly and newly-industrialised countries (NICS) to slower growing and predominantly rural societies; it embraces the cultural and religious traditions of all the major thought-systems, including Islam, Hinduism, Confucianism, Buddhism and Christianity; and it incorporates a complete continuum in state-policy approaches to birth control ranging from one-child to pro-natal programmes. Such is the lack of homogeneity that hypotheses developed to explain son preference or daughter discrimination in any one South or East Asian society rarely hold for another. Yet disparate and diverse as the societies of East and South Asia are, there is a demographic, development and gendered coherence combining rapid and progressive fertility decline, rising and sometimes rapid economic development and a common culture of gender, all of which have contributed anew to high masculinity ratios with continuing or even more pronounced son preference.

According to demographers one of the most remarkable global changes in recent centuries has been the shift from high to low fertility in Asia. If this fertility decline had its beginnings in Europe (first in France, followed by almost all European countries and countries of European settlement such as the USA, Canada, Australia and New Zealand in the second half of the nineteenth century), it is Asian societies that have shared in the sharpest and most dramatic decline of the twentieth century. The magnitude of change can be gauged by comparing world-wide fertility of 115 million births in 1965 with that of 139 million births in 1986 which, although representing a rise, is one far below the extra 40 million births which would have taken place if natural fertility levels had remained constant at the 1965 level.[4] Densely populated Asia with just under 60% of the world's population was responsible for 80% of this decrease. According to John Caldwell, a well known demographer, what is even more remarkable is that about 60% of the total global reduction and over 75% of Asia's reduction was made by just two countries: China, with 22% of the world's population accounting for 40% of the reduction, and India with 16% of the world's population accounting for 19%. Indeed, demographers have described this Asian fertility decline as 'the greatest single demographic change in the second half of the century'[5] and 'one of the most significant events of modern times'.[6]

Although the timing, onset, pace and magnitude of this fertility decline varies within the Asian region, in most Asian societies there have been two similar and striking changes in fertility behaviour which began in the 1960s: a substantial decline in post-marital fertility rates and a dramatic rise in the mean female age of first marriage by two years. It has become less common to find females married at ages 15 to 19 years,[7] although almost all women in Asia also eventually marry and commonly share in the substantial decline in post-marital fertility which has almost halved family size or numbers of children per couple — from six to three or so children. For Asia as a whole, the total fertility rate, or the average number of children per women, is estimated to have fallen from 5.7 in 1960–65 to 3.4 in 1985–90.[8] These continent-wide figures mask large variations in fertility trends between and within sub-regions. Within Asia, the decline in total fertility rate between 1950 and 1985 and projected into the twenty-first century can be seen to be greatest in East and Southeast Asia, followed sluggishly but nevertheless increasingly by South Asia.[9] Fertility declined between 1960 and 1990 first in East Asia, rapidly from 5.3 to 2.3; in Southeast Asia there were lesser but sustained reductions from 5.8 to 3.6; and a more modest but still significant decline took place in South Asia from 6.0 to 4.7. In the 1990s the total fertility rates in Korea and China dropped to around 1.7–1.8, and in India and Bangladesh to new lows of 3.1–3.2.[10] Indeed, the overall decline of fertility in Asia, the variations in pace within that continent and their correlations with levels of socio-economic development, degrees of political control and types of cultural beliefs have attracted much demographic attention.

A substantial decline in fertility presupposes a desire for fewer children and the means to limit family size, and it is a common assumption that both these conditions can be achieved with increasing levels of socio-economic development. The assumed interdependence of fertility decline with socio-economic development has been such that identifying prerequisite socio-economic factors making for fertility decline became a development priority. In studies of Europe, the socio-economic indicators associated with fertility decline were identified as industrialisation, urbanisation, the proportions of non-agricultural labour force and per capita levels of income, education and health care and female employment opportunities. In forecasting and investigating these same fertility trends in developing countries, demographic studies have emphasised the importance of literacy and in particular female education; female labour force participation and in particular female independence and autonomy; infant survival and in particular nutritional levels and health care delivery; familial resources and in particular the value or costs and benefits of children or the direction of wealth flows between parents and children; and the availability and use of contraceptive technology which permits the limitation of family size. As for Europe, several decades of demographic research on fertility trends and determinants in the various sub-regions in Asia have suggested that all these factors are pertinent and that to no one factor can be attributed an overall or overarching significance in explaining or causing fertility decline.

However, if recent demographic studies confirm that there is no single path from high to low fertility, the onset or accumulation of fertility decline in Asia did roughly coincide with some and usually very substantial socio-economic development. Indeed, much of East Asia has experienced an economic growth the pace, scale and scope of which is such that the terms 'newly industrialised' and 'take-off' are most usually deployed to describe either their present or anticipated economic status. In many respects the coincidence of rapid fertility decline and rapid economic development in many parts of East Asia and pockets of South Asia lend support to a primary correlation between general levels of socio-economic development and fertility decline. However, this rough correlation does not sufficiently account for the magnitude of the fertility decline in the poorer regions of Asia, and especially in the populous and predominantly rural populations of East and South Asia. The dramatic decline in fertility in still poor regions has drawn attention to the importance of political interventions, in the form of state-led family planning programmes, in effecting a reduction in fertility. Faced with dense populations and projected population growth rates that are high, some governments in East and South Asia took the view that economic development itself continued to be impeded by continuing high rates of population growth. Hence many Asian governments opted to intervene directly and took the lead in creating state-led national birth control programmes which advocated or insisted upon birth control, encouraged or imposed limits on family size, advanced contraceptive technology, and made free and cheap contraception widely available or even compulsory. These national birth control programmes have been somewhat distinctive in that the type of contraception offered is heavily reliant on 'one-off' methods, such as IUD insertion and sterilisation, which make delivery more easily organised and controlled by government action and less reliant on continuous co-operation on the part of the recipients. In the absence or failure of contraceptive methods these control programmes also rely heavily on abortion. Among the most studied birth control programmes in Asia are those in China, India, Indochina, Thailand and Bangladesh; these have all shown that government intervention, even if it merely makes contraception widely available, can have a powerful influence in inducing or accelerating fertility decline either in the absence of or accompanied by rising levels of socio-economic development.

If the strength of government involvement in birth control programmes has proved to be a more recent but major determinant of fertility decline in some Asian societies, most demographic studies also suggest that cultural or religious factors have played an important role in determining fertility trends, although these are less often investigated, perhaps because they are less easily measured. Demographers increasingly have drawn attention to the importance of cultural factors in exploring demographic behaviour in Asia where the long-standing and powerful religious traditions of Islam, Confucianism and Hinduism play a major role in influencing beliefs and behaviour. It has to be said, however, that few such demographers have taken their research a step further and examined in more detail the relations between culture and demographic behaviour although they have all recommended that such a study take place. One cultural feature identified by analysts as common to these traditions is the value attached to sons. Most demographers early concluded that son preference, one of the most common features of Asia's religions and culture, would either impede or at least delay fertility decline until socio-economic development reduced gender bias or rendered son preference unnecessary. However, more recent studies have shown that son preference, instead of declining in East and South Asia, has increased alongside lower fertility and rising economic development and it is these important new correlations that call for further analysis of the nexus of economic, social and cultural factors underlying son preference.

Son preference

Son preference and its effects on the survival and development of daughters can be demonstrated by collating demographic data on contraceptive use in relation to sex composition of surviving children, sex ratios at birth and gender-disaggregated infant and child mortality rates, nutritional status, physical development and differential access to education and health facilities. In addition, ethnographic enquiry based on local field-studies, life-histories and informal observations contribute to qualitative data on gendered values attached to children, ideal family size and composition, the demand for and spacing of additional children and differential allocation of familial resources to boys and girls affecting their physical development, health and education. A near universal insight derived from both quantitative and qualitative studies is that this preference for sons over daughters is a striking feature of most East and South Asian societies. Indeed in East and South Asia there is a reversal of the established biological norms of lower mortality of the female foetus, the infant and the child which can be directly linked to a familial preference for and biased resource allocations favouring sons.

The general preponderance of males over females in the population and the differential familial treatment of sons and daughters at birth and in childhood has been a subject of concern since the late eighteenth century in India and early nineteenth century in China. One of the most enduring features of missionary and traveller reports from both countries was their observations of gender bias, including female infanticide and abandonment, bound feet and widow death which became potent symbols of the 'backwardness' of the nineteenth-century Asian continent. In the twentieth century it is the adverse female to male sex ratios that have continued to be investigated and documented. As Table 1.2 shows, Asia, and in particular South Asia, continues to stand out for the lesser proportions of females to males,[11] and according to data collated by the United Nations in 1985 there were 95 to 97 males for every 100 females in Europe, the USA and Japan; 88 males per 100 females in the Soviet Union; 99 males per 100 females in Africa and 105 males to 100 females in Asia.[12]

Masculinity ratios can be affected by differences in the ratios at birth, differences in gains and losses through migration and differences in mortality, but of greatest contemporary concern are the elevated female death

Table 1.2 World sex ratios, 1980

Region	Sex ratio (female/male)
World	0.990
Western Europe	1.064
Eastern Europe	1.056
United States	1.054
Latin America	0.999
Asia	0.953
India	0.931
Pakistan	0.929
Bangladesh	0.939
Western Asia	0.940
Eastern and South-eastern Asia	1.008
China	0.941
Africa	1.015
Northern Africa	0.986
Non-Northern Africa	1.024

Source: A. K. Sen, *Africa and India: What do we have to learn from each other?*, WIDER Discussion Paper No. 19, 1987.

rates due to discrimination in infancy and childhood which offsets the natural lower mortality of females. Indeed, as Ansley Coale has argued, the high masculinity of some populations is traceable to this single cause with the most notable examples all in Asia: China (1.074), India (1.066), Pakistan (1.105), Bangladesh (1.064) and Sri Lanka (1.040).[13] In all these populations demographic studies show that the higher female death rates mainly take place in the first five years of life and that gendered discrimination in resource allocation is sufficiently adverse to daughters to cancel out their normal advantage in survival rates.

Ethnographic studies, reporting on gender preference or parental bias and its consequences for the survival and development of children in the early years of their lives, have also shown that bias towards sons has been greatest in East and South Asia. In her cross-cultural survey of parental sex preferences in the 1970s, Williamson found that parental preference for sons was most pronounced in the Asian countries of China, India, Pakistan, Taiwan and Korea. In her world-wide ranking of parental sex preference, these East and South Asian societies were rated, on a scale ranging from −3 to +4, as either +3 (strong son preference) or +4 (very strong son preference).[14] In another analysis of son preference based on the World Fertility Survey data in which countries were ranked into four categories according to ratios of women's son to daughter preferences, the South and East Asian countries surveyed were all allocated to the strong-son preference group.[15] Given the importance of son preference in East and South Asia, and given that an average of six or so births is necessary to ensure two surviving sons, many demographic studies subsequently investigated the degrees and ways in which son preference might be expected to affect contraceptive use and limitation of family size. Most of these studies suggested that parents continue child bearing until they have their desired or preferred number of sons and that only then do they practise contraception. Birth spacing is also narrower and the use of contraception less likely following the birth of a daughter until there are the desired numbers of sons, and in all the countries excess female infant and child mortality persists. Thereafter much attention has been given to investigating factors which might reduce son preference and therefore hasten fertility decline. These included raising the literacy and educational levels of mothers, increasing female employment and economic autonomy which might lessen their dependence on fathers, husbands and sons, and reducing the degree of familial reliance on sons' economic support for parents in old age. This emphasis on economic factors in reducing son preference was based on prior experience in Europe; this suggested that son preference would decline with economic development incorporating improvements in female education, employment and independence and the growth of social security and employment benefits reducing familial risks and spreading sources of support.

What recent studies of son preference in East and South Asia show, however, is that son preference, far from being eroded by economic development, remains a feature of the most developed regions of East and South Asian societies and that son-support has been incorporated into most national strategies for economic development. Son preference remains an observable characteristic not only of their poorer and less developed rural regions still characterised by high fertility and competition for scarce resources, but also a demonstrable characteristic of regions and societies which have 'taken off' economically and where the material basis for son preference might be expected to have ended. The notion that son preference will decline or disappear with rising economic development and cumulative changes in the role of women and status of mothers is aptly challenged by the studies cited in this book, which show that in post-fertility-transition Asia such changes have been accompanied by an unexpected continuation or even exacerbation of son preference and the associated phenomenon of 'missing girls'. Such was the evidence accumulated on this phenomenon in the early 1990s that a special international symposium on Issues Related to Sex Preference for Children in the Rapidly Changing Demographic Dynamics in Asia was convened in Seoul in November 1994.[16] The papers presented there uniformly challenged the notion that gender bias before, during and after birth declines with economic development — even where the fertility transition has been completed and the material basis for son preference seriously eroded. This book looks at the evidence in each Asian society, and particularly in China and India, for continuing son preference and the reasons why gender bias may be exacerbated in circumstances of economic development and fertility decline. In doing so, however, it seeks not so much to emphasise son preference as to draw attention to prejudice against daughters.

Daughter discrimination

This book aims to shift the focus of discussion from son preference to daughter discrimination. Much of the existing literature uses phrases such as son preference, abnormal sex ratios, masculinity rates, gender bias and preferential treatment for boys, rather than directly referring to their consequences for the physical survival, growth and emotional well-being of girls or daughters. If the problem is recognised it is often defined in terms of 'others' and projected into the future. For example, there has been more anxiety expressed about the fate of the nation's bachelors as a consequence of the future shortage of brides and about the consequences for the physical and educational qualities of tomorrow's women than about the nation's daughters or today's girls. What has rarely been considered or even defined as a problem is the physical suffering and death of daughters, or the effects of excessive female mortality on the self-esteem and self-image of surviving girls as they learn of extreme forms of discrimination on the lone grounds of gender. One of the aims of this book is to make visible such self images of young and growing girls in Asia. This is an important question given that cross-cultural studies of gender relations suggest an important linkage between the socialisation and self-esteem of daughters and women's empowerment, now one of the most common and long-term goals of development programmes.

Thus this book is concerned to highlight the mirror image of son preference, namely, daughter discrimination and to emphasise how a strong preference for sons in and of itself actively entails discrimination against daughters. As Barbara Miller, the author of *The Endangered Sex*, which is one of the few existing country-specific monographs on discrimination against daughters, argued in 1981: 'The problem is that son preference is so strong in some areas of India and amongst some classes that daughters must logically suffer in order that families' perceived and culturally mandated needs are fulfilled.'[17] This logic, previously underplayed by many demographers and anthropologists, implies that 'moderate strong' or 'very strong' son preference is co-existent with and entails 'moderate strong' or 'very strong' discrimination against daughters. Hence the greater the scale of son preference the more intense the discrimination against daughters is likely to be. This book is a study of how the quest or desire for sons, be it moderate or intense, is directly tied to daughter discrimination and neglect which in its most extreme form results in their demise. In India and China during preceding centuries, it was the practice of female infanticide which most dismayed foreign observers.[18]

Although definitions of infanticide are rarely precise and quantitative

Table 1.3 Frequency of infanticide in 112 societies: World area[a]

Frequency of infanticide	Asia		Africa		North America		Oceania		South America		Totals	
	n	%	n	%	n	%	n	%	n	%	n	%
Common	6	100	7	58	11	48	12	22	4	25	40	3
Occasional	0	—	0	0	3	13	4	7	7	44	14	1
Not common	0	—	0	—	1	4	1	2	0	—	2	
Not practiced	0	—	0	—	3	13	6	11	1	6	10	
No information	0	—	5	42	5	22	32	58	4	25	46	4
	6	100	12	100	23	100	55	100	16	100	112	10

[a]Table constructed from Human Relations Area Files data compiled by Divale and Harris (1976, pp. 533–5).

Source: Susan Scrimshaw, 'Infanticide in human populations: societal and individual concerns', in G. Hausfater and S. Blaffer Hrdy, *Infanticide: Comparative and Evolutionary Perspectives,* Aldine Press, 1984, p. 451.

data sufficiently available to discuss its incidence with any confidence, cross-cultural comparisons suggested that infanticide, almost always female sex selective, was practised in most societies in East and South Asia. Susan Scrimshaw estimated the scale of female infanticide for the world's major geographic regions using the large amount of ethnographic material summarised in the Human Relations Areas Files collected from 112 cultures or 561 populations, and assumed to be reasonably representative. In categorising societies according to whether infanticide was 'common', 'occasional' or 'absent', she listed all Asian societies as 'commonly' practising female infanticide[19] (See Table 1.3). Just as for son preference, it was assumed that female infanticide along with other threats to daughter survival, growth and development would also disappear with economic development, lower and controlled fertility, improvements in income levels, nutritional levels and health care delivery and with female education. However, although the overall physical well-being and education of both male and female children may have improved with economic development and declining fertility, recent studies of female infanticide, alongside new biases in sex ratios at birth and infant and child mortality rates, reveal that extreme forms of daughter discrimination resulting in death have persisted and even increased despite the socio-economic and demographic trends that might have been expected to eradicate this gender difference. It is this exacerbation of daughter discrimination and increased threat to daughter survival accompanying both economic development and lower fertility in some parts of Asia that, clearly identified by demographers, has received less attention in other disciplines and arenas.

There are probably two reasons why threats to the survival and development of female infants have received less attention outside of the demographic literature. Gender and women's studies have shown a greater concern with the social construction of gender, gendered divisions of labour and adult women in terms of status, employment conditions, reproductive health and rights and domestic violence, than with girls. Yet all the demographic evidence suggests that the very first path to girlhood may be threatened by parental bias, lack of nurture, nutrition and disadvantaged resource allocation, each of which may affect her survival and physical and emotional development into adult womanhood. It is not just girls in difficult or vulnerable circumstances who are at risk, rather it is girlhood itself which may be a difficult and even perilous path to traverse. Given the still precarious points in young female lives in East and South Asia today, before and at birth and in infancy and childhood, it is still the case that today's girls are not necessarily tomorrow's women or, to paraphrase the well known first sentence in Simone de Beauvoir's 'The Second Sex', even if one is born female one does not necessarily become a woman.[20] The second reason for the relative neglect of girls and daughters is that the term 'children' is rarely gendered. During the 1990s there has been a much greater development interest in children and in the especially disadvantaged categories of child labourers, street children, child soldiers and child victims of war, trafficking and prostitution. Sometimes girls are added to this list, but despite an extensive demographic literature on the subject of children, their costs and benefits, their health, nutrition and their education, only now is there some recognition that the experience of childhood may be gendered, with a child's survival, physical development and emotional well-being primarily linked to their gender. Although there have been some international moves to collect gender-disaggregated statistics on children, it is still difficult to find comprehensive and routine data which permits analysis of the differential life chances and experiences of girls and boys or for different categories of girls. Girls too can be differentiated with not all daughters at equal risk.

Recent demographic research including that undertaken by Monica Das Gupta, has shown that while in some circumstances parents may even prefer a first-born daughter or at least not discriminate against her, it is second and subsequent parity daughters who are most at risk from parental discrimination.[21] A recent number of studies across many cultures in East and South Asia suggest that, with some exceptions, there may be a preference for one daughter, although this does not mean that parents will continue child bearing in the hope of a daughter in the same way as they continue to bear children in the quest for a son. Correlatively, in the absence of sons, it is daughters in the second and higher parities who are at the receiving end of the most extreme forms of discrimination. Certainly, as Das Gupta's comparative study shows, the abnormality of sex ratios at birth and rates of female infant and child mortality rises steeply in the absence of sons and with increasing parity of birth. Ethnographic studies too suggest that, in the absence of sons, the continuing birth of daughters draws forth loud expressions of dismay and condolence, and is widely and openly commented upon by family members often resulting in dramatic expressions of gender bias. It is also a common feature of female autobiography in Asia that it is second and subsequent daughters, with or without brothers, who write most vehemently about discrimination within the family. Statistical and ethnographic data on daughter discrimination suggests that daughter discrimination may not be as generalised or 'unconscious' as it is sometimes argued, instead it may be calculated consciously and managed selectively within family planning as parents exercise choices in the planning of child numbers, spacing, gender composition and decide for and against the resourcing of their daughters.

Family planning

One of the reasons for emphasising the term daughter, as opposed to girl, girl child or female infant, is that it is within natal, or birth, families that decisions about reproductive behaviour are planned and managed; thus the restraints that deprive a young girl of her legitimate claims to a birthright and girlhood may be due less to poverty, inadequate resources or entry into school than to the exercise of familial or parental choice reflecting gender bias exercised before conception or during infancy and childhood. It is the intention of this study to focus on the process of family planning and the agency of the family implied by the use of this phrase. It is true that the phrase 'family-planning programmes' is once again being used internationally to reflect a broader concern than that represented by the term 'population control', which primarily refers to remedial measures to counter rapid population growth identified as a principal cause of poverty, under-development and more recently environmental degradation. If the population problem itself is narrowly defined then the narrow targeting of women's fertility via contraception and sterilisation is forwarded as a single and simple solution. Indeed, several governments in Asia identified population growth as one of the main obstacles to economic development and established such narrowly defined population control programmes. Their unidimensional encouragement or imposition of strict fertility control has led to a concern with women's or human rights within a reproductive health framework and it is a change to this broader approach which has led to a re-emphasis on more inclusive family planning programmes. These take account of an individual or couple's right to plan freely and take responsiblity for the number and the spacing of their children. Although there has been a welcome shift in political emphasis to parental agency and women's rights which is signalled by the shift to 'family planning programmes', this study uses the term 'birth control' to refer to the mechanics of contraceptive limitation and attempts to shift the new emphasis on family planning from programme to process by emphasising strategies for family building.

Although demographers have been responsible for much of the

research relevant to macro-population trends and concerns, less research has been conducted at the level of the family to explore how family members relate to 'birth control' programmes and the role of economic factors, political interventions and cultural norms in the planning and building of their families. Demographic research has been more concerned to correlate macro-level or national-level demographic data with individual parental characteristics such as the age, income, education and occupation of mothers. Over the years this research has yielded interesting insights into the factors which may both induce or accelerate fertility decline and reduce son preference, but this approach best reveals a correlation of variables at a highly aggregate level and does little to explain individual and familial responses to changing circumstances at the micro-level. More recent research, both demographic and ethnographic, has suggested that it is at the level of the family that macro-economic, social and political variables interact and where individuals, as family members, make and manage reproductive choices and decisions. In the periodical *Demography*, a recent article argues the case for family demography as a new sub-field of that discipline to mediate macro-level economic, political and social factors and reproductive choices and behaviour which influence the micro-level environment of the family.[22]

In anthropology many of us have continuously studied the ways in which inter-generational and gendered relations shape and are shaped by reproductive behaviour and have long been much intrigued by the ways in which demographic processes affect and are affected by family size, structure and intra-familial relations within and between households. We have very much felt ourselves to be inter alia family demographers. Ethnographies of India and China have drawn attention to the fact that in the final analysis it is couples or parents rather than nations or individuals that prefer, plan for and bear children. It is individual couples and parents who vocally express their preferences and their rationales for numbers, the spacing and gender of each child and normally these preferences and rationales are expressed in relation to family needs and interests. This shift in focus from individual or nation to the family context or environment involves not only a study of family formation, building or aspirations but also beliefs about the family structures and relations influencing the reproductive choices and behaviours of its members.

While it can be argued that in any society family demography plays a crucial role in understanding both the determinants and consequences of familial reproductive behaviour and, in turn, wider demographic trends and processes, this is especially so in Asia. Although there are many different models of familial aspirations and expectations in Asia today, family systems feature large and determine types of social organisation, parents are tied into family needs, activities and schedules more than in many continents, and the notion of the family embraces a wide range of social obligations across kin, generation and gender hierarchies. In Asia too one of the most common aims of family planning or building is the short and long-term reduction of risk and the maintenance of economic and social security of the family unit; to achieve these important ends families accumulate and divide resources, allocate roles and distribute activities. On this continent the concept of the family has a contemporary significance which is not only underpinned by inherited traditions, but beliefs and customs to do with the family and familial relations have been re-asserted via new emphases on Asian values. It is the aim of this study to explore family aspirations, family formation and family building strategies as the environment in which the management of reproductive choices and behaviour takes place and, at the same time, examine the many dimensions of parental choice at conception, at birth and during pregnancy, infancy and childhood.

Historical and cross-cultural research in demography and anthropology shows that not all children are wanted and that the value of children or the costs and benefits involved in child bearing and rearing are such that families have generally attempted to plan and limit the size of their families by controlling or limiting births, spacing children and trying for a particular gender composition or sibling configuration. To these ends parents have long utilised birth control methods such as withdrawal, abstinence, abortion and infanticide. Ethnographic research has revealed that most societies have a repertoire of fertility strategies based on folk beliefs, customs and remedies which attempt to limit birth and influence the gender of the unborn and, that where these means are unsuccessful, parents may resort to infanticide or neglect. The most remarkable change in the planning and management of familial reproductive behaviour came with the widespread availability of relatively safe and cheap contraception so that the limiting and spacing of births was no longer left to chance but could be controlled. Henceforth, parents could themselves decide with some accuracy whether and when to have a child, bringing familial control over the number and spacing of births within 'the calculus of conscious choice', to use Ansley Coale's apt and memorable phrase.[23]

This control has been extended to most societies in Asia and, except for some of the poorest and most populous regions of South Asia, the availability of contraception has been an important factor in bringing about a radical decline in fertility. The most common forms of contraception include IUD, the pill, injection, abortion and sterilisation, and much demographic research in Asia has focused on measures of and factors inducing contraceptive use. Much of the earlier research concentrated on exploring the match between desired and actual numbers of children born, but increasingly research has pointed to the importance of family planning as a process made up of not just of an initial blueprint but also sequential adjustments. In other words, although family size might be planned at the outset and expressed in terms of desired number, spacing and sex of preferred children, family planning was found to constitute an iterative process of decision-making with each successive outcome dependent on the birth, survival and, most importantly, the gender composition of previous births or surviving children.

Gender reasoning

Evidence from many country studies in Asia suggests that contraceptive acceptance and usage was most influenced by the gender composition of surviving children and parental gender bias. That is, couples set out to achieve the desired number of sons and daughters and will only employ contraception to limit the size of their family if they have achieved their preferred gender composition of children. In these terms conception is as much a cognitive as a physical act by parents. It has been argued by anthropologists and demographers that both infanticide and selective but avoidable child mortality are means whereby parents traditionally attempted to determine or manage the gender composition of their families. Studies of sex-selective infanticide and infant and child mortality directly link these practices to gender determination and the reduction of surplus or unwanted girl children. Hence it is the gender composition of existing children which is increasingly identified as a key factor determining the birth and survival of additional children, and which gives rise to high or otherwise avoidable excessive morbidity and mortality rates of young girls. What has constituted an important development in family planning and building is that, while in the past gender composition has been an important chance factor in this iterative process of family planning, now parents in much of East and South Asia can exercise greater control over the gender composition of their families in addition to the number and spacing of their children.

In Asia both infanticide and fatal female neglect have been newly supplemented or replaced by sex identification and sex-selective abortion. In many regions of East and South Asia the widespread use of advanced technologies has permitted the identification of the sex of the foetus before birth and this, followed by sex-selective abortion, has given families a new means to determine the gender configuration of their children. Although new technologies may have played a role in increasing discrimination it is important to note that patterns of discrimination are not always contingent upon the availability of new technologies; this suggests that these are still a means or an outcome rather than a cause of discrimination. Nevertheless, the introduction and widespread use of these technologies and control has meant that it is daughters who are most and at increasing risk in a new trade-off between smaller family size and controlled gender composition. In times past, a larger family size was the most common means of accommodating gendered preference but now, rather than repeatedly bearing daughters in the attempt to produce a son, smaller family size and reduced fertility have meant that unborn daughters are the first to be sacrificed. What these family strategies imply is that, although women may be educated, enter the labour force and have a modicum of independence from fathers, husbands and sons, young daughters still cannot substitute for sons, and indeed are increasingly traded for sons, and this is so whether familial resources are plentiful or scarce and environments developed or less developed. In contemporary East and South Asia, then, gender planning has given rise to a new trade-off which is not that between size and composition, as in the past, but between sons and daughters with daughters increasingly and openly sacrificed for sons. This new trade-off based on the unsubstitutability of daughters for sons emphasises all over again that, even where there are national and open campaigns to the contrary, daughters still are not interchangeable with sons and that the process of family planning and reproduction management in Asia is rooted in cultural assumptions about gender difference and hierarchy.

The persistence of son preference and escalation of daughter discrimination in contemporary Asia, which covers wide-ranging levels of economic development and socio-economic contexts and includes the most economically developed regions and societies, has again drawn attention to culture as a very significant causal factor explaining reproductive behaviour. Most studies analysing son preference in Asia first looked to the socio-economic indicators of development including income and educational characteristics of parents or mothers, the economic value of children, types of familial support and the reduction of economic risk, and to types of political intervention in birth control programmes rather than cultural factors. However, the survival and exacerbation of son preference in Asia despite economic development, fertility decline and small family size has confounded previous demographic assumptions, which, based on European experience, had suggested that these trends would lead to increased security for and investment in female infants and children equal to that of their male siblings and peers. Most of the studies have concluded that not only is son preference economically based, but it is also deeply rooted in cultural assumptions about gender identity and relations although there have been few detailed examinations of the linkages. Yet in looking at how families or parents assign resources, roles and activities, ethnographic evidence suggests that it is cultural assumptions about gendered differences and gendered exchanges or transactions between parents and their children which are important determinants of daughter discrimination. Contemporary ethnographies also suggest that this gender reasoning is based not so much on biological attributes as on anticipated gendered divisions of familial labour and activities. As future men and women, boys and girls are also differentiated by their expected daily and ritual life-cycle roles which both reiterate and are rooted in notions of gender difference.

All the ethnographic evidence suggests that girls and boys are expected to and indeed do exhibit different behaviours, undertake different physical and emotional tasks, and participate in and perform different practical and ritual activities within family and kinship groups. Yet there has been little attention given to gender-differentiated experiences of families. Female autobiographies in Asia document in great detail the secondary position of daughters as temporary members or outsiders estranged from the permanence of the family line and future, their own sense of exclusion from family genealogies and from ritual and practical definitions of the family, and the repercussions this has for representations of daughters and their own self-perceptions and self-representation as lesser or secondary beings. The most important and immediate factor underlying this familial exclusion is the movement out of daughters upon marriage, so that the most common idioms which associate daughters with loss or double-loss are compounded by the burden of the expenses of her upbringing and marriage. These are compared negatively to sons who as assets are worthy of short- and long-term investment. Although a daughter may in fact make substantial labour or financial contributions to her parents before and after marriage, which often subsidise the schooling of her younger brothers, there still remains a congruence of perceptions mutually reinforcing and sanctioning parental choices to rear sons rather than daughters. Many of these choices are rooted in notions of gender difference and complementarity which distinguish many Asian cultures and derive from both ancient philosophic texts and current re-assertions within the commercialism, consumerism and culturalism which characterises much of Asia today. This study argues that it is these contemporary and continuing assertions of gender difference, divisions and complementarity which emphasise gendered divisions of labour that are also hierarchical and most assuredly contribute to the cognitive conception that daughters cannot substitute for sons. It is such gender reasoning that has to be challenged if agendas and campaigns to reduce discrimination against girls or daughters are to be successful.

Targeting daughters

It has long been assumed that if women's status was improved then mothers would be less reliant on sons for income and support and that the consequent reduction in son dependence and preference would benefit daughters. This assumption has resulted in long-standing emphases within the development context on women's education and employment opportunities or income generation to effect an increase in women's status and a correlative increase in girls' status. What recent research has shown however is that, while the evidence is mixed, there seems to be no over-arching or direct correlation between a rise in women's education and employment status and reductions in son preference. Although there is a direct link between an increase in women's education and employment status and fertility decline this is not necessarily translated into more balanced sex ratios at birth or improved female infant and child mortality. Overall, the simultaneous increase in women's status and in daughter discrimination suggests that the status of daughters may be different from or independent of that of female adults, be they daughters-in-law, wives or mothers. This study concludes that, although the parallel improvements in women's access to education, employment and other public services undertaken within the women or gender and development rubric may be necessary, they are not sufficient to reduce daughter discrimination. Daughters should therefore be targeted separately in any equity initiative.

The continuing and rising discrimination against young girls during the 1990s has very recently attracted world-wide policy concern, with new agendas and campaigns in favour of girls instigated in both China and India and by United Nations and non-government agencies. Since the beginning of that decade international attention increasingly has been drawn to discrimination against the girl child. In 1989 the Convention on the Rights of the Child and the 1990 World Summit for Children singled out the situation of girls for remedial actions. In 1990 the Executive Board of UNICEF recommended that their programmes and strategies explicitly address the status of girls with a view to eliminating gender disparities and organisations such as Save the Children have followed suit. UNICEF explicitly recognised that the survival and growth of the female gender was largely determined at the moment of conception when her biological sex was ordained. Thus in addition to general programmes to publicise and improve pre- and post-natal care, survival at birth, access to health care, immunisation, access to education and exclusion from the worst abuses of child labour and exploitation, UNICEF singled out the girl child for special attention. This international campaign has included moves to collect gender-disaggregated statistics and to create international and regional profiles of the girl child, and at the same time publicise her perilous path from birth to girlhood with its consistent pattern of discrimination in health, nutrition and education.

In addition individual governments have taken a number of initiatives some of which predate these international campaigns. In the 1990s in South Asia, girls received special attention during 'The Decade of the Girl Child' when numbers of longer-term national research, policy and practical initiatives were set in motion. In India a survey-based national project on the Girl Child and the Family aimed to generate comparative data on the condition of girls which would help in the planning and implementation of remedial programmes. Additionally, there have been numbers of attempts by women's organisations and women activists writing in the media and periodicals to draw attention to the 'silent' violence against daughters and the types and degrees of discrimination which shadow the growing girl child. To counter new trends in discrimination before birth, the use of ultra-sound to determine the sex of the foetus has been banned while, after birth, the emphasis of programmes has been to encourage the education of girls. In China too, there have been a number of initiatives to raise awareness about discrimination against girls and its causes. Several years ago the State Family Planning Commission expanded its birth control planning programmes not just to reduce the numbers and extend the spacing between children, but also to reduce son preference and gender bias. It has sponsored discussions on whether or not girls can carry on the family line and name and have equal filial abilities to care for aged parents. The Chinese government has also banned the use of technology for sex identification purposes, while throughout the past decade the State Education Commission and the All-China Women's Federation (ACWF) have consistently placed a high priority on girls' education and helped girl drop-outs return to school. The ACWF expanded its interest in the girl child as a result of the Fourth United National's Women's Conference held in Beijing in 1995 and, since that time, it has introduced and supported initiatives in aid of the girl child by organising a recent Conference on the Girl Child in Poverty Stricken Regions, establishing a National Expert Group on the Girl Child and initiating a new joint project with UNICEF to draw up national guidelines for a public education strategy in support of the girl child.

While these country-specific initiatives and international expansion of concern for the girl child are welcome, an analysis of their agendas and campaigns suggests that these campaigns are still limited in scope and less than effective in targeting the main forms of discrimination. This is largely because much of their emphasis has been on girls' education in the interests of both equipping tomorrow's women and of economic development, rather than with a wider concern for gender reasoning or bias in thinking about daughters and sons within familial environments. Until the agendas and campaigns designed to improve the status of girls and daughters embrace issues to do with family and gender they are likely to be limited in their effectiveness. Indeed, both the demographic and ethnographic studies of East and South Asia cited in this book suggest that in the meantime it is still, at the end of the twentieth century, a most important question at conception and birth: 'Will it be a boy or a girl?' If a second or higher parity daughter is born in the absence of a son then, in South and East Asia, she will remain fortunate if her survival chances and development opportunities equal those of her brothers. This is the major reason why in this book the focus is on 'missing girls', on family planning as an iterative process and on interpretations of gender, for they all contribute to prolonged or exacerbated daughter discrimination alongside fertility decline and economic development at the beginning of the twenty-first century.

2   Demographic narratives
'Missing girls'

For analytic purposes it is convenient to divide the diverse societies of Asia into the four sub-regions of East, South, Southeast and West Asia, each of which constitutes 43, 39, 14 and 4% respectively of Asia's 1990 population. Their growth rates between 1985 and 1990 ranged from 1.3% in East Asia to 2.8% in West Asia.[1] Within East Asia, China comprises 85% of the region's population, in South Asia, India (72%), Bangladesh (10%) and Pakistan (10%) together make up 92% of the total, while in Southeast Asia, Indonesia comprises 42% of the population.[2] These six countries, all among the world's ten most populous countries, together totalled 82% of Asia's population in 1990, which means that demographic processes in any of these countries greatly influence aggregates and Asia-wide trends. This study is confined to East and South Asia, where there has been a coincidence of socio-economic and demographic trends including rising economic development, reduced fertility, new birth control technologies and continuing or exacerbated son preference, which have all led to persistent or increased daughter discrimination. Although these correlations are common to both East and South Asia, patterns of discrimination take different forms. In East Asia it has been the dramatic increase in abnormal sex ratios at birth or interventions before or at birth which has drawn attention to discrimination against daughters plus, but to a lesser extent, rising trends in female infant and child mortality. In contrast, in South Asia it was excessive female infant and child mortality which first drew attention to daughter discrimination although, in recent years, there has been an increased concern with sex ratios at birth as a result of sex selective abortion. Combined, these patterns have led to the phenomenon of 'missing' girls in both East and South Asia and, most especially, in the two most populous countries of China and India.

China

China, with a population of more than one billion persons, has attracted much demographic attention over the past few decades, largely because of rising life expectancy now around 70 years or so, a population growth rate averaging 0.9% each year[3] and a rapid fertility decline from 5.7 in 1960 to 2.2 in 1990 and 1.8 in 1997.[4] This steep decline in family size was mainly due to a decrease in the incidence of third and higher order parity births which fell from 30% or so of all births in 1979 to 19.32% in 1989.[5] Much of this decrease in higher-parity births was due to stringent birth control programmes centring on the one-child policy which, introduced in 1979, reinforced anew the age-old secondary status of daughters. With the establishment of the one-child rule, the sex of the single child became a very important issue: 'The question of having boys or girls is a common social problem that at present faces most families'.[6] It is not an exaggeration to suggest that over the past 20 years the single-child family policy has been one of the most unpopular policies, largely because it challenged the age-old preference for sons. Indeed, the ensuing scale of discrimination against daughters was deemed so unacceptable that the government felt that it had no choice but to amend the policy to permit two children in certain circumstances. The first major modification of the one-child policy was taken in 1984 when the government extended the range of conditions under which a second child was permitted.[7] A second major modification occurred during the late 1980s when in most rural areas 'daughter-only' households were permitted to have a second child if the first child was a daughter.[8] In the late 1990s 'one couple, one child' was still encouraged, but the rigorous application of the one-child rule is applied almost exclusively to urban residents, and then only very stringently in the three municipalities of Beijing, Tianjin and Shanghai, and the two most populous provinces of Jiangsu and Sichuan. Currently, in 18 of the 23 provinces general regulations allow a second child for couples whose first child is a daughter while, in the remaining five provinces, two children are permitted in most rural areas whatever their sex. In addition for some non-Han ethnic populations there are special birth control regulations which are more lenient.[9]

Despite these modifications to the one-child policy which explicitly aim to reduce bias against female infants, discrimination against daughters has continued to rise. Strong son preference was evident in a number of surveys conducted in the 1980s, including one in Hebei province which revealed in 1981 that 95% of the population wanted two or more children of which one at least was a boy. If only one child was to be permitted then a mere 2.2% wanted a daughter.[10] Subsequent surveys in Hebei province and elsewhere during the 1980s, showed that a continuing and marked son preference was sufficient to cause couples to ignore birth regulations, to refuse to accept the one-child certificate and to bear the burden of heavy financial penalties. Even in the cities in the 1980s, where son preference could be expected to be much less evident, surveys, including my own in Beijing, revealed that parents of single daughters were more reluctant to support the policy, took longer to sign the single-child family certificate and constituted the majority of the couples defying the policy and proceeding with additional births, even in the face of stringent rules and great government pressure.[11] Evidence of a general increase in discrimination against daughters, rural and urban, was revealed in new imbalances in sex ratios at birth which from the mid-1980s could be directly correlated with the stringency of China's birth control policies and whether or not the policies permitted one or two children. Indeed, discrimination against daughters did not lessen with the two-child policy for while this shift might lessen the risk to first-born daughters, it merely transferred the risk to second daughters. The new wave of discrimination against daughters reflected in abnormal sex ratios at birth and in the numerical estimates of 'missing' girls from population figures aroused increasing disquiet among China's demographers.

Sex ratios at birth

Both Chinese and foreign demographers have argued that levels of and trends in sex ratios at birth are among the most puzzling and disturbing of demographic issues in China.[12] Uniformly their studies have shown an increasing imbalance in the number of boys born per hundred girls over past decades, thereby confirming the fears of some that millions of girls are 'missing' from the statistics. The following discussion relies almost entirely on the findings of China's demographers who have drawn attention not only to a growing imbalance in sex ratios, but also to new forms of discrimination against the female infant that may take place before, during or after birth.[13] Reported sex ratios at birth rose from those close to the norm of 106 male births per 100 female births in the 1960s and 1970s to 108.5 in 1981, 110.9 in 1986, 110.0 in 1987, 111.3 in 1989, 111.8 in the first half of 1990 and 118 in 1995.[14] As Table 2.1 shows the exact figures calculated may vary slightly, but the trends reported are similar.[15] According to demographers within and outside China the 1990 census eliminated any doubt that sex ratios were high and rising in excess of 112:100. At the end of the decade there were periodic reports that nationally the sex ratios have reached 120 males per 100 females, but the most complete and accurate data set on sex ratios remains that of the 1990 census which also reveals considerable regional variations.

Data from the 1990 census shows that provinces with the highest sex ratios of children between 0 and 14 years and therefore the most striking dearth of girls are along the richer southern and eastern coasts; that the proportions of girls missing in most provinces of central and north-central China are almost as severe; and that, in contrast, the provinces on the periphery of China display lower sex ratios and smaller proportions of girls missing than elsewhere in more densely populated Han province (see Map 2.1). Yet even in Southern Manchuria, Inner Mongolia and the far southwestern provinces discrimination against female infants can be serious. For example in southwestern Yunnan province, the female infant

24 *Endangered Daughters*

Table 2.1 Reported total fertility rate, sex ratios at birth and of infant mortality, China 1960–93

Year	TFR	SRB	SRIM[b]
1960–64[a]	5.40	107.9	1.09
1965–69	5.96	106.4	1.11
1970–74	4.99	106.2	1.12
1975	3.57	106.4	1.10
1976	3.24	107.4	1.07
1977	2.84	106.7	1.11
1978	2.72	105.9	1.15
1979	2.75	105.8	1.12
1980	2.24	107.4 (106.4)	1.04
1981	2.63 (2.69)[c]	107.1 (108.5)	1.05
1982	2.6 (2.84)	107.2	1.04
1983	2.42	107.9	1.06
1984	2.35	108.5	1.07
1985	2.20	111.4	1.10
1986	2.42	112.3	0.96
1987	2.59	111.0	1.05
1988	2.52	108.1	—
1989	2.35 (2.25)	113.9 (111.3)	0.87
1990	2.31	114.7	—
1991	2.20	116.1	—
1992	2.00	114.2 (113)	—
1993	—	114.1	—

[a] Five year intervals for 1960–74 are arithmetic averages of the corresponding values for these five single years.
[b] SRIM = Sex ratio of male to female infant mortality.
[c] Figures in brackets show discrepancies between sources.

Sources: *Dual Effects of Family Planning Programme on China's Women*, Research Report of Institute of Population and Economy, in Xi'an Jiaotang University, 15 December 1955, p. 51, Table 4.4; Gu Baochang and Krishna Roy, 'Sex ratios at birth with reference to other areas in East Asia: What we know', *Asia–Pacific Population Journal*, Vol. 10, No. 3, September 1995. pp. 20, 24 (Tables 1 and 3).

mortality rate is 2 to 5 times higher that of the male rate.[16] As Table 2.2 shows, there is considerable regional variation between the provincial administrative units, with only 6 of the 30 provinces having a ratio of boys to girls that is less than the norm of 105.5. These are the western and minority provinces of Xinjiang, Tibet, Qinghai and Ningxia, the northeast Manchuria province of Heilongjiang and China's most advanced city of Shanghai. Twenty of the thirty provincial-level units have a sex ratio of 108 or higher; these include both poorer and richer densely populated provinces, including Guangxi, Zhejiang, Anhui, Henan, Hainan, Shandong and Sichuan.[17] At lower administrative-level units, incomplete data sources suggest that 232 out of 334 prefectural units (70%) and 1301 of 2067 counties (63%) have higher than normal sex ratios at birth.[18] Some of the available figures for still smaller local-level units show ratios well in excess of the national average. For example in one city in Jiangsu

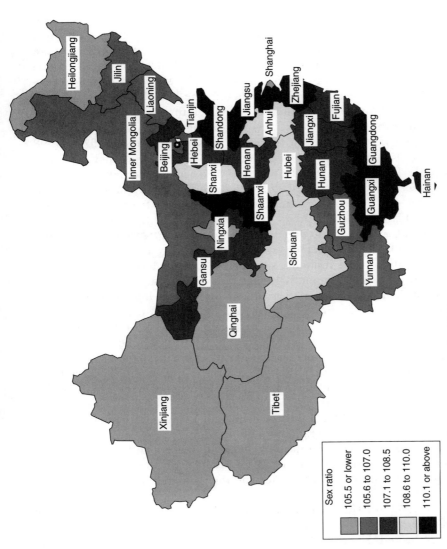

Map 2.1 China, ages 0–14 provincial population sex ratios 1990

Source: Judith Banister, personal communication, later published in 'The PRC: End-of-century population dynamics', *PRC Tomorrow*, Chong-Pin Lin (ed.), Graduate Institute of Political Science, National Sun Yat Sen University, Kaohsiung, Taiwan, p.77.

Sex ratio

- 105.5 or lower
- 105.6 to 107.0
- 107.1 to 108.5
- 108.6 to 110.0
- 110.1 or above

province, the figures suggest that the ratio had risen from 105 to 119 per 100 female births between 1988 and 1990,[19] while the ratio in one city in Shandong province is estimated to have reached 163.8 to 100, which is higher than the norm reported for the surrounding rural areas, estimated to be a serious 144.6 to 100.[20]

When sex ratios at birth are correlated with total fertility rates, provinces having a high total fertility rate are more likely to have a normal sex ratio at birth; correlatively those with declining total fertility rates are more likely to show rising sex ratios at birth.[21] This direct linkage between total fertility rates and sex ratios at birth is also shown in Susan Greenhalgh's study in Shaanxi province, which in the late 1980s had an overall ratio of 111 boys to 100 girls. Her study of three small villages there showed that the sex ratios fluctuated according to the stringency of birth control programmes, ranging from 114 boys to 100 girls in 1979–83, 98 per 100 girls in a locally lenient period (1984–87) to a very high 145 male births per 100 girls in 1988–93, a period of strict enforcement and reductions in fertility.[22] This suggests that the drive to reduce the birth rate has coincided with increasing numbers of missing girls from these villages. Nationwide, as Table 2.2 shows, sex ratios are likely to be higher in the countryside, although whether a household has an agricultural or non-agricultural registration is more strongly correlated with sex ratios at birth than is rural or urban residence per se. Sex ratios at birth for county-level cities and towns are frequently higher than for the surrounding countryside probably, because of the greater availability of interventionist technologies. Higher sex ratios at birth tend to be found among the Han rather than among the minority nationalities, which is not surprising given that the latter experience less strict birth control policies. Lastly, and contrary to expectations, increasing education has not necessarily resulted in lower sex ratios at birth, although mothers in the most professional and skilled occupations are likely to have a higher proportion of female births. In 1989, the sex ratios at birth were 112.5 for mothers with some primary school education, 114.2 for those who had completed primary school, 116.2 for middle school graduates and a relatively lower one of 110.7 for women who had college education.[23] Despite these trends, abnormal sex ratios at birth cannot be correlated so directly with the characteristics of parents as with parity or birth order and the gender composition of surviving children.

From 1953 to 1978, sex ratios at birth showed little difference per parity largely because couples continued child bearing till they had the number of sons desired. Since 1981, as Table 2.3 shows, the sex ratios at birth for parity 1 over the years have remained near normal, while the sex ratios at birth for parity 2 or higher have risen abruptly over the decade, although it also has to be remembered that the number of higher-parity births declined during the 1980s. China's 1990 census revealed that while sex ratios at birth were 105 males to 100 females at parity 1, they reached

Table 2.2 Sex ratio at birth by province and residence: China 1989

Rank	Province	Total	City	Town	Country
	China	111.3	108.9	111.9	111.7
1	Guizhou	103.4	99.4	109.0	103.7
2	Tibet	103.6	112.4	106.0	102.8
3	Xinjiang	104.1	106.6	104.6	103.6
4	Shanghai	104.1	103.9	104.0	104.7
5	Qinghai	104.6	115.3	92.5	103.9
6	Beijing	107.1	106.1	105.8	108.9
7	Yunnan	107.3	103.9	105.3	107.6
8	Heilongjiang	107.3	105.5	106.4	108.6
9	Jilin	107.8	106.0	107.3	108.5
10	Gansu	108.4	106.6	112.6	108.5
11	Inner Mongolia	108.5	105.2	105.3	110.1
12	Hubei	109.5	108.8	115.0	109.4
13	Ningxia	109.7	111.8	110.0	109.4
14	Fujian	109.9	109.4	124.0	108.9
15	Shanxi	110.1	111.5	109.3	109.9
16	Hunan	110.1	105.6	111.1	115.4
17	Shaanxi	110.3	113.6	116.7	109.9
18	Tianjin	110.4	106.4	107.6	110.5
19	Jiangxi	110.4	112.8	112.1	109.6
20	Liaoning	110.5	107.5	107.0	113.2
21	Hebei	110.9	104.0	108.4	111.9
22	Anhui	111.3	108.9	107.8	111.0
23	Guangdong	111.3	114.0	120.5	109.1
24	Sichuan	112.1	108.9	106.0	112.8
25	Jiangsu	113.8	112.0	107.3	114.5
26	Shandong	115.0	113.3	117.2	115.2
27	Hainan	116.1	111.1	136.2	114.7
28	Henan	116.2	113.0	113.9	116.6
29	Zhejiang	116.7	107.5	119.2	118.2
30	Guangxi	117.4	113.2	110.4	118.1

Original source: State Statistical Bureau, 1991, pp. 45, 427–29; quoted in Gu Baochang and Li Yongping, 'Sex ratio at birth and son preference in China', Paper presented at UNFPA Symposium on 'Issues related to sex preference for children in the rapidly changing demographic dynamics in Asia', Seoul, Korea, 21–24 November 1994.

120.9, 124.6 and 131.7 respectively at parities 2, 3 and 4 if the first-born was a girl, and that this pattern appeared to be similar in urban areas, townships and rural areas throughout most provinces.[24] Further scrutiny of data on sex ratios at birth shows that parity-specific ratios were directly affected by the gender composition of surviving children or the presence of a son, and that this was a crucial factor in determining whether parents wanted or planned to have another child and proceeded to do so whether or not there were restrictions on their childbearing. One study shows that sex ratios at each parity rose dramatically after 1980 for those couples with only daughters but less so for those with a combination of sons and daughters or only sons, despite strict birth control policies.[25] It can be seen from

Table 2.3 Sex ratio at birth by parity: China 1981–89

Year	Parity of women				
	1	2	3	4	5+
1981	105.1	106.7	111.3	106.5	114.1
1982	106.6	105.2	109.4	112.9	109.9
1983	107.8	107.2	109.5	104.7	112.1
1984	102.5	113.3	113.0	115.3	127.3
1985	106.6	115.9	114.1	126.9	117.3
1986	105.4	116.9	123.1	125.3	123.5
1987	106.8	112.8	118.9	118.6	124.6
1988	101.5	114.5	117.1	123.1	108.7
1989	105.2	121.0	124.3	131.7	129.8

Original sources: 1. 1970–88 from SFPC (1990).
                   2. 1989 from SSB (1991).
Source: Gu Baochang and Li Yongping, 'Sex ratio at birth and son preference in China'.
Paper presented for the UNFPA Symposium on 'Issues Related to Sex Preference for Children in the Rapidly Changing Demographic Dynamics in Asia', held in Seoul, Korea, 21–24 November 1994.

Table 2.4 that overall in 1990 the sex ratios at birth for surviving children between birth and 18 months were a high 115.3 (male) per 100 (female) in 1990; that sex ratios at birth tended to be normal for women with no children or one son; that the sex ratios of surviving children for women with no son but only daughter(s) were as high as 200+ males to 100 females; and that the sex ratios of surviving children for women with son(s) but no daughter tended to be too low to be in the normal range.[26] More detailed information on sex ratios of surviving children shown in Table 2.4 shows that women with no sons tend to have extremely high sex ratios at birth whether they are resident in city, town or countryside or whether they have received little or more than 9-years' schooling. This strongly supports the hypothesis that the imbalance between male and female births occurs not only among the births of high orders but more specifically among women in all locations and levels of education with daughter(s) but no son.[27] While high and rising sex ratios at birth provide hard evidence of shortfalls in the numbers of female infants, a most important question and one which has vexed demographers within and outside China is whether these girls are permanently missing from the statistics or temporarily hidden and perhaps under-enumerated.

Under-reporting of female births

It is generally agreed that births are under-reported in China in that infants may not be registered at birth and therefore do not become part of the statistics. There is certainly evidence of local instances of serious

Table 2.4 Observed sex ratio of surviving children born in 1989 and the first half of 1990, by number and sex of surviving children, residence and education: China 1990

	0	1		2			3		Total
Sex	0m 0f	1m 0f	0m 1f	2m 0f	1m 1f	0m 2f	3+m 0f	1+m 1+f	0m 3+f	
SR	105.6	101.4	149.4	74.1	116.4	224.9	64.4	121.9	219.4	115.3
Residence										
County										
SR	105.1	101.1	152.9	73.1	114.6	226.6	63.6	119.7	215.9	116.0
Town										
SR	106.0	100.1	143.6	79.4	120.4	215.2	71.7	125.3	215.6	115.5
City										
SR	106.0	103.8	147.7	69.7	116.4	233.5	52.1	125.4	237.0	113.8
Education										
<1 year schooling										
SR	99.2	99.2	129.5	74.8	115.0	209.2	66.8	119.0	186.0	111.9
1–5 year schooling										
SR	104.3	99.5	148.0	74.3	116.9	223.7	62.8	117.0	237.3	115.0
6–8 year schooling										
SR	107.5	105.3	159.9	73.5	118.2	239.2	68.8	146.7	245.8	117.4
9+ Year Schooling										
SR	108.1	100.1	157.2	71.6	111.3	228.9	41.2	131.3	223.3	114.1

Note: 1. Calculated from a 1% sampling of China's 1990 census data, some figures may disagree with those of published in 10% tabulations.
　　　2. Twins are not considered due to poor sex identification.
Original sources: 1. 1970–88 from SFPC (1990).
　　　　　　　　　2. 1989 from SSB (1991).

Source: Gu Baochang and Li Yongping, 'Sex ratio at birth and son preference in China'. Paper presented for the UNFPA Symposium on 'Issues Related to Sex Preference for Children in the Rapidly Changing Demographic Dynamics in Asia', held in Seoul, Korea, 21–24 November 1994.

under-reporting or non-registration of births in order to evade penalties and/or to obtain official permits for a second birth. In a random check on the registration data in one county in Shandong province, the registration figures showed a birth rate of 12 per 1000 while the subsequent check revealed a birth rate of 24 per 1000.[28] There is also evidence that under-reporting is more likely to take place for female and for higher parity births, which are more likely to be concealed or penalised. One study showed that in 1989 approximately two-thirds of the under-reported births were female.[29] Another showed that under-reported rates of female births exceeded twice those of male births in most years between 1983 and 1988, and that the rates of under-reported male and female births for the 18-month period preceding the survey were 2.6 and 5.5% respectively.[30] One study shows the differences between reported and expected numbers of births for the 1989 birth cohort and reveals that the 1990 census omitted at least 625 thousand female births and 241 thousand male births leading to a decline in the calculated sex ratio at birth from 114.7 to the lower but still significant 110.8. Demographers concluded that sex differential under-reporting of births in the 1990 census inflated sex ratios at birth by at least 3.9 male per 100 female births and that the under-reporting of female births was more serious than for male births in 25 of the 30 provinces. Altogether the sex differential in under-reporting of births accounted for between 42.6% and 70.4% of the difference between normal ratios and those reported by the census.[31]

However, calculations by Chinese demographers also show that sex ratios at birth remain quite high even after adjustments for the under-reporting of female births. When Peng Xizhe adjusted the sex ratio at birth to take account of under-reporting, his calculations revealed that the differences between his amended figures and those based on the 1990 census were around 5%.[32] What is more important in the context of this study is his finding that child sex ratios do not appear to revert to normal, which might have been expected if previously concealed or unregistered children were enumerated as they entered older age groups. The fact that there has been little if any re-emergence of girls into the cohorts born in the last half decade suggested to demographers that, while under-reporting of female births did exist, this did not explain the observed high sex ratios at birth. While concealment or non-registration was held responsible for the shortfalls in girls during the late 1980s, the 1990 census with its amnesty on hidden births and new attempts at accuracy cast doubt on the degree to which shortfalls were due to under-enumeration or under-registration. It is the opinion of China's demographers that, unless female infants have been concealed with a tenacity that is hard to imagine, the 'missing' girls are truly missing and do not survive pregnancy or birth. Because hypotheses based on under-reporting have appeared much weaker than they did several years ago, attention has shifted to more serious forms of discrimination which may affect daughters before, during and after birth. These include abandonment, infanticide, sex-selective abortion and infant and child neglect.

Female abandonment and adoption

Both abandonment and formal or informal adoption have been identified by researchers as possible causes for the apparently high sex ratios at birth. In 1991 Johansson and Nygren concluded that around half of the reported abnormal sex ratios at birth could be attributed to child abandonment and adoption. As a result of the surveys in 1980, they claimed that in the aftermath of higher-order births parents may attempt to abandon children at birth, or at an older age, or send them elsewhere to reside with either relatives or friends on either a permanent or temporary basis. They surmised that children were not so much hidden by parents as 'temporarily mislaid' or sent away only to be brought back later and recorded in the statistics as 'in-migrants'. That is, if a boy was born outside the village he was more likely to return with his mother and be registered locally, but if a girl was born she was either abandoned, loaned or given to relatives or friends outside the neighbourhood.[33] The Women's Federation also found in one of their investigations that there were a number of cases where women had given away their first-born daughters in order that 'they might have a son to continue the family line'.[34] This hypothesis rested on the very high proportions of females recorded among children 'adopted in' which might account for the females 'missing' from the birth cohorts reported for previous years. Although this also seemed a likely explanation in the late 1980s, the 1990 Census data subsequently cast doubt on this hypothesis too. Certainly all females who were subsequently adopted should have reappeared in that census and in the household records of their adopted families, but when the sex ratios of birth cohorts are compared with successive ages of children in subsequent surveys, the missing females again do not seem to reappear in the statistics. Until they do, it is difficult to sustain arguments that shortfalls in the numbers of girls mainly derive from under- or mis-reporting.

There is evidence, however, to suggest that the numbers of children abandoned or adopted-out have risen and that girls are more likely than boys to be abandoned or put up for adoption. Although again it is difficult to find the statistics to document overall trends, there is some data to confirm reports and observations that the numbers of abandoned children have risen. In 1991 the Ministry of Civil Affairs registered 140,000 orphaned and abandoned children, with tens of thousands of abandoned children being cared for in over 5000 welfare homes. Although official adoptions were reported to number between 10,000 and 15,000, sample survey data suggested that the real figure may be much higher, perhaps amounting to 500,000 if private and unregistered adoptions are included, and that these cases increased steadily during the 1980s.[35] In Hunan and Hubei provinces, local data suggests that there were escalating numbers of children abandoned and that these were mainly girls. For instance, in Hunan province between 1986 and 1990 more than 16,000 abandoned children, of whom 92% were girls and 25% handicapped, were brought to the civil affairs department of the province. The increase in proportions of children and healthy girls as opposed to disabled boys abandoned can be seen in the following figures for Wuhan city, where 233, 352 and 854 children were abandoned in 1988, 1989 and 1990 respectively.[36] In one orphanage alone, as Tables 2.5 and 2.6 show, the intake between 1966 and 1975 hovered between 50 and 80 children per year; in 1988 the number climbed steeply to 300 and between 1988 and 1992 the numbers escalated sharply, doubling every two years to reach 1200 in 1992.[37] A study of the children abandoned and taken into this single

Table 2.5 Annual intake at the Wuhan Orphanage, 1950–92

Year	Numbers of children received	Year	Numbers of children received	Year	Numbers of children received
1950	139	1964	126	1978	96
1951	57	1965	109	1979	150
1952	37	1966	56	1980	161
1953	72	1967	49	1981	144
1954	82	1968	52	1982	252
1955	149	1969	47	1983	261
1956	305	1970	42	1984	246
1957	177	1971	60	1985	187
1958	166	1972	67	1986	—
1959*	120	1973	77	1987	—
1960*	125	1974	68	1988	300
1961*	67	1975	86	1989	—
1962	127	1976	89	1990	590
1963	54	1977	102	1991	895
				1992	1200+

*During these years, twelve other temporary orphanages were opened, housing 3929.

Source: Kay Johnson, 'Chinese orphanages: saving China's abandoned girls', *The Australian Journal of Chinese Affairs*, No. 3, July 1993, p. 69, Table 1.

Table 2.6 Percentage of girls in the Wuhan Orphanage, 1951–92

Year	% girls	Year	% girls
1951	89.2	1984	83.0
1958	99.0	1985	76.0
1960	88.2	1988	
1980	75.0	1989	
1981	81.0	1990	90+
1982	80.0	1991	
1983	85.0	1992	

Source: Kay Johnson, 'Chinese orphanages: saving China's abandoned girls', *The Australian Journal of Chinese Affairs*, No. 3, July 1993, p. 72, Table 2.

orphanage alone revealed that girls accounted for upwards of 90% of the children and that there was a direct correlation between the stringency of birth campaigns and numbers abandoned. For instance, in the latter months of 1991 campaigns to sterilise women with two children caused up to ten children, including an unusually large number of older girls between ages 2 and 5, to be abandoned each day. In neighbouring Hubei province, while in the early 1970s over 90% of those abandoned were disabled, increasing numbers of healthy daughters were abandoned during the 1980s. In one county in Southern Zhejiang province, a total of 2,928 infants were abandoned between 1982 and 1991 of whom 95.4% were females.[38]

Some of these abandoned children became available for adoption, but figures for child-adoption between 1950 and 1988 remained relatively steady at around 0.6–0.7% between 1950s and 1970s; however, that percentage rose to 2.32% in 1988 or nearly four times higher than for earlier decades.[39] Although these figures may include fictitious adoptions registered to avoid birth control regulations they do represent a trend. Certainly there is firm evidence of this in the growing number of children available for foreign adoption who, almost without exception, are girls. The sex ratio of adopted children for the same period also reveals that the sex ratios widened steadily so that, in the 1980s, three-quarters of all adopted children were girls.[40] It can be argued that adopted children are among the fortunate for, as Kay Johnson notes in her study, there is some evidence that abandonment itself may have serious life-threatening consequences given the high mortality rates of foundlings.[41] Many arrive in a critical condition at orphanages where they do not necessarily receive the medical care that they need. Officials have estimated that a majority of infants abandoned in the countryside die before they are found and that orphanages located in small towns have high mortality rates. One orphanage in Hebei province was found to have a death rate of 90% among its predominantly female foundlings, while widely publicised foreign film and media reports suggest low survival rates in orphanages. Some of these reports quite wrongly suggest that institutional neglect is intentional, but there is evidence that there are considerable shortfalls in the levels of care required by these children, largely because of a lack of local funding sources. On the basis of her extensive studies and first-hand experience Kay Johnson concludes that, while abandonment and infanticide may only be sufficiently widespread to contribute to a minority of the rapidly growing number of 'missing girls', female infant abandonment is still severe in some regions and likely to amount to many tens of thousands or perhaps hundreds of thousands of cases each year.[42] These figures suggest that this form of female disadvantage and discrimination is widespread and deserving of further attention.

Female infanticide

Although there is a congruence of opinion that the practice of female infanticide at birth is less responsible for the current rise in sex ratios than other discriminatory practices, field investigations suggest that the incidence of female infanticide probably rose during the early 1980s when it became the subject of media concern. Female infanticide has a long history in some regions in China, but there is general agreement that the practice, while not unknown, was probably not widespread in China after 1949. However, the introduction of the one-child family policy in 1979 caused an immediate increase in incidence of the practice after which it has declined once again. Although it was only after the introduction of the single-child family that concern became apparent, the practice probably became more common in the late 1970s as birth control programmes pressed couples into having widely spaced two- to three-child families. There were occasional reports in the media of female infanticide, with sex ratios obtained in a number of villages producing some puzzling discrepancies. The first serious suggestion that female infanticide again might be a factor to be reckoned with occurred when detailed data for three counties in Zhejiang province suggested that the lower proportion of females born in 1978 should attract attention, since it 'reflected the recurrence in recent years in some places of abandoning and killing infants, for the most part girls'.[43] In 1980 it was noticeable that the new Marriage Law continued to incorporate prohibitions against infanticide even though reference to other long-established practices thought no longer to be relevant had been dropped. Even so, a year later, it still came as something of a surprise to most observers within and outside of China that female infanticide should become the subject of emotive headlines in the Chinese press. At the end of 1981, the national youth newspaper ran the headlines 'Save Our Baby Girls' because it deemed it necessary to draw attention to the numbers of baby girls abandoned and the sharp increase in female infanticide which was occurring in China in response to the introduction of the one-child policy.[44]

Once reports in the media suggested that the first years of the new policy had been marked by a sharp increase in female infanticide, the government charged the All-China Women's Federation with ascertaining the scale of female infanticide throughout the country. It initiated a nation-wide survey designed to investigate and document cases of female infanticide and other forms of discrimination against female infants and their mothers. In interior Anhui province, where previously a long history of infanticide had given rise to large numbers of unmarried men over the age of 40 years, it found that a disproportionate number of newborn and young female infants had died in the last few years. In some areas the ratio of female to male infants was reported to have dropped to a low 1 in 5; in one production team more than 40 infant girls had been drowned in 1980 and 1981; and of the eight babies born in another brigade in the first quarter of 1982, the three boys survived and the five girls were all drowned or abandoned. Further comparisons with nearby villages revealed that these patterns were not unique. In one of the neighbouring counties, the percentage of male over female infants had risen from 3.2 to 5.8% within one year, so that in 1980 the percentage of males born was 53% compared to 46% female. In yet another county, the problem was shown to be even more serious, for the ratio of males born had risen from 112.6 to 116.4 between 1980 and 1981, so that the percentage of males born was 58.2% compared to 41.8% female. There were also reports of similar trends in female infant deaths from Henan, Hebei and Hunan provinces. A national newspaper published these findings of the Women's Federation to draw attention to the intolerable behaviour of drowning and forsaking baby girls which is 'still rampant in some rural areas' and 'a major problem worthy of serious attention'.[45]

It is my own view that the practice is clustered and more likely to persist in the poorer inland regions and regions where the tradition of infanticide meant that it was rarely perceived as a crime, and that there is little evidence to suggest widespread female infanticide. China's demographers also argue that female infanticide is not likely to explain the 'missing girls' phenomenon. The 1990 census data on infant deaths in the preceding 18 months showed mortality sex ratios at birth between January 1989 and July 1990 to be 98.6 males per 100 females nationwide and 109.7 in the cities, 98.8 in the towns and 97.5 in rural counties which, they concluded, do not suggest that 'widespread female infanticide is the main cause of the high reported sex ratios at birth seen in China today'.[46] In support of their argument, China's demographers cite the legal strictures, the difficulty of keeping such births and deaths hidden, the considerable psychological costs and, above all, they suggest that there are now alternative pre-natal options including sex-selective abortion.

Sex-selective abortion

Before the 1980s contraception was commonly used to prevent births, with a heavy reliance on intra-uterine devices (IUD) and sterilisation. From the 1970s and before the single child family policy, China had a strict birth control programme limiting families to two to three children and encouraging or enforcing contraceptive use with legal abortion a widely used back up for failed contraception. Some rural and most urban parents used contraception to space their children and to stop child bearing after having both their preferred number and gender composition. The widespread use of contraception only after the desired gender configuration of previous children — a son and daughter, two sons, two sons and a daughter or three sons — suggested that parents were only prepared to intervene after the desired number of sons were born. Thus the spread of contraception in the 1970s had only a minor effect on sex ratios at birth, even at higher parities, although it did lead to a cessation of fertility after the birth of wanted sons.[47] However, once the one- or two-child policy was widely implemented, parents could no longer continue to bear children until they had their desired number of sons; instead they increasingly traded daughters for sons via sex-selective abortion.

Ironically it is the improvements in the standards of pre-natal care and, in particular, the development of new technologies that have been responsible for permitting an increase in sex-identification before birth. The now widespread availability of ultrasound B machines has made it technically feasible for sex-selective abortion to take place in many regions in China. In 1979 the first Chinese-made ultrasound B machine was produced and in 1982 a large volume of imported and Chinese-made ultrasound B machines began to enter the Chinese market. In 1985, a sample survey in 101 counties and 37 districts revealed that 67 counties had ultrasound machines with a total of 70,169 people annually examined and a ratio of around 1000 patients per machine. If these statistics were in any way representative of the national situation, they indicated that ultrasound machines were widely available by 1985 and moderately to intensively used. By 1987 the number of ultrasound B machines used in hospitals and clinics was estimated to exceed 13,000, that is about six per county or enough to supply every county and many townships in China.[48] It was also estimated that China had the capacity to produce more than 10,000 ultrasound machines annually, or enough to provide all China's counties with four additional machines each year. Surveys, my own observations and those of others suggest that since 1985 most county and township clinics have acquired ultrasound machines advanced enough to screen for birth defects and pre-natal sex identification.

Government policy has forbidden the use of new technologies for sex identification; however, their widespread use for this purpose is difficult to police, and the lack of local funding for health encourages this misuse because the fees levied for ultrasound services have been used to finance an otherwise under-funded local health service and supplement incomes in the many new forms of private and semi-private medical practice. Strong son preference, gifts and bribes make back-door options likely and it is rumoured that the deployment of pre-arranged informal or unwritten signs such as a smile for a son and a frown for a daughter make prohibited verbal or written confirmation unnecessary. At present, China's demographers agree that the most likely explanation for rising sex ratios at birth is that it has now become possible for parents to determine the sex of the foetus and for pregnant women to have an abortion if they so wish. What lends weight to the importance of sex-selective abortion as the cause of rising sex ratios at birth is that the sex ratios of aborted foetuses and of births in urban hospitals where surveillance is greater also show high sex ratios, which additionally suggest that numbers of women have undergone prenatal sex identification. A study of medical records of 1,243,284 pregnancies after the 28th week of gestation surveyed for birth defects at 945 hospitals in 29 provinces, municipalities and autonomous regions by the Western China Medical University showed that the sex ratio for live births delivered in 1988, 1989, 1990 and 1991 were 108.0, 108.3, 109.1 and 109.7 respectively. The study concluded that because of hospital surveillance and record-keeping there could be few undue practices at birth and thus the only plausible explanation for high sex ratios above 108 for 1.2 million live hospital births is that some of the women had previously undergone prenatal sex identification and sex-selective abortion.[49]

Induced abortion is legal and a frequent form of birth control where access to contraception is difficult and failure rates high. It is estimated that there is about one induced abortion per two live births and, given this ratio, demographers have argued that even a small proportion of 11 million induced abortions is enough to result in a high sex ratio at birth. For example, Li Yongping argues that if only 10% of 11 million induced abortions are gender-related and there is a selective efficiency of 80%, then the resulting sex ratio at birth will be around 110 instead of the norm of 106.[50] The sex of the foetus is not recorded for most induced abortions in China, but one survey in 1986–87 of 1726 aborted foetuses for which the sex was identifiable, showed that sex ratios were 94.6 and 96.8 in rural and urban areas suggesting that 10.2% of induced abortions were sex-selective.[51] More recently, a survey of the sex ratios of 10,782 aborted foetuses in ten counties in Southern Zhejiang in 1993 was conducted jointly by the China Population Information and Research Center and the Zhejiang Family Planning Commission.[52] Table 2.7 shows that, among the more than 10,000 cases recorded, the overall sex ratio of foetuses was 86.7 female, which is lower than the normal foetus sex ratio, and that the sex ratio of aborted foetuses for women with one child was a low 72.3 female.[53] The interference becomes more evident when the sex ratio of aborted foetuses is set alongside the gender of surviving children, so that the sex ratio of aborted foetuses for women who have only one daughter reach a low 51.0 for females.[54] Judith Banister reports that during 1983–90 at least 1.5 million sex selective abortions of female foetuses were carried out in China, with the numbers escalating sharply in the late 1980s.[55] If demographers are agreed that fertility strategies such as sex identification followed by sex-selective abortion have been responsible for the rise in sex ratios at birth in the 1990s, they have also drawn attention to new increases in female infant and child mortality rates.

Table 2.7 Sex ratio of aborted foetus by number and sex of surviving children: Southern Zhejiang, 1993

Surviving Children		Total aborted	Male foetus aborted	Female foetus aborted	Sex ratio of aborted
Male	Female				
0	0	4,518	2,345	2,173	107.9
1	0	2,559	1,329	1,230	108.0
0	1	3,124	1,055	2,069	51.0
2+	0	81	40	41	97.6
0	2	105	38	67	56.7
0	3+	15	4	11	36.4
1+	1+	380	196	184	106.5
Total		10,782	5,007	5,775	86.7

Source: Gu Baochang and Li Yongping, 'Sex ratio at birth and son preference in China'. Paper presented for the UNFPA Symposium on 'Issues Related to Sex Preference for Children in the Rapidly Changing Demographic Dynamics in Asia', held in Seoul, Korea, 21–24 November 1994.

Infant and child health and mortality

As a result of rapid economic growth and economic reforms since the late 1970s there have been substantial improvements in the quality of most children's lives, and most especially of their shelter, food supply, nutrition, health and education. However, not all children have benefited from new and recent socio-economic policies to the same degree, with certain categories of children remaining at risk. These groups include children in poor and remote regions and among the new urban poor, those physically or mentally incapacitated and female infants and children who remain at greater risk than their male siblings and peers. However, any discussion of these vulnerable groups should take cognisance of the overall improvements in the health of children in recent years which is reflected in the lower infant and child mortality rates. Although as Table 2.1 shows, the infant mortality rate for both males and females declined rapidly from over 80 per 1000 in the 1960s and the 1970s to less than 40 in the 1980s the decline has been less dramatic for girls.[56] Excess female infant and child mortality has been observed in most provinces and some minority populations since the late 1980s, and is all the more serious given that in most developed and developing countries natural causes contribute to higher rates of male infant mortality. Table 2.8 shows that the infant mortality for boys decreased by 3.34 per thousand between 1981 and 1989, female infant mortality increased by 3.53 per thousand. This means that while the infant mortality rate for girls was lower than that for boys in 1981, the reverse is observable by the end of the decade, with the infant mortality rate for girls higher (40.4 per 1000) than that for boys (35.5 per 1000).[57] Not surprisingly, these and other estimates suggest that this trend is more pronounced in rural areas.[58]

Studies of child mortality rates show similar downward trends but excess female child mortality was observed in the 1960s, or more than 20 years earlier than for infants.(59) The causes of child deaths have rarely been broken down by gender, but the incidence of the most common diseases

Table 2.8 Comparison of estimated infant mortality rates by sex and residence: China 1981 and 1989 (per thousand)

Year	China		City		Town		County	
	Male	*Female*	*Male*	*Female*	*Male*	*Female*	*Male*	*Female*
1981	38.88	36.87	25.05	25.85	24.27	22.60	41.41	39.37
1989	35.54	40.40	25.33	29.36	27.83	32.17	43.42	49.41

Source: Adapted from Sun Fubin, Li Shuzhuo and Li Nan, 'A study of the under-reporting of deaths in the 1990 Census', *Population Science of China*, No. 2, 1993, pp. 20–5; and quoted in Gu Baochang and Li Yongping, 'Sex ratio at birth and son preference in China'. Paper presented for the UNFPA Symposium on 'Issues Related to Sex Preference for Children in the Rapidly Changing Demographic Dynamics in Asia', held in Seoul, Korea, 21–24 November 1994.

show there to be no sharp differentiation between the sexes that is not compensated elsewhere. Additionally, the gendered data available on heights and weights do not seem to show significant differences in the nutritional status and food intake of boys and girls. Similarly data on disability rates show no apparent differences that could be attributed to female neglect.[60] While there is some evidence to suggest that girls may suffer from a number of micro-nutrient deficiencies, there is little evidence to suggest that this shortfall is attributable to gendered practices or results in death. However, there is growing evidence to suggest that more boys than girls receive hospital care and that parents pay more for the medical treatment of boys. These differences will be discussed in the next chapter, but recent studies in Yunnan province suggest that the proportion of boy-patients whose parents paid above 10 yuan for their medical fee was slightly higher than for girl-patients, that boys were more likely to be taken to hospital before girls and that more girls were likely to die on the way to hospital.[61] A very recent field study in richer regions undertaken by myself and a team of researchers from the All-China Women's Federation and UNICEF also found significant differences in the numbers of boys and girls admitted to city, county and township hospitals and in the costs of their treatment. A growing number of studies have found direct and indirect evidence of such discrimination; it is a matter of concern that this trend is likely to be exacerbated as health services are increasingly fragile and costly as a result of the introduction of higher standard facilities, but concentrated at greater distance from the patient and at higher medical fees. What is surprising is that rising trends in female infant and child mortality are confined to increasingly younger age groups. Studies of successive censuses show that age-specific death rates of girls were higher from birth through age 11 in the years prior to 1953, through ages 0–6 prior to 1964, ages 0–4 in 1981 and only through ages 0–2 in 1989.[62]

Data from the 1990 census allowed for more detailed estimates of the number of missing girls who should be alive at each cohort. Ansley Coale and Judith Banister, in their article 'Five Decades of Missing Females in China', argue that the number of missing girls changes greatly from cohort to cohort. For instance, 2% of girls are missing from children born in the mid-1970s, 3% from those born in the years 1979–82 and even higher proportions are missing from the 1990 census cohorts younger than age 8. Of those born between 1982 and 1987 or aged 3 to 7 years in 1990, 4% are missing, 5% are missing from those aged two years and, of those born between 1988–90 and aged 0 to 1 year, a total of 6% of girls are missing.[63] With totals such as these, it is difficult for demographers to escape the conclusion that there is a large and growing number of female infants missing from the birth registers. Ansley Coale and Judith Banister have concluded that the high numbers of missing girls are the result of excess female discrimination before birth and very early in infancy and childhood and that, although female survival rates generally are a little higher than for males, they are not as high as they should be under non-discriminatory conditions.[64] Demographers within and outside of China consistently suggest that the numbers of girls 'missing' amount to a total of close to 40 million, with one Chinese newspaper estimating in 1992 that by the end of the century this figure would rise to some 70 million.[65] More detailed analyses of the statistics not only shows wide variations in the proportions of girls missing between provinces but that this discrimination can take different forms. In 1990 in Anhui and other provinces there was no evidence of the use of sex-selective abortion, but there was a major shortage of girls due to excess female infant mortality and selective neglect of older girls. In contrast, Liaoning is an example of a province which displays a rapid escalation of sex-selective abortion,[66] which it is commonly agreed now results in an increase in the numbers of missing girls not only in China but also in the Republic of Korea, Taiwan and Vietnam.

Republic of Korea

What has attracted the attention of demographers to Korea is the dramatic decline in the total fertility rate and the country's continuing reputation for an 'extremely strong, pervasive and persistent' preference for sons.[1] In Korea the term 'precipitous' is usually used to describe the pace of fertility decline. The introduction of a birth control programme in the early 1960s had given women immediate access to contraception and, by the 1970s, it was estimated that about 30 to 50% of women used contraception.[2] Over the decades the total fertility rate dropped from 6.0 in the early 1960s to 2.1 or near replacement level at the beginning of the 1980s and a low 1.7–1.6 in the 1990s.[3] The decrease in the total fertility rate for the capital city of Seoul occurred earlier and more rapidly, with a decrease from an estimated 5.4 in 1955–60 to just 3.0 in 1966.[4] In the 1960s large families were still the norm and, as in China, most parents continued to have additional children until two sons were born. Then the sex ratio at birth was near normal except for the birth of the last child and the number of sons determined differential contraceptive use.

In her 1970 cross-cultural study of sex preference, Williamson[5] placed Korea in +3, or strong son preference category, on a scale of −3 to +4, and in the 1970s there is evidence that tension between family size and son preference appeared as the total fertility rate dropped from five or six to a more moderate three or four children. In Seoul between 1968 and 1974 there is increasing evidence of a sudden imbalance in sex ratios occurring as family size was reduced to three to four children.[6] Further it was becoming apparent that desired fertility, birth intervals, abortions and the length of breastfeeding were all linked to the gender composition of previous children, with the sex ratios of last-born, usually the third or fourth child, markedly higher due to contraceptive use following the birth of sons and some sex-selective abortion. The World Fertility Survey in 1974 also showed that parents tended to stop childbearing when certain sex preferences and configurations were achieved and that there was a strong preference for sons, particularly at the second parity. At both second and third parities there were more than twice as many families with all boys than with all girls, indicating that women with all daughters were much more likely to continue childbearing in the hope of bearing a son.[7] Not surprisingly smaller families tended to have greater number of boys and larger families greater number of girls.

The World Fertility Survey data for 1974 also suggested that there was higher female mortality among infants between ages 0 to 5 years; this again was linked to birth order and birth interval.[8] Infant mortality was high for parity one and for males, while child mortality was lower for parity one and for males.[9] At the same time, studies showed that succeeding birth intervals were also an important factor in sex specific mortality at young ages.[10] Not only was the proportion of women progressing to a subsequent birth much higher following that of a daughter, but there was also a shorter average birth interval following a daughter's birth.[11] Female child mortality was also higher for births of higher order and after shorter gaps, while male child mortality was not affected by a shorter preceding interval.[12] However, figures in later years suggest that excessive female mortality between the ages of 1 and 5 years is less common now and has been replaced by higher sex ratios at birth resulting from sex-selective abortion.[13] It was forecast in a number of early demographic studies of Korea that if couples were ever able to identify the sex of their unborn children and actively achieve their ideal gender composition, then the total fertility rate would drop, abortions would rise and sex ratios at birth would become extremely high.[14] These trends resulted in a sudden rise in sex ratios for almost all parity births after 1985.[15]

Over the previous two decades family size has reduced dramatically to one or two children, while at the same time the sex ratio at birth has risen suggesting that sex preference has been exacerbated as family size has decreased (see Table 2.9). Table 2.10 shows that sex ratios at birth have risen not only for higher parity births but also for first and second parity births in one- to two-child families.[16] Park and Cho examined the recorded sex ratios of children by single year of age through age 4 and concluded that, although they were around normal before the mid-1980s, they increased in 1985 and have remained at a level around 113.[17] Park and Cho found that the sex ratios of children under 5 years of age rose earlier in large cities reaching a consistent level of 110 or more for cities in 1985, for towns in 1986 and for rural areas in 1988, although by 1990 the ratio had become uniformly high irrespective of population concentration and location (see Table 2.10).[18] In 1990 Taegu, which is one of the largest cities in Korea and with its surrounding rural areas is noted for

Table 2.9 Sex ratios at birth and total fertility rate in Republic of Korea 1980–93

Year	Republic of Korea	
	SRB	TFR
1980	103.9	
1981	107.0	
1982	106.9	2.7
1983	107.7	
1984	108.7	2.1
1985	110.0	
1986	111.9	
1987	109.0	1.6
1988	113.5	1.6
1989	112.1	
1990	116.9	1.6
1991	112.9	
1992	114.0	
1993		

Source: Adapted from Table 1 in Gu Baochang and Krishna Roy, 'Sex ratio at birth in China, with reference to other areas in East Asia; What we know', *Asia–Pacific Population Journal*, Vol. 10, No. 3, September 1995, p. 20.

conservative ways, sex ratios at 0–4 years ranged from a high 122 to 130 males per 100 females.[19]

In the 1980s the sex ratios at birth by parity showed that while those at parity 1 were near normal in the 1980s and at parity 2 near normal until 1986, the sex ratios for other parities exceeded 200 for parity 4 and above in the 1980s.[20] Table 2.10 shows the systematic rise in the sex ratios according to birth order: prior to 1981 there was no specific association, between 1982–85 there was an abrupt decline in girls born in families with two to three children or in birth order 3, while after 1985 there was an abrupt decline from birth order 2.[21] Table 2.11 shows sex ratios at birth by birth order and the gendered sequence of previous births between 1974 and 1991. It confirms that since 1989 there has been a systematic rise in the sex ratios at birth and not just for higher birth orders.[22] It also shows that the sex ratio for birth order 4 and above exceeded 200, the sex ratio at birth of third children born to women with two daughters was 136.3 while ratios at all birth orders other than second births remained high.[23] The high sex ratio of first born children suggested to Park and Cho that Korean women now apply sex selective technology to ensure the outcome of first order births.[24] Table 2.11 shows that there is some preference for girls among Korean couples in that the sex ratio of second-born children following a male birth was 94.0 while that following a female birth was 103.9, implying that if a first-born child was male then women may choose to have a daughter second.[25] Sex-selective abortion appears prevalent in families having only daughters while the sex ratios for last-born children are extremely high regardless of family size.[26]

Table 2.10 Sex ratio by birth parity, Republic of Korea 1980–92

Year	Total	Parity of women				
		1	2	3	4	5+
1980	104	106	104	103	102	96
1981	107	106	107	107	113	115
1982	107	106	106	110	113	118
1983	108	106	106	113	121	128
1984	109	107	108	119	132	134
1985	110	106	108	133	157	154
1986	113	108	112	143	161	161
1987	109	105	109	137	150	163
1988	114	108	114	170	199	187
1989	113	105	114	190	217	214
1990	117	109	117	196	234	215
1991	112.9	106.1	112.8	184.7	212.3	
1992	114.0	106.4	112.8	195.6	229.0 (4+)	
Cities						
1980	108.0					
1985	110.9					
1990	112.3					
Towns						
1980	107.8					
1985	108.6					
1990	111.1					
Rural						
1980	109.4					
1985	109.7					
1990	115.3					

Sources: Adapted from Table 3 in Gu Baochang and Krishna Roy, 'Sex ratio at birth in China, with reference to other areas in East Asia; What we know', *Asia–Pacific Population Journal*, Vol. 10, No. 3, September 1995, p. 24, (Table 3); and Chai Bin Park and Nam-Hoon Cho, 'Consequences of son preference in a low fertility society: imbalance of the sex ratio at birth in Korea', *Population and Development Review*, Vol. 21, No. 1, March 1995, p. 63.

All the evidence correlating sex ratios and birth order between 1974 and 1991 suggests a growing conflict between smaller family size and son preference although the family size distribution has changed. In 1974 33% of women had five or more children, whereas in 1991 fewer than 5% had five or more births, 31% of women had one or two births in 1974 while in 1991 two-thirds of the entire sample and more than half the women with completed fertility had only one or two births.[27] Within this context rising sex ratios at birth also suggest that female births have been steadily suppressed after a first or second child so that the desired number of sons may be attained within the new small family norm.[28] The widespread substitution of sons for daughters within the small family coincides with the introduction and spread of sex identification technology which also explains the sequential bias in sex ratios between cities, towns and

Table 2.11 Sex ratios at birth by birth order following specified sex sequence of previous births: Korea 1974 and 1991

Birth order	Preceding sex sequence	1974		1991 Full sample		1991 Completed fertility	
		Number	Sex ratio	Number	Sex ratio	Number	Sex ratio
1		4978	106.5	6857	110.1	2770	117.9*
2	M	2196	104.7	2802	103.2	1350	94.0*
	F	2068	111.2	2681	102.2	1199	103.9
3	MM	869	105.4	466	105.3	237	107.9
	MF	875	113.4	567	98.9	354	110.7
	FM	868	110.7	482	104.2	264	100.0
	FF	821	111.2	839	136.3*	456	135.0*
4	MMM	306	109.6	73	135.5	28	250.0
	MMF	302	100.0	74	76.2	30	76.5
	MFM	301	96.7	74	146.7	36	140.0
	MFF	318	116.3	127	115.3	59	118.5
	FMM	310	118.3	77	120.0	37	117.6
	FMF	313	100.6	117	88.7	60	100.0
	FFM	337	100.6	129	101.6	62	106.7
	FFF	318	100.0	242	130.5	130	154.9*

M = male; F = female.

* Difference from a ratio of 107 is statistically significant (p < 0.05).

Original sources: For 1974, Korean World Fertility Survey; for 1991, Fertility and Family Health Survey.

Source: Chai Bin Park and Nam-Hoon Cho, 'Consequences of son preference in a low fertility society: imbalance of the sex ratio at birth in Korea', *Population and Development Review*, Vol. 21, No. 1, March 1995, p. 68, Table 7.

countryside. The lag in the rise of adverse sex ratios in rural areas may be largely explained by a lesser availability of sex identification facilities than in the urban areas.[29] As early as 1988, the National Fertility and Family Health Survey suggested that sex identification tests were conducted in 1.2% of the pregnancies surveyed that year. More than 90% of the tested pregnancies indicating male foetuses resulted in normal births while more than 30% of those indicating female foetuses were terminated by induced abortion.[30] While Park and Cho have argued that sex-selective abortion appears especially prevalent among families having only daughters, Cho and Kim have noted that the abortion rate tends to increase with parity and is also much higher among families having at least one son, which indicates the changing preferences toward even smaller families while maintaining son preference.[31] In sum, sex-selective identification followed by abortion has been identified as the single most important cause of rising sex ratios at birth in Korea and demographers also concur that the possible failure to report female births is not a factor in Korea.[32] Other sources of information, such as the school enrolment statistics, also reveal a discontinuous but consistent rise in the sex ratios

Table 2.12 Estimated number of female births averted, assuming three levels of the normal sex ratio at birth, Korea 1986–90

Normal sex ratio	1986	1987	1988	1989	1990	Total
105	19,300	12,800	18,400	19,800	21,300	91,600
106	16,100	9,800	15,300	16,700	18,300	76,200
107	13,000	6,800	12,200	13,600	15,400	61,000

Source: Chai Bin Park and Nam-Hoon Cho, 'Consequences of son preference in a low fertility society: imbalance of the sex ratio at birth in Korea', *Population and Development Review*, Vol. 21, No. 1, March 1995, p. 74, Table 11.

of pupils born after April 1984.[33] As in China the coincidence of smaller family size, continuing son preference and new technologies have contributed to a rise in the number of 'missing girls'. If the normal sex ratio of 106 is taken as a yardstick, then it has been calculated that the annual number of female foetuses aborted appears to range between 10,000 and 18,000, amounting to nearly 80,000 between 1986 and 1990, which makes for a total of 5% girls 'missing' from the numbers of expected female births (see Table 2.12).[34]

Taiwan

As in other East Asian societies, Taiwan has also experienced a rapid reduction in the total fertility rate from 6.51 in 1956 to 2.16 in 1983 and by a further 22% to 1.68 in 1986 (see Table 2.13). In 1991 the total fertility rate was 1.72, ranging from 1.37 in Taipei, 1.54 in other cities, 1.84 in urban townships to 1.94 in rural townships.[1] This drop in fertility rate is reflected in the decline in family size and the mean preferred number of children, which decreased from 4 in 1965, to 2.7 and 2.4 in 1983 and 1991 with one son and one daughter the preferred composition.[2] There was also evidence of a new conflict between a decreased family size of only 2 to 3 children and the continuing desire for at least one son.[3] Since the early 1960s Taiwan has had an effective birth control programme in place and the first island-wide surveys in 1965 estimated that 43% of married women in the five largest cities and 28% of all women used contraception while, 20 years later, contraceptive prevalence among women aged between 20 and 39 years was estimated to be 78%.[4] Five years after this first survey, Williamson's study of urban and rural townships found that the number of living sons was the most useful predictor of contraceptive use and that the decline in preferred number of children mainly resulted from a drop in the preferred number of daughters rather than sons.[5] Generally women with at least two sons were more likely to use contraception than those with only one son or daughters. A study of contraceptive use in 1973 found that women preferred 3.2 children made up of 1.9 sons and 1.3 daughters giving an ideal sex ratio of 146.[6]

In a more recent study Freedman, Chang and Sun correlated contraceptive use, number of living children, and sons born to married women aged between 22 to 39 years in 1965, 1980, 1985, and 1991.[7] Their study not surprisingly revealed that the percentage of women who wanted no additional children and were currently practising contraception increased with numbers of living sons rather than surviving children and here too preference for more than one son visibly declined between 1965 and 1991. The proportion of women perceiving either sons or daughters to be 'alright' rose from 11 to 22% between 1985 and 1991, but the data also showed that one quarter of the married women in their twenties and one third of those in their thirties still preferred to have two or more sons and fewer daughters.[8] These studies indicated that preference for sons, although diminished, had persisted into the 1990s alongside declining family size and fertility trends.[9] The continuing conflict between preferences for two to three children and the desire for a son is reflected in the rising sex ratios at birth, resulting from the increasing number of couples using prenatal sex identification and selective abortion to manipulate the sex composition of their small families.[10] Such manipulation became possible in the 1980s with the widespread introduction of prenatal sex screening followed by sex-selective abortion. Abortion itself, though not part of the birth control programme, has been easily available; the proportion of women reporting that they have had an abortion increased from 9% in 1965 to 34% in 1991.[11] According to a 1992 survey, most of the pregnancies with reported prenatal sex screening turned out to result in male live births with a sex ratio of 295, or 72% male births as opposed to 24.4% female live births.[12] This increase in the use of prenatal sex screening followed by sex-selective abortion since 1987 is directly reflected in Taiwan's recent sex ratios at birth.

Table 2.13 shows that sex ratios for registered births before 1986 was near normal but increased to 108.3 in 1987 and to 110.2 in 1990.[13] Again sex ratios at birth became increasingly imbalanced as the total fertility rate decreased and were most imbalanced in urban areas and for higher parity births. In 1990 the sex ratios at birth were 112 for Taipei city, 109 for Kaohsiung city and for provincial cities, and 110 for rural areas.[14] In one city, sex ratios for children aged 0 to 4 years were even higher, ranging from 122 to 130 in 1990.[15] Park and Cho's studies have revealed that the recorded sex ratios of children under 5 years' of age also show that the sex ratios for those less than 1 year have risen since 1987.[16] As in other East Asian societies sex ratios at birth rise substantially with birth order. As data for 1991 presented in Table 2.14 shows, sex ratios at parity 1 were normal, for parity 2 a little higher than normal, but for parity 3 and 4 sex ratios at birth had risen to 118 and 130 respectively.[17] Again there are geographical variations with sex ratios for parity 3 and above reaching 138 for the capital city Taipei, 123 for Kaohsiung city, 121 for other cities and 119 for rural counties. This pattern probably reflects the spatial distribution of

Table 2.13 Sex ratio at birth and total fertility rate, Taiwan 1980–93

Year	SRB	TFR
1980	106.4	
1981	107.0	
1982	106.9	
1983	106.7	2.16
1984	107.3	
1985	106.6	
1986	107.2	1.68
1987	108.3	1.70
1988	108.2	1.85
1989	108.6	1.68
1990	110.2	1.81
1991	110.0	1.72
1992		
1993		

Source: Adapted from Table 1 in Gu Baochang and Krishna Roy, 'Sex ratio at birth in China, with reference to other areas in East Asia; What we know', *Asia–Pacific Population Journal*, Vol. 10, No. 3, September 1995, p. 50.

Table 2.14 Sex ratio at birth by parity, Taiwan 1980–93

Year	Parity of women					
	Total	1	2	3	4	5+
1987	108	107	108	110	114	
1988	108	107	107	112	111	
1989	109	107	107	113	121	
1990	110	107	109	119	128	
1990 (Taipei)	112	108	110	134	156	
1990 (Kaohsiung)	109	106	107	122	130	
1990 (Cities: all)	109	105	108	119	131	
1990 (Rural: all)	110	107	109	117	121	
1991	110	107	109	118	130	

Source: Adapted from Table 3 in Gu Baochang and Krishna Roy, 'Sex ratio at birth in China, with reference to other areas in East Asia; What we know', *Asia–Pacific Population Journal*, Vol. 10, No. 3, September 1995, p. 24.

sex-screening technologies[18] which simultaneously have permitted both continuing son preference and new smaller family norms. As in China and Korea any tension between the two has been resolved in Taiwan and Vietnam by the substitution of sons for daughters.

Vietnam

The total fertility rate for Vietnam has almost halved during the past 40 years, declining from 6.01 in 1960 to 3.8 in 1990 and 3.0 in 1997.[1] The small family norm has been growing in popularity since the 1970s with the two- to three-child family encouraged by the government first in the 1960s and then again following reunification of the north and the south in 1975.[2] In the 1980s, nation-wide programmes provided free contraception and abortion services and a comprehensive birth control policy was introduced in late 1988 as it became evident that 37% of Vietnam's population was aged between 0 and 14 years and that the growth rate was more than 2%.[3] The government then committed itself to a new birth control programme which raised the minimum child-bearing age to 19 and 21 years of age for the general population and to 22 and 24 years of age for government officials, encouraging parents to have no more than two children with a spacing of 3 to 5 years and incorporating a series of fines and penalties for excess births.[4] One study indicated high levels of awareness of both modern and traditional methods of fertility regulation in 1988 and revealed that around 60% of women with two or more children and close to 40% with one child practised contraception.[5] The main contraceptive used is the IUD which, with its greater risk of failure, led to an abortion rate of 2.5 abortions per woman which is unusually high by international standards.[6] This study also found that Vietnamese women desired an average total family size of 2.6 children (2.7 rural and 2.3 urban) and that desired family size was also higher in the south (2.8 children) than in the north (2.4 children), thus suggesting that preferred family size was slightly higher than the two-child family norm advocated by the government.[7] Allman's interviews in the late 1980s confirmed that the decision of couples to have more than two children was often related to persistent son preference.[8]

More recent research by Goodkind, who employed a variety of indicators to measure gender preference, such as the stated preference of parents, sex combination preferences in two-child families, birth spacing and sex ratios in child mortality, found a strong preference for sons, with parents who had yet to bear a son apparently willing to part with a few month's earnings as fines.[9] After examining evidence for continuing son preference in the Living Standard Measurement Survey of 1992–93, Dominique and Jonathon Haughton concluded that couples continue to prefer at least one son surviving to childhood and that couples who do not have a son are more likely to continue childbearing than couples who already have a son. This study suggested that son preference remains strong despite the numbers of women with education and in the workforce, but that preference is now for one rather than several sons. They also looked for signs of child malnutrition, still widespread in Vietnam, but found no apparent gender bias against girls in access to nutrition, medical care and in education although there may be some discrimination evident at higher order parities for both males and females.[10] However Goodkind found that the sex ratios of death probabilities at ages 1 to 14 shifted strongly between 1979 and 1989 from a surplus of male deaths to a surplus of female deaths, suggesting decreasing survival probabilities for female relative to male children.[11] This finding suggested that son preference was entirely consistent with lower overall fertility and small family size, although there is a trade-off and it is that between daughters and sons. Again in Vietnam, one of the most important implications of continuing son preference is that couples may well avail themselves of new sex-identification technologies now available; these permit greater control over the gender composition of smaller families, which can be expected to increase the ratios of male to female births in the future so that within a few years there will be considerable numbers of girls missing from the younger population cohorts in Vietnam. If in East Asia as a whole a combination of new technologies and old strategies are placing daughters at increasing risk, in South Asia new technologies are also supplementing age-old strategies of neglect discriminating against daughters.

India

India is a country of striking demographic diversity, of high but declining fertility and of spasmodic economic development due first to the Green Revolution of the 1970s and then to economic reform in the 1990s. India's regions vary widely in their pace and levels of economic development, with the main divisions those between northern and southern states. The north has lower levels of literacy and higher levels of agricultural development than the south although pockets of industrialisation and urbanisation are scattered throughout the country. Demographically too the country is not a single unit. At one end of the continuum lies the southern state of Kerala, much famed for its demographic features more typical of a middle-income country, with a life expectancy at birth of 72 years, an infant mortality rate of 17 per 1000 births and a total fertility rate of 1.8 births per woman.[1] On the other hand the large northern states reflect trends typical of the world's least-developed countries. In Uttar Pradesh, for instance, the infant mortality rate is six times as high as in Kerala and the total fertility rate is a high 5.1.[2] However, for the country as a whole there has been a decline in fertility and infant and child mortality rates but an overall rise in sex ratios. In 1960 the total fertility rate was 5.9, in 1990 it was 3.7 and it then declined to 3.1 in 1997.[3] One of the southern states, Tamil Nadu, showed an even greater decline in the total fertility rate from 3.5 to 2.2 during the 1980s.[4] Within the same period the country's overall infant mortality rate also decreased by about 50%.[5]

The factors that contributed to a reduction in fertility include the widespread availability of contraceptive techniques and an overall decline in the country's infant mortality rate. As in East Asia, studies of contraception use in India have concluded that once parents have at least two surviving sons they are prepared to use contraceptives to limit family size,[6] so that again it is the number of surviving sons rather than any parental characteristic that has the largest influence on contraceptive rates.[7] However, anticipated child-loss has been high so that the chances of conceiving two sons who survive into childhood are less than they might have been in more developed circumstances. For example, May and Heer estimated in the 1960s that for an Indian couple to have a 98% probability of raising one son to adulthood they had to have over six births, and that to ensure the survival of two sons the number of births had to be even higher.[8] Although there has been a substantial decline in infant and child mortality, the number of pregnancies required to fulfil this preference is still high. It is also evident that some couples with only sons may proceed to have further births in the hope of bearing a daughter, but rising contraceptive rates have meant that fewer daughters have been born once son plans were achieved. In 1981 this trend was welcomed by those studying female neglect in the hope that this 'would have the highly beneficial effect of reducing the number of unwanted daughters born and thus of reducing their suffering and wastage through neglect and discrimination'.[9] However, this reduction in higher-parity female births has not prevented India's ratios of females to males continuing to constitute the highest masculinity ratios in the world.

Throughout the twentieth century, census reports have recorded a steady decline in the proportions of females in the population. As Table 2.15 shows, the ratio of females to males in 1961 was 941 to 1000 males, but in 1971 it had decreased to 930; in the 1981 census the figure rose to 934 but the increase was short-lived, as the ratio reached its lowest recorded level of 927 in the most recent census of 1991.[10] The ratio of females to males was lowest in the northern states of Punjab, Haryana, Western Uttar Pradesh, Rajasthan and Bihar which all had averages of less than 930 girls per 1000 boys, while in southern states lesser adult differentials derived from average female child sex ratios ranging between 951–970.[11] Basu who has studied these trends argues that with little under-reporting of births and little reason to expect any increase in the selective under-enumeration of females, these figures do suggest a century-long widening of the gap between male and female mortality.[12] If Sen estimated there to be 30 million missing women, Agnihotri's more detailed study of missing females from Indian population totals between 1961 and 1991 showed a rise from 13 to 32 million, with the sharpest rise between 1981 and 1991 (see Table 2.15).[13] As early as 1961 Visaria undertook a systematic analysis of the imbalances in census sex ratios between 1901 and 1960; he suggested that the imbalance in sex ratios was due to neither the under-enumeration of females nor to any imbalance in sex ratios at birth, but rather could be attributed to differentials in mortality rates between males and females, with excess mortality among young girls and maternal mortality the major factors underlying higher female than male mortality.[14]

> Evidence on excessive female mortality is indeed impressive. The magnitude of such female disadvantage in chances of survival seems to be

Table 2.15 Female–male ratios and missing females, India 1961–91

	Female–male ratios	Population totals (millions)		
		Males	Females	Missing females
1961	941	226.3	212.9	13.4
1971	930	284.0	264.1	19.9
1981	934	343.9	321.4	22.6
1991	927	435.2	403.4	31.8

Source: Adapted and summarised from Tables 2 and 3 in S. B. Agnihotri, 'Missing females: a disaggregated analysis', *Economic and Political Weekly*, New Delhi, pp. 2075–9.

large enough to explain a major part and sometimes the entire excess of males in a population in the Northwestern areas of the sub-continent. There is suggestive indication of regional differences in sex ratios of population being associated with differences in the sex pattern of mortality. Additional evidence will probably accumulate over time.[15]

Visaria identified both the higher mortality of girls, perhaps due to their mistreatment, and maternal mortality of women as the major factors causing higher female than male mortality and deserving of further study. While maternal mortality is a factor contributing to excessive female deaths, subsequent studies have drawn greater attention to excess female mortality among younger girls. In 1981 Barbara Miller argued that excess female mortality in several regions, among some groups and among certain categories of daughters was so great that it must be concluded that females can be deemed to be 'endangered'.[16] Kishor concluded in 1993 that one of the best indexes of active gender discrimination in India is the relative survival rates or differences in the 'right to live' of sons and daughters.[17] Studies in South Asia have since demonstrated that 0–10 years and especially 0–4 years are the age ranges with the most imbalanced sex ratios, the highest mortality differentials and therefore most pronounced female disadvantage resulting in excessive female mortality. Agnihotri's analysis of female mortality rates recorded in the 1981 census showed an unusually low (below 910) and alarmingly low (below 900) female to male ratios for the younger age groups of 0–4 and 5–9 years, suggesting high female mortality rates at very young ages. Agnihotri also argued that, even where the ratios were more favourable to female, this should not be taken to signify an absence of female discrimination but rather to be seen as a sign of excess male mortality before birth and in infancy due to poor maternal nutrition and health care.[18] For children under the age of 7 years the average sex ratio for the whole of India in 1991 was 950 females per 1000 males, which is above the figure of 930 for the entire population because it does not include the mortality figures for women of reproductive age.[19] Government statistics on sex ratios reveals that excess female mortality is most pronounced even earlier in life, in that the all-India death rate in 1991 for the 0–4 year age group was 25.6 for males and 27.5 for females per 1000 population.[20] An overview of the data shows that the female to male ratios in child mortality continues to exceed 1.00 in over 60% of India's districts, that 54 districts in the country have sex ratios below 900 for the 0 to 6 year age group, and that these are located mainly in northern states or clustered in some southern states.[21] Of the practices that result in excess female mortality, infanticide and neglect are the most important, although increasingly they are supplemented by sex-selective abortion.

Infanticide

The most immediate form of female discrimination at birth, and one long observed in India, is the practice of female infanticide which has customarily been deployed to limit the number of births and determine the gender composition of families. In the nineteenth century, although female infanticide was universally practised neither across regions nor among all groups, it was the main cause of disparities in sex ratios revealed by the 1872 census. Even at this early date, sex ratios at birth were identified as the main cause of high sex ratios among older age groups with some juvenile sex ratios of more than 120 males to 100 females. Again these are located in the northwest provinces or more particularly the western plains portion of Uttar Pradesh.[22] More detailed studies revealed variations across regions ranging from a normal 107 to a high 121.8 males per 100 females for children under 10 years and between 114.1 and 129.7 males to 100 females for children under 12 years.[23] While in general there were seven boys for every six girls, the proportions of girls among groups practising female infanticide were more imbalanced. For instance, in the district of Mainpuri which had the highest sex ratios, roughly 25% of the population was charged with practising infanticide in 50% of female births.[24] Nineteenth-century records show that in large groups of villages comprising several hundred households in Rajputstan and Gujurat no female child had been allowed to reach adulthood for many generations.[25] At first female infanticide seemed to be confined to the north-western part of India from Gujurat in the west to the eastern border of present day Uttar Pradesh. The 1881 Northwest Provinces Special Census Report, one of the first official sources on female infanticide, named seven caste groups among whom the practice was suspected to be common and these were all groups of northern middle- and upper-level castes, but there were also additional references to female infanticide among two or three groups in southern regions.[26] As a result of her studies of nineteenth-century records, Miller argued that the rather extreme assumption that roughly one quarter of the population kills half of their female offspring may in fact be accurate.[27] However, studies of sex ratios in each subsequent census suggested that sex ratios at birth might be more balanced than sex ratios in infancy and in childhood and, in the absence of detailed data, female infanticide was assumed in past decades to be a localised practice of decreasing importance. However, contemporary scholars such as Patel, Sabu and Harriss-White do not discount the possibility that in some instances female infanticide may have been given new vigour by socio-economic changes wrought by the Green Revolution of the 1970s and the economic reforms of the 1990s.

Patel is one of several scholars who have found that the practice of female infanticide continues in parts of Western Gujarat, Rajasthan, Uttar Pradesh, Bihar, Punjab and Madhaya Pradesh, which are all northern and western provinces.[28] In addition some of the most detailed recent evidence suggesting that female infanticide is a continuing practice today derives from studies in south India. For example, a report in *India Today* in 1986 drew attention to the 'shocking' incidence of female infanticide among the Kallars, a caste of small farmers and agricultural labourers in the Madurai district in the southern state of Tamil Nadu.[29] A report from a government hospital nearby estimated that a high 70%, or more than 450 of the 600 females born there, were victims of infanticide, which implied that around 70% of infant girls did not survive birth, although such figures need to be confirmed.[30] In the same year (1986) Sabu, Abel and Miller began a four-year study of child growth and survival in a rural southern population in Tamil Nadu state. They found that, in six of the twelve villages studied, female infanticide was practised and affected 10% of new-born daughters. Of 773 live births there was a total of 759 or 378 males and 381 female births, so that the sex ratios at birth were near the norm of 105 males to 100 females; but in the case of the 21 still births, 8 were male and 13 female with infanticide apparently accounting for the disproportionate number of female stillbirths. Of the 33 female and 23 male infants who died in the period of the two and half-year study, more than half (19) of the 33 female deaths were confirmed infanticides, with 17 of these taking place within 7 days of birth and the remainder within 16 days of birth. While more than half of the female deaths in the 12 villages were due to direct and confirmed infanticide, they all occurred in six of the 12 villages, so that a total of 72% of the female deaths in these villages were infanticides. Thus in the six villages where female infanticide was practised in the late 1980s, female infanticide accounted for 9.7% of all female deaths at birth, and this was in a region where juvenile sex ratios were near equal at the provincial and district levels. Given that in the 12-village study, the overall sex ratio of females per males was 977.5, and in the six villages where female infanticide was practised it was 939.8, Sabu, Abel and Miller argue that to ignore infanticide overlooks the significance of clustered female deaths at birth.[31] Their findings pointing to the concentration or clustering of female infanticides were confirmed in more recent studies.

A Report on Structural Adjustment Policy and the Child (1992) incorporated summary evidence suggesting that female infanticide was widely practised in some districts, with more than 51% of the 2350 families interviewed having practised it within the past 2 years and 70% admitting that they knew it was being practised in their own village, making for village sex ratios of 742 compared to 972 for the state.[32] In a study of eight villages in a northern district of Tamil Nadu state, Sargent, Harriss-White and Janakarajan found that the entire population of children under 6 years, comprising 555 boys and 475 girls with a sex ratio of 856 girls to every 1000 boys, was much lower than the state average of 946. In four of the villages restudied by Harriss-White comparisons drawn between sex ratios in 1981–82 and 1993–95 suggested that the survival chances of young girls in this district had fallen sharply during the 1980s.[33] In the mid-1990s Chunkath and Athreya were alarmed to find that in the state of Tamil Nadu, a state with higher levels of health and education, the practice of female infanticide was recent in origin. The practice had spread from a core region of four districts to three districts in a belt running north-south along the western half of the state and, most disturbing, to a further nine districts on the periphery.[34] In another region, that of rural Bihar, a recent report in the mid-1990s estimated that the number of female infanticides in seven districts there amounted to 1.6 million each year. It also noted that the practice is spreading to new geographic regions resulting in the spread of female infanticide across India's rural population and across the social spectrum from Rajput and Brahmins to other caste groups for whom it was also a new practise.[35] In sum, recent research suggests that infanticide continues to be practised in India today and perhaps increasingly so in both clustered populations in the south and more generally in northern states. However, if infanticide has attracted new attention in contemporary analyses, it is the practice of female neglect in infancy and childhood which has been identified as more widespread and significant in accounting for higher female mortality at a young age.

Daughter neglect

In India most analyses focus on juvenile sex ratios rather than on sex ratios at birth because of the concern that excess female mortality manifests itself in childhood years rather than at the time of birth. It was long believed that a decline in infanticide was accompanied by an increase in excess female mortality at early years due to neglect of female children. 'Neglect' is a term which usually refers to shortfalls in the supply of food, nutrition or medical care which threatens survival and development. Although female infanticide has long been openly observed as a form of birth control, the similar effect of child neglect was less well recognised. It was not until Barbara Miller's path-breaking book-length study in 1981 that female-specific neglect was acknowledged as an additional or even the main form of fertility regulation and discrimination against daughters in India. Barbara Miller's study of the neglect of female children in rural north India drew on her own and preceding studies to point out the ways in which an intense desire for sons was directly tied to the fatal neglect of daughters, and how this fatal neglect could be interpreted as an indigenous method of birth or family-size and gender control so serious that young females could be deemed 'endangered'.[36] Regional distributions of female neglect similar to those for female infanticide in the nineteenth century can be identified; this suggested to analysts that by the twentieth century the biased allocation of food and nutrition and medical care had replaced infanticide in reducing the total number of surviving daughters.[37] Perhaps it is not surprising, given that children under 5 years comprise 13% of India's population, to see geographic patterns of adult sex ratios closely following those of child or juvenile sex ratios.

For juvenile sex ratios, a well known regional pattern is observed in the so-called 'Bermudan triangle for the female child' which embraces the states of Punjab, North and Northwestern parts of the Haryana, Western Uttar Pradesh, some of Rajasthan and the ravine area of Madhaya Pradesh. Kelly in her 1975 study of sex ratios in Punjab and Kerala concluded that the excessive young female mortality to be found in the northern states gave rise to the very high sex ratios and was the result of lesser medical care for girls.[38] In her review of mortality rates in two northern and southern districts, Miller found that in northern Punjab, female infant mortality rates were much higher than for males, although in one of her southern studies infant female mortality was slightly lower than for males. Female child mortality in the northern two studies was also almost twice as high as male child mortality rates, but again in the south the difference was less with infant male mortality proportionally higher during the first 5 months of life after which female deaths become preponderant.[39] These early studies identified the different patterns of mortality for boys and girls in north and south India: girls die at much higher rates than boys in the north while the differentials are less in the south. For northern states both Kelly and Miller argued that fatal neglect of daughters went some way to mitigate the high birth rate in the quest for sons and, that if it were not for the effects of daughter neglect, population growth spurred by the desire for sons would have been greater. For example, Kelly estimated that sex differences in infant mortality in the Punjab were responsible for reducing the population growth rate by 7.78%.[40]

Subsequent demographic studies have confirmed these north-south differentials in sex ratios and in female infant and child mortality rates. In 1983 Dyson and Moore found that sex ratios in child mortality were much higher in the north than in the southern states, and several years later, Basu also argued that India-wide patterns are best understood by dividing the country into northern and southern regions with the states in the north characterised by higher levels of female child mortality between birth and exact age 5 years.[41] Kishor's later study of the 1981 census showed that the number of female deaths per 100 male deaths between ages 0 and 5 years across India's 366 districts averaged 106.4, but ranged between 81.6 to 144.9 with the northern Indian states having the highest excess of female mortality and child mortality.[42] A government report also based on the 1981 census showed that for the death rates in the 0–4 age groups, the female mortality rate was lower than the male rate in the southern states of Andhra Pradesh, Kerala and Tamil Nadu but higher in other major states with the exceptions of Assam and Himachal Pradesh. Female disadvantage resulting in mortality was most pronounced in the north-central and north-western states of Bihar, Madhya Pradesh, Punjab, Rajasthan, and Uttar Pradesh (see Map 2.2).[43] Several years later Das Gupta found that for girls between ages 1 and 4 years in the Punjab female mortality rates were far higher than for males. Between 1 and 23 months, when a large proportion of childhood deaths occurred, the female rates were nearly twice those of males.[44] In perhaps the most detailed of regional studies, Agnihotri calculated in 1991 that the most adverse sex ratios were to be found in north India with the prosperous Jat-dominated wheat-growing states of Punjab, Haryana and Uttar Pradesh all registering sex ratios of under 900 females per 1000 males, while Rajasthan and Bihar had sex ratios of 910 and 911 respectively. In the southern states, Kerala registered a sex ratio of 1036 females to 1000 males, Tamil Nadu was the second highest with a low 974 and Andhra Pradesh followed closely with a sex ratio of 972.[45]

A number of studies have questioned this rigid divide between northern and southern states and shown that analyses disaggregating districts and development blocks show some variations or clustering within northern and southern states. For example, Malhotra revealed that female to male rates of child mortality are below 1.00 in some of the hill districts of north India despite a general pattern of higher female child mortality in north-ern states. Similarly in the mid-south, a pocket of districts shows higher female child mortality despite more normal sex ratios of the south.[46] Mal-hotra also drew attention to differences between the coastal, frontier and interior districts, and the more favourable sex ratios to the female child in the coastal districts of southwest India.[47] Barbara Harriss-White, on the basis of a review of previous studies together with her own field studies, argues that the overall sex ratio of 927 females per 1000 males in the 1991 census camouflages some very interesting differentials even within south-ern states. She used the 1991 census data to construct the sex ratios for the under-6 age groups in each of its districts and development blocks of Tamil Nadu state where, despite an overall sex ratio for this age group of 945 females to every 1000 males, five districts exhibited average sex ratios of 849, 905, 918, 929 and 934 which were lower than the state average.

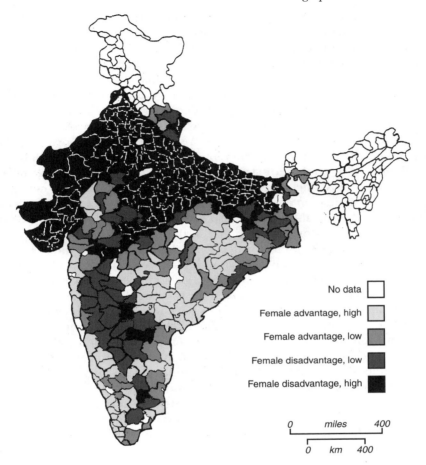

No data

Female advantage, high

Female advantage, low

Female disadvantage, low

Female disadvantage, high

0   *miles*   *400*

0   *km*   *400*

Map 2.2 Gender bias in under-five mortality rates, by district, India 1981

Notes: Female disadvantage, high FD > 5; female disadvantage, low 0 < FD < 5; female advantage, low −5 < FD < 0; female advantage, high FD < −5.

Source: M. Murthi, A. Guio and J. Dreze, 'Mortality, fertility and gender bias in India: a district-level analysis', *Population and Development Review*, Vol. 21, No. 4, December 1995, p. 751.

When the data was further disaggregated for development blocks, the variation was even wider, ranging between 614 to 1113 females for every 1000 males, with those at the lower end of the continuum mainly, although not exclusively, located in rural clusters.[48] What has emerged from such studies of infant and child mortality is not only a localised picture of excessive female mortality greater in the south than expected, but that not all categories of daughters are at equal risk.

In examining differential infant and child mortality, a more recent and significant demographic finding in India has been the increased risk to daughters at higher birth orders. As early as 1976 Beals suggested that daughters of higher birth order were given very little medical treatment,[49] and in rural Uttar Pradesh, Simmons found that 'females ... are vulnerable, especially when the family perceives itself as having enough daughters'.[50] More recently Monica Das Gupta's studies in Punjab have confirmed that neglect might be applied selectively with second or higher parity daughters having a 70% greater risk of death before reaching the age of 5.[51] Her studies of sex differentials in child mortality by birth order in Punjab, a north-western state which historically had the most imbalanced sex ratios due to excessive female mortality, showed not only greater discrimination against all daughters relative to sons in the allocation of food and health care but also that the burden of excessive mortality fell most heavily on girls at higher birth orders. There was a steep rise in mortality of girls at birth order 4 and higher, with daughters having elder sisters most at risk. Boys born with older male siblings had a slightly higher child mortality than only sons, girls with no sisters experienced child mortality rates that fell between the two rates for boys, and there was a sudden jump in the mortality of girls born with sisters who experienced 53% higher mortality than other children. Moreover, daughters of older women aged 30–59 had a 45% higher mortality than their siblings, with this gap increasing to 71% among the daughters of younger women aged 15–29; this suggests rising disparities against elder daughters in recent years.[52] A notable feature of Das Gupta's study is that while there has been an overall and substantial decline in young female mortality, the mortality levels of daughters with elder sisters is almost unchanged. It appears then that even where daughters are born and survive, discrimination does not cease and that neglect is applied selectively, with the burden of excess mortality falling on girls born into families that already have a surviving daughter. Monica Das Gupta argues that such selective intent requires a degree of conscious and voluntary behaviour far greater than if discrimination was random.[53]

In the past 10 to 15 years it has become quite clear that there has been a rise in discrimination against young females resulting in increased rates of female infant and child mortality. Agnihotri has argued that the steepest rise in missing young females was between 1981 and 1991.[54] Again just as this book was being completed, Sudha and Rajan published a very interesting paper showing that excessive female mortality was increasing in contemporary India. Their examination of sex-specific mortality probabilities shows that young girls who had experienced heightened risk in 1981 continued to experience increasing risk in 1991, and that in 1991 excessive female mortality had extended to include girls in regions not so disadvantaged in 1981 (see Table 2.16). Their map shows the spatial distribution of trends in mortality sex ratios across 1981–91 identifying

Table 2.16 Sex ratios of child mortality, India 1981–91

State/region	1981		1991	
	Sex ratio of child mortality q5 m/f		Sex ratio of child mortality q5 m/f	
	Rural	Urban	Rural	Urban
India	93	98	89	95
North/Northwest				
Himachal Pradesh	104	107	108	110
Jammu and Kashmir	97	102	—	—
Punjab	87	92	92	92
Rajasthan	89	89	85	90
Haryana	81	89	81	82
Delhi (UT)	85	95	89	96
Chandigarh (UT)	88	99	107	110
Uttar Pradesh	83	86	79	82
Central				
Bihar	87	90	72	79
Madhya Pradesh	96	98	92	92
Maharashtra	101	106	100	104
Orissa	103	101	93	86
Gujarat	92	94	80	82
Goa	106	103	96	91
East/Northeast				
West Bengal	99	99	92	152
Assam	—	—	103	108
Mizoram	107	111	113	116
Nagaland	106	132	100	107
Meghalaya	105	126	104	105
Arunachal Pradesh	106	152	104	91
Tripura	105	108	102	104
Manipur	104	103	90	94
Sikkim	120	128	110	106
South				
Kerala	113	101	94	88
Andhra Pradesh	105	107	103	108
Tamil Nadu	101	104	88	100
Karnataka	101	102	96	97
Union territories				
Andamans	107	92	112	102
Lakshadweep	121	105	136	91
Dadra Nagar Haveli	113	97	133	136
Pondicherry	103	104	107	103

Note: For all cells other than for Kerala, any value <100 can be considered to indicate female disadvantage.

Original sources: 1981: Government of India (1988); 1991: Irudaya Rajan and Mohanachandran (1998).

Source: S. Sudha and S. I. Rajan, 'Female disadvantage in India 1981–91, *Development and Change*, Vol. 30, No. 3, July 1999, p. 613.

rural and urban areas of the states with ratios showing bias against young females (see Map 2.3) Sudha and Rajan concluded that the phenomenon of excessive female mortality had not only persisted over the decade and spread across India, but that sex ratios of mortality between 1981 and 1991 indicated that, with the exception of a few areas, mortality fell more for males than for females and that, in addition, higher female mortality rates for females may reflect the increasing availability of sex identification techniques.[55]

Sex-selective abortion

The scale of son preference was still such that, in the 1980s, scholars such as Barbara Miller feared that the very future of female births in India might be jeopardised if it ever became possible to identify the sex of a child before birth. She forecast that 'if such a choice were ever made widely available to the Indian population, there is no doubt that people would get far many more sons than daughters particularly in the North . . . [where] there might be villages without a single daughter'.[56] Her predictions that sex identification followed by sex-selective abortion would lead to further increases in the already high masculinity rates in the population have been confirmed by widespread and increasing use of sex-selective abortion, not only to reduce the number of unwanted daughters but to trade daughters for sons within smaller families. Throughout the past 20 years, local studies and surveys made for serious concern as they reveal the wider distribution, privatisation and commercialisation of sex identification and abortion facilities, a greater awareness and use of relatively cheap facilities in clinics and hospitals, and the absence or partial absence of regulation which have allowed sex identification facilities to mushroom and intensify already low female survival rates.

As early as 1974, when the All India Institute of Medical Sciences in Delhi began using amniocentesis to determine foetus abnormalities, it found itself inundated with requests for abortion services as soon as the parents were told that the foetus was a girl.[57] In 1979 this test was introduced in Punjab on a commercial basis and since that time open advertisements in the newspapers and on roadsides have appeared increasingly in many regions. In 1986 a survey of gynaecologists revealed that 84% were performing amniocentesis, that most had begun to do so in the 1970s and that they performed an average of 270 amniocentesis tests per month for women, predominantly of the middle and lower classes.[58] Although amniocentesis tests were first conducted in government hospitals on an experimental basis, they became popular in the mid-1980s with ensuing abortions taking place in private clinics or private and government hospitals. According to conservative estimates based on six hospitals in Bombay, a research team found that ten women per day underwent the test in 1982 and that the demand was such that tests and abortions in

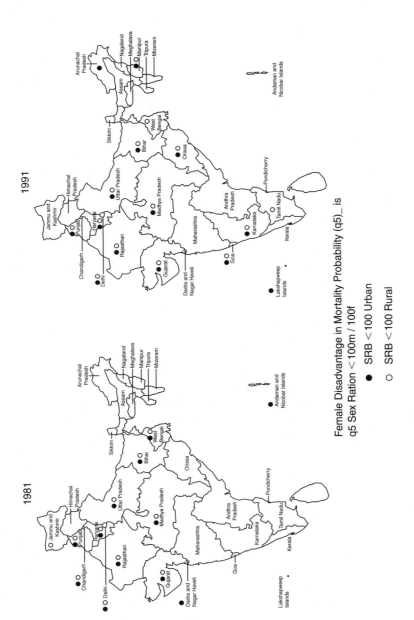

1981

1991

Female Disadvantage in Mortality Probability (q5)_ is
q5 Sex Ration < 100m / 100f

● SRB <100 Urban

○ SRB <100 Rural

Map 2.3 Spread of female disadvantage in mortality probability, India 1981–91

Source: S. Sudha and S.I. Rajan, 'Female disadvantage in India 1981–91', *Development and Change*, Vol. 30, No. 3, July 1999, p. 603.

hospitals and clinics had to be booked one month in advance.[59] An equivalent survey of several slum districts in Bombay showed that, of the many women who had undergone the test and found that the foetus was female, a high proportion had an abortion in the eighteenth and nineteenth weeks of their pregnancy.[60] One study in 1990 revealed that in Bombay, 7959 out of 8000 aborted foetuses were female, and in another city, Ludhiana, the sex ratio for hospital births and nursing-home births increased from 105 to 122 between 1981–88.[61] In one hospital in a city of Western India 430 out of 450 of medically tested foetuses were identified as female while not one of the 250 foetuses that had been identified as male was terminated.[62] Interviews in villages selected at random in two community development blocks on the outskirts of a town in Uttar Pradesh convinced three sociologists in the early 1980s that the clinical services offering sex-identification facilities which had appeared 10 years previously were now prevalent in all communities.[63]

In the 1980s several investigative reports were published in popular newspapers and magazines; one report that shocked many was featured in the *Times of India* in June 1983. It stated that 78,000 female foetuses were aborted after sex determination tests between 1978 and 1983.[64] In 1986 an article in the same paper revealed that almost all the 15,914 abortions conducted by a well-known abortion centre in Bombay in 1984–85 were undertaken after sex determination tests.[65] Between 1986–87 some 30,000 to 50,000 female foetuses were estimated to have been aborted. By 1987 the number of clinics for sex determination had risen from 10 in 1982 to 248, while between 1987 and 1988 13,000 sex determination tests were estimated to have been undertaken in seven Delhi clinics alone.[66] The increased interest and growing use of new techniques becomes apparent from the way these facilities came to be advertised in newspapers and pamphlets, in trains, buses and on city walls and roadside hoardings. Indeed, in 1989 Patel reported that the words ionography, foetoscopy, needling, chorionic biopsy (CVP) and amniocentosis had all become household words in urban India, with amniocentosis by far the most favoured technique in India, for determining the sex of the foetus. Also gaining in popularity were pre-planning gender determination techniques based on diet, centrifuging of chromosomes, drugs and vaginal jellies, in addition to more traditional methods deploying herbs and sacred beads which had long been administered in the hope of begetting boys. Patel claims that although Bombay and Delhi had become major centres for the deployment of new technologies, their open use had spread from the largest cities to clinics in the small towns of Gujarat, Uttar Pradesh, Bihar, Madhya Pradesh, Punjab, Tamil Nadu and Rajasthan where there has been 'a rush to abort female foetuses'. Indeed Patel argues that whereas infanticide might have been confined to certain regions, new sex identification facilities are now available and used in all districts.[67]

In the 1990s demographers began to argue that increasingly it is important to take into account sex ratios at birth as a factor contributing to the high masculinity rates in India as a whole. They speculated that although better health conditions and consequent falls in intra-uterine mortality may increase naturally the number of live male births, prenatal sex identification may newly skew sex ratios at birth.[68] In the absence of official figures for sex ratios at birth and of reliable statistics on sex ratios in abortions, it is only recently that there has been any interest in India in ascertaining or calculating sex ratios at birth. Using reported sex ratios among infants aged 0 to 1 year, as well as sex ratios of child mortality probabilities, to calculate sex ratios at birth, Sudha and Rajan show a stark shift towards excessively masculine sex ratios at birth between 1981 to 1991 from near normal to a range of 107 to 118 boys per 100 girls in urban areas and 99 to 117 in rural areas (see Table 2.17).[69] They speculate that ratios of less than 103 boys to 100 girls born are due to the numbers who die after birth and who are mostly boys and probably not enumerated, leading to uncommonly 'feminine' sex ratios at birth. They argue that the increasing masculinity and some very high sex ratios at birth in north and north-western states and in urban areas in some central states suggest the growing use of prenatal sex identification (see Map 2.4). However, they conclude that the numerical magnitude of its impact is not as great as it might be largely because it is unclear whether prenatal controls are additive or substitutive strategies. In the mid-1990s Monica Das Gupta and Mari Bhut referred to a consequent 'intensification' effect leading to fast-declining rates of female births,[70] but Sudha and Rajan are not yet so sure. They cite the example of a rapidly urbanising and changing rural area near New Delhi where local parents of the Jat community had an ideal family composition of two sons and one daughter and thus formed the clientele of the flourishing local sex identification clinics. Although in this case the community would show a total fertility rate of 3.0 and sex ratios at birth of 200 : 100, the subsequent infant or child mortality rates among their children no longer revealed female disadvantage.[71] How far the use of new sex identification techniques either supplements or substitutes for older methods of female infanticide and neglect remains to be seen. In the meantime, as in East Asia, this rising bias against females in India co-exists with greater economic development, a reduction in fertility and is aided and abetted by new technologies. Additionally, this rising bias is likely to be duplicated in the still poor countries of Bangladesh and Pakistan which, although displaying similar trends in son preference, have yet to experience the same rates of economic and technological development or, in the case of Pakistan, the same rate of fertility decline.

Bangladesh

Bangladesh is in the midst of a significant fertility decline in which the fertility rate has halved from 6.7 in 1960 to 3.2 in 1997, with a continuing

Table 2.17 Sex ratios at ages 0 + 1 and estimated sex ratios at birth, India 1981–91

State/region	1981 Sex ratio (m/f)				1991 Sex ratio (m/f)			
	Observed ratio 0 + 1		Estimated SRB		Observed ratio 0 + 1		Estimated SRB	
	Rural	Urban	Rural	Urban	Rural	Urban	Rural	Urban
India	103	104	103	104	106	108	106	108
North/Northwest								
Himachal Pradesh	105	105	105	105	108	113	109	114
Jammu and Kashmir	105	110	105	110	—	—	—	—
Punjab	107	108	105	107	117	119	117	118
Rajasthan	103	103	101	102	108	111	107	110
Haryana	109	107	108	106	114	117	113	116
Delhi (UT)	105	104	105	106	111	111	110	110
Chandigarh (UT)	112	103	111	107	110	109	110	109
Uttar Pradesh	104	102	103	102	107	109	106	108
Central								
Bihar	102	104	101	103	107	108	105	107
Madhya Pradesh	101	102	102	101	103	108	102	107
Gujarat	105	108	104	107	107	112	106	111
Maharashtra	102	101	106	105	103	108	106	109
Orissa	101	103	102	104	104	104	103	103
Goa	104	105	104	105	103	106	103	107
East/Northeast								
West Bengal	102	104	103	103	104	105	103	104
Assam	—	—	—	—	105	108	104	107
Mizoram	103	100	104	100	102	104	103	104
Nagaland	101	103	102	103	99	103	99	102
Meghalaya	102	104	102	104	101	103	101	103
Arunachal Pradesh	100	105	102	105	101	109	101	109
Tripura	105	104	106	104	104	104	104	104
Manipur	101	101	101	100	103	105	102	105
Sikkim	105	99	104	98	105	123	105	124
South								
Kerala	102	107	103	106	106	106	105	106
Andhra Pradesh	101	102	102	102	103	104	103	103
Tamil Nadu	103	102	104	101	105	105	105	105
Karnataka	102	104	103	104	105	105	105	105
Union territories								
Andamans	102	94	104	95	100	104	100	103
Lakshadweep	109	110	109	108	102	106	102	106
Dadra Nagar Haveli	98	100	99	103	101	94	101	101
Pondicherry	102	102	103	103	103	105	103	106

Note: Any value above 107 can be considered 'excessively' masculine. The census was not conducted in Assam in 1981, or in Jammu and Kashmir in 1991.

Original sources: Censuses of India 1981 (Government of India, 1988); and 1991 (Government of India 1991).

Source: S. Sudha and S. I. Rajan, 'Female disadvantage in India 1981–91; sex selective abortions and female infanticide', *Development and Change*, Vol. 30, No. 3, July 1999, p. 612.

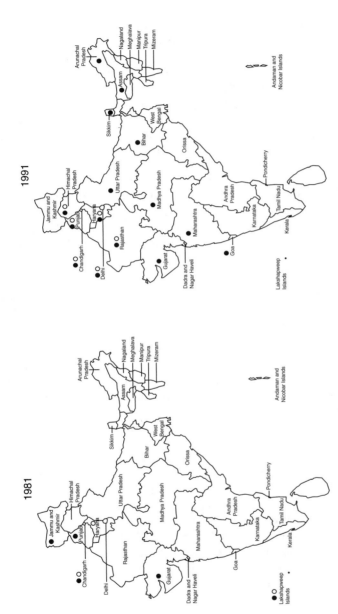

Map 2.4 Spread of 'masculine' sex ratio at birth, India 1981–91

Source: S. Sudha and S.I. Rajan, 'Female disadvantage in India 1981–91', *Development and Change*, Vol. 30, No. 3, July 1999, p. 606.

preference for at least one to two sons and a daughter.[1] Twenty-five years of complete and accurate population registration data for the Matlab District, a rural area 35 miles south of Dhaka, suggests that there is a clear preference for male children and that knowledge of modern contraceptive methods has been widespread since the 1980s, largely due to government-supported birth control programmes which have been in place since the 1960s. However, another study showed that although contraceptive use among married women increased steadily it was still as low as 18% in 1986.[2] Again, as in other East and South Asian societies, there is strong evidence that it is the gender composition of surviving children which influences contraception use. In the Matlab district, studies which examined the effects of fertility preferences and behaviour on contraception use between 1977 and 1988 all revealed that couples still clearly express a preference for several sons and one daughter. An early study in rural Bangladesh concluded that 90% of the women in the study could be classified as having a preference for sons with only 5% having a preference for a balanced gender composition, in that they also showed a desire for a daughter following several sons.[3] Bairagi and Langeston also observed in their study of 1986 that more than 98% of women desired at least one daughter following the birth of sons and that couples were more likely to stop childbearing if they had reached their preferred family size — normally composed of three to four surviving children made up of two to three sons and one daughter.[4] A more recent study of the effect of gender composition of surviving children on contraceptive use in the Matlab district showed that in four- and five-child families acceptance rates among couples with no surviving sons were 24 and 8% respectively. If families had one or more surviving sons, more than 50% of couples accepted contraception; in families with three or fewer children, contraceptive rates were consistently lower where there were no surviving sons; and in families of any size where there were no sons the proportion contracepting decreased.[5]

If contraception is deployed to limit births once preferred size and composition have been attained, it does little to influence sex ratios at birth, largely because couples continue to bear children until they have achieved a preferred or acceptable gender composition and only then cease childbearing. Thus sex ratios at birth in Bangladesh have fluctuated between 103.5 and 107 males to 100 females which is almost within the norm, and hence do not explain disparities in the sex ratios at later ages.[6] As for India, demographers have concluded that high mortality rates are due to the differential survival ratios among boys and girls in infancy and childhood. During the 1980s infant mortality declined in Bangladesh, although it was still in excess of 100 deaths per 1000 births in 1989.[7] Earlier studies of child nutrition had shown that, using height for age as a measure of chronic deprivation, a higher percentage of girls were severely or moderately under-nourished and stunted,[8] and that the nutrient intake relative to requirements was lower among female children.[9] Data from the Matlab district found that the most marked differences in survival occurred in the age group 1 to 4 years when female mortality exceeded male mortality by as much as 50%. During the first year of life when 12% of infants died there was no clear evidence of excessive female deaths, except at age 1 year when female deaths were some 50% higher than for males, while at age 2 years they were some 60 to 80% higher. In subsequent years through to 14 years of age female deaths were mostly higher than male deaths. The main causes of infant and child death were tetanus, respiratory diseases and diarrhoea and, in the age group 1 to 4 years, females had a 20–50% higher death rate than males for measles, respiratory diseases, for 'fever' and 'other' diseases.[10] However a number of subsequent studies analysing sex differential survival chances found that the risks to girls can be linked more directly to the gender configuration of their siblings.

When Mahuri and Preston examined the effect of gender composition of older siblings on the mortality of male and female children, they found abundant support for the premise that female child mortality is concentrated in families with more than one daughter.[11] Girls who have surviving older sister or sisters had higher death rates at each age than daughters without sisters, while there was only a mild hint of excess mortality among sons with older brothers. Their study shows the death rates of girls rise much more steeply with birth order than do the death rates of boys, which are largely unaffected by the presence of older siblings of either sex. That is, the average death rates of girls aged 0.5 to 5.0 years is 54.2% higher than for boys, for girls without older sisters it is 14.5% and for girls with older sisters it rises to 84.3%. Thus they conclude that 73% of excess female mortality is attributable to added disadvantage faced by girls with sisters. In life-table terms this means that 10.8% of girls with no older sisters who reached 0.5 years died before aged 5, while the corresponding figure for girls with older sisters is 15.8%. There was some discrimination against later-born boys but not until there were two older brothers, and then at only a fraction of the female equivalent rates. Boys with older sisters, like girls with two or more older brothers, showed unusually low mortality.[12] Such studies all conclude that selective neglect or discrimination against daughters is the most important determinant of excessive female infant and child mortality and the introduction of new interventionist technologies may well continue this trend and disadvantage daughters at an earlier age, thus contributing to rising sex ratios at birth and increasing numbers of 'missing girls'.

Pakistan

Pakistan society is also characterised by the high masculinity rates of its population,[1] but it has had a slower fertility decline, moving from a total fertility rate of 6.9 in 1960 to 5.8 in 1990 and 5.1 in 1997.[2] In 1993 Shah and Cleland concluded that recent trends in marital fertility for women aged between 20 and 49 years have remained fairly stable, largely due to desired family size and new pro-natalist attitudes. They suggest that there have been few changes in reproductive behaviour in recent years and that much of the reduced fertility is due to rising age of marriage rather than widespread awareness about contraception.[3] The country's first birth control programme was implemented in the early 1960s when a target-oriented programme initiated by the government attracted international endorsement and donor funding. However, the high-level cash programme faltered and there were no further serious campaigns until 1983–88 when the government adopted a much broader and more cautious strategy linking birth control programmes with health and women's welfare. At the time it was anticipated that the outcome of such programmes in Pakistan might bring the level of fertility down to an average of three to four births per woman, but most studies anticipated that the fertility rate was unlikely to decline much further, largely because of continuing son preference.[4]

There have been fewer demographic studies of Pakistan than other South Asian societies, but a national survey in 1968–69 analysed by Khan and Siragilden showed there to be a strong son preference on the part of both husbands and wives, and that it was the number of living sons which primarily influenced additional child bearing, although parents might also desire a daughter following a number of sons.[5] As in earlier studies,[6] more recent data confirms that son preference continues to be an important factor in the use of contraception and child survival ratios. For instance, the differential care rendered to sons and daughters is confirmed by survey data published in 1987 which showed that neonatal mortality of two girls born in succession was much higher than for combinations of boy-girl, girl-boy or of two boys.[7] A Pakistan Demographic and Health Survey of 1990–91 showed that for the women with no children, preference for daughters was negligible and that among those who had two daughters and no son 93% wanted their next child to be a son.[8] It is a fair guess that should there be further up-to-date studies similar to those conducted more recently in neighbouring South Asian societies, parallel demographic trends would emerge made up of a continuing demand for sons and perhaps one daughter, the rare deployment of contraception before the birth of a son or two sons, and higher female infant and child mortality rates with particular risks for second and later-born daughters who will be placed at greater risk by the introduction of new technologies.

For South and East Asia as a whole, recent research shows that although quite distinctive patterns of discrimination against girls are responsible for their high masculinity rates, the trends in each country are converging and resulting in overall and increasing excess of female mortality before birth, at birth and in infancy and childhood. While the statistics which reveal these common demographic trends speak eloquently at a societal level and illustrate demographic outcomes, the investigation and further understanding of this rising discrimination against daughters requires a shift from macro- to micro-studies, or from statistics to voices, to look at how populations and parents in particular talk about the beliefs and behaviours associated with daughter discrimination. If researchers look to demography for numbers or outcomes it is via ethnographies that they seek to identify the behaviours and beliefs which characterise the demographic process or narrative. Generally more familiar with words than numbers, anthropologists have long turned their ethnographic eye and ear to ascertain the varieties of perceptions, assumptions or norms that underlie economic, political and social trends. If ethnographic observations accord with demographic statistics, then a new status can be ascribed to ethnographic observation and case study as not merely anecdotal but as representative of growing and widespread trends. As ensuing chapters will show, when words are matched with numbers or processes with outcomes then the statistics are not a surprise and it is possible to arrive at an enhanced and multifaceted understanding of the process of daughter discrimination and its outcomes.

3   Ethnographic voices
Disappointing daughters

An extensive perusal of ethnographic field studies and personal narratives suggests that in the two largest societies of East and South Asia, China and India, there is a pervasive theme which punctuates everyday conversation, interview and life-cycle event or ritual and that is – that children are gendered. In both societies, among urban and rural, secluded and employed, literate and illiterate or rich and poor populations, differential characteristics and values attached to boys and girls are assumed, articulated and unquestioned, so that in daily practice girls and boys are categorised, welcomed and represented quite differently. In China, I had only to enter a household to observe the visible differences in the introduction of sons and daughters and the smiling response to the presence of sons by friends, neighbours and officials. In India, ethnographers Patricia and Roger Jeffery also found that sons were listed and introduced before daughters and that, whatever the topic of conversation, discussion spilled over into crucial differences between the characteristics and values of sons and daughters. In both countries the gendering of children is quite explicit in men and women's statements about conception, pregnancy, birth, infancy and childhood, and in their discussions of support in old age and at marriage and funeral ceremonies. In these discussions the significance attributed to sons contrasts with that accorded to daughters, who are frequently greeted with disappointment and almost always relegated to a secondary position. What the ethnographies cited in this chapter show is that in both China and India couples go to enormous lengths to have sons and, in the absence of sons, they may have many more children than they want. Alternatively they may defy government stricture or nature by taking radical measures against daughters during pregnancy, at birth or in infancy and childhood. Ethnographic observation and record confirm that conception is as much a cognitive as physical act and that, despite economic development, technological advance and women's movements for equality, the most important question before and during pregnancy and at birth is still the gender of the child. For the majority of girls born, their welcome into families and communities in China and India will be quite different from that accorded to their brothers.

China

'May you have many sons' has long been a common felicitation and references to sons or a son as 'the greatest of blessings' punctuate everyday language and ceremonial occasions, such as weddings. Customarily each generation has been exhorted anew to have a son and continue the family line, so that the greatest of unfilial acts has been the failure to produce a son and the most venomous of curses has been: 'May you die without sons'. Although such phrases are less likely to be openly articulated in present-day China, prestige and stature are still linked to sons and it is often said that the birth of a son causes a house 'to grow by three feet'. In contemporary China, with its stringent birth-control and single-child policies, the quest for sons has been magnified with the result that, in the absence of sons, the birth of a daughter not only remains a disappointment but more than ever before means a 'lost opportunity' for a son.

What impresses observers and ethnographers alike is the open enjoyment and privileging of children but, how often in speech, gesture and ritual, it is sons who are welcomed and especially valued, so that daughters by overt or open implication come to be either directly devalued or deemed a disappointment. In field investigations, children are rarely referred to as a collective ungendered category; rather they are divided by gender with sons and daughters identified and presented in quite different ways. In my own field work in Chinese villages in many different provinces over the past 25 years, one of my most pervasive observations has been the contrasting status openly accorded to sons and daughters within the family, so that even the ways in which they are introduced constituted both a measure of the secondariness of daughters and a message for those daughters that was unmistakeably clear.[1] Although it was once the custom for rural families to count only their sons, it is no longer the practice to reckon daughters of so little account that they are omitted from tallied lists of family members. However, in hundreds of households interviewed over many years sons have been enumerated and/or presented before daughters whatever the birth order. How many times have I sat in rural and urban households where the smiles gradually broadened and the cheer heightened among both family and visitors as more than one son was introduced. Many sons have been cause for congratulations and a sequence of only daughters occasion for commiseration. The only time that I can remember when a son was not listed first he had been adopted, and it was only this unique reversal of order in presentation that had alerted me to question further.

Wishing for a son

If son preference and privilege has continued to be openly expressed in everyday practice, it is also evident at significant life-cycle and ceremonial moments of birth, marriage and death. From the marriage ceremony and celebrations until the first birth of a son there are felicitations and rituals which reflect age-old dreams of sons and grandsons. During the marriage ceremony itself there are references to procreation in the hope that the couple will bear a son — or two — to continue the family line or, as it used to be said, 'continue the incense smoke at the ancestral shrine'. The bride and groom are openly wished 'blessings' and 'posterity', both euphemisms for sons, and fertility symbols such as ripe rice are timely reminders to the bride and groom, should they need it, that it is the common expectation in both rural and urban China that a birth will closely follow, preferably within the first year of marriage. Thereafter there are many social practices and rituals performed in the hope of obtaining sons and celebrating their arrival into the world. In one of my most recent field experiences in 1998, I visited a newly married household of a young professional and wealthy couple in a rich Shandong county city. There the bedroom was adorned with a wall-sized photograph of their infant nephew facing the marital bed, while beside the bed was a smaller photograph of the same baby boy with legs splayed emphasising his 'maleness'. After marriage a new bride is likely to be watched and wondered at, and this period of 'waiting' is frequently accompanied by a degree of anxiety and pressure. Indeed the new bride has only to look around her to see the fate of the childless or sonless who, avoided at weddings, are represented as objects of sadness and pity by kin and neighbours. It is often said that 'if you have no son you will be pitiful'.[2]

In one village in northern Guandong province recently studied by a graduate student of mine from Hong Kong, it was the plight of sonless 80-year old Grandma Xiao which constituted a perpetual and timely reminder to all in the village of the misery of old age in the absence of sons. Recently when she had fallen and broken her bones the villagers were reminded once again of that age-old lesson.

> If we don't have a son, we will be very sad in our old age. The state won't take care of our livelihood. Do you know Grandma Xiao? Her experience shows us that having your own son is very important. Although she adopted a son, the son isn't her own. Last time while she was hurt, he didn't come to visit her. I don't want to follow in her footsteps.[3]

They contrasted her plight with that of fellow-villager Granduncle Liu who, when he died aged 75 years, had an elaborate funeral at which the attendance of four sons and four grandsons had reminded the villagers once again of the importance of having descendants:

What is the greatest blessing of Grandpa Liu! Full of posterity.
Luckily he has so many sons and daughters. If not, how can they afford the large expenditure? Nowadays, it isn't easy to pay for a death.

Granduncle Liu's funeral was so lively. Now every family only has two children. I wonder if the funeral can be done like that.
Sons are the greatest blessing of Granduncle! If there were no sons, who
can handle all these things for him.[4]

Another funeral in the same village at which the weeping was not for the
father but for a son also reminded the villagers of the vulnerability of
having just one son and losing the potential for more. When Brother
Hua's 2-year younger son died of asthma and the parents were heard
'crying for a son', all the villagers shook their head and heaved a collective
sigh.

What a pity! I think Hua must be very sad. He loved this son more
than anyone else. You know, today everyone can only have two children. Nobody can afford to lose one. A son is as precious as a heart.

Other villagers reflected the prevailing village view that 'the saddest thing
is that Hua's wife has been sterilised after she had a second birth.

I think after Hua's case, nobody will be so foolish as to accept sterilisation just after a second birth. The government never considers the difficulty of the peasant. How can a castrated cat still give birth?[5]

The ethnographer Marjorie Wolf also noted the pity reserved for those
without sons. To her a 30-year old woman said: 'No sons is bad. There is
nobody to take care of them when they are sick. Nobody to bring them
food or boil water for them. That is a bad thing.' Another woman also
young shook her head and muttered: 'Nobody to see them to the moun-
tain [a euphemism for a proper funeral].'[6] These sentiments were not
confined to rural villages. One young woman working in a city factory who
did not conceive directly after marriage found herself to be the subject of
intense speculation and innuendo suggesting that she was being punished
for having been promiscuous before marriage. Quickly she felt herself to
have been looked down upon and labelled 'an inferior person'.

A hen can lay eggs when it is the right time. A woman who can't give
birth after she gets married is not even as good as a chicken. A person
with no sons or grandsons — what has she got to be so proud about?[7]

It is still true today that if there is no imminent sign of pregnancy then
marriage can be followed by a period marked by pressure and anxiety.
The prayers offered to Guanyin, Goddess of Women, at any temple testify
to the rising fears and desperation of women who have difficulty in
becoming pregnant. It is the view of several ethnographers that such
watching and waiting, and the accompanying pressure and innuendo, are

such that it is a cause for some wonder that the young couple conceive at all!

During pregnancy there may be many consultations and prayers in the quest for auspicious signs that the outcome will be the birth of a boy. There is evidence to suggest that the exacerbated wish for a son within smaller families has resulted in the open use of traditional methods for identifying, if not influencing, the sex of the foetus. Some couples use a sex prediction table that purports to indicate the sex of the unborn child according to the timing of conception, others consult the gods or more worldly fortune tellers, while others rely on the intake of herbal medicines to guarantee a son.

> Because of my desire to have a son when my wife became pregnant last February I asked someone to consult a 'sex prediction chart'. In addition a child who had just learned to talk wished me luck and I engaged in several other superstitious activities. All of these indicated that my wife would bear a son. My wife even dreamed that she gave birth to a son. So I believed that it was almost certain that we would have a son, and I was extremely busy. Everyday I brought her special food, and I did not let her do any work. I even went to Shenyang, especially to buy 700 eggs for her to eat during the first month after delivery.[8]

Others relied on diet to guarantee a child's sex. As a young woman from north Anhui with two daughters said: 'If you require me to go three days without eating I'll do that to have a son'[9]

Another young woman who does not yet have any children recently described the elaborate dieting measures taken by some women to have a son:

> Pay attention to diet. If you eat different things you will have a child of a different sex — you can even change the sex of the foetus. If you eat iron chain and white chicken together you will have a son. The chicken shouldn't come from your husband, you must find it yourself. You should eat it alone without anyone seeing you. That you are doing so should not be known to anyone. When you are pregnant, you should let people look at your shape to tell if you have a boy or girl. If you want to decide the sex of the foetus, you need to think about what sex you want. Someone who has a son will then get sterilised. But if you have a daughter you won't get used to it. One woman went to see a fortune-teller after her second pregnancy. The fortune-teller asked: 'How old are you and when did you get pregnant?' The fortune-teller said it was a girl. But when she aborted it, it was a boy. If you have a daughter as a second birth, you must have a sterilisation, so that is your last chance.[10]

As more stringent birth control programmes, including the one- or two-child rule, have become more widespread, research has suggested that there has been an increase in anxiety during pregnancy and a correlative increase in intervention before birth.[11] For example in Zhejiang province, recent field work by Chinese ethnographers showed that those couples who already had a girl and were permitted to have a second birth wished so strongly to have a son that some women privately made every effort to have the sex of the foetus identified and underwent an abortion if it was found to be female. Even in group discussions, the villagers admitted that many were driven by the desire for a boy and have secret ultrasound examinations, with an estimated 80% of those carrying a girl in their second pregnancy having an abortion.[12] In similar investigations in north Anhui, focus groups also discussed the lengths women would go to have a son by using ultrasound machines to determine the sex of the foetus and having a sex-selective abortion, even though it is illegal.

> People use an ultrasound B machine. If it is a female foetus, they don't want it. People will usually go elsewhere to check — for example, in Henan province. No matter how much money they have to spend, they think it is worth it.[13]

Welcoming a son

With more stringent birth control programmes it is not surprising to find that there is an increasing disappointment upon the birth of a daughter, especially if it is the only or final birth permitted. There is much historical evidence that it was a normal occurrence for daughters to be welcomed into the world with less ceremony and pleasure than sons, and several literary sources contrast the age-old differences in the births of sons and daughters. It is not always true, in the much-quoted ancient words of the poet Fu Xuan, that 'no one is glad when a girl is born and by her the family sets no store',[13] but *The Book of Poetry*, one of the richest and most authentic source materials depicting social life in ancient China, did record the unequal treatment likely to be accorded to sons and daughters from the moment of birth:

> When a son is born
> Let him sleep on the bed,
> Clothe him with fine clothes
> And give him jade to play with
> How lovely his cry is!
> May he grow up to wear crimson
> And be the lord of the clan and the tribe.

When a girl is born,
Let her sleep on the ground.
Wrap her in common wrappings,
And give her broken tiles for playthings.
May she have no faults, no merit of her own
May she well attend to food and wine
And bring no discredit to her parents.[14]

There is much ethnographic evidence in the late twentieth century that such attitudes have persisted and there is now an equivalent poem which suggests that, although many centuries and changes have intervened, the birth of a daughter is still less welcome than that of a boy:

Times have changed
Men and women are equal
Then why in a certain family
Do they respect boys and look down on girls?
If a baby boy is born the mother is happy
If a baby girl is born she does not like it.[15]

In China today contemporary ethnographic research and literature also suggests that, while a girl is still welcomed into the family, community and society with fewer expectations and less ceremony than a boy, this is not necessarily the case for all daughters. Where a two-child family is permitted, a first-born daughter may be tolerated or even welcomed and, conversely, where a son is first-born then a second-born daughter may be welcomed or even desired. The ideal gender composition for most parents is a son and a daughter. Just as the word for 'good' (hao) is made up of characters for male and female, most of the sex preferences expressed by parents, whatever the composition of their own family and however stringent the birth control policy, are made up of two children comprising a boy and a girl or two sons. In my own case I experienced at first hand a sequence of responses: pity because I was voluntarily childless following my decision to continue working for nearly 10 years after an early marriage, shared joy at my first-born son, and openly expressed envy upon the subsequent birth of my daughter.

Much pity is reserved for those who give birth to successive daughters. Margery Wolf writes that in traditional China, the birth of a daughter was a disappointment, the birth of a second daughter brought grief and perhaps death of the infant, while the birth of a third daughter was a tragedy for which the mother was most assuredly blamed.[16] Again a poem published in 1997 expressed a sentiment that was not so very different:

One year after my marriage
I was going to give birth

Haven't experienced the happiness of new marriage,
My eldest daughter came into the world.
The whole family was content,
I too happily took care of her.
When she was one year and a half,
I got the second daughter in 1985,
But her father disliked her,
Because he longed for a boy.
At once he left home to work outside,
Nobody cared for me when I was confined.
I was in tears all day long,
which were as bitter as medicine.
Times flies so fast. . .
And finally I gave birth to my third child.
This time it was a boy,
The father was filled with happiness.[17]

What is clear is that in much of China the introduction of stringent birth control policies and in particular the one- or two-child policy has escalated the differential value attached to sons and daughters. Whereas before the 1980s village voices made it quite clear that birth control was not considered to be a viable option until after the birth of a son, now the ceilings on numbers of children meant that both the quest or struggle for a son has been magnified and that the birth of a daughter is not only still a disappointment but also 'an opportunity lost' to try for and bear that desired son.

In China there are fewer first-hand accounts of birthing culture compared to India, where several ethnographers have been present at births or reported verbatim the conversations and first-hand responses of new mothers, their female kin and the midwives. Nevertheless there is sufficient indirect evidence to suggest that a girl is still born into the family, community and society with fewer expectations and less ceremony than a boy. In conversation, urban friends have often told me that the birth of a daughter is more subdued compared to the greater excitement surrounding the birth of a son, and that this joy is magnified now that normally only one child is permited in the cities. In my own conversations over the years with mothers and grandmothers of new-born sons in hospital obstetric wards, it has been noticeable that the smile is wider, the 'voices' are lighter and the decoration of the cribs sometimes more colourful and elaborate. In circumstances where son preference is deemed politically incorrect, a wider and broader smile, laughter and congratulations assume greater significance and such signs have assumed a quasi-official status. During ultrasound and amniocentesis when it is illegal to provide information on the sex of the foetus, a smile has become the accepted sign that the unborn child is a boy. In some circumstances the disappointment or ambivalent response to the birth of a girl may be such that it leads to rejection, abandonment or violence, and in extreme cases infanticide.

Although the statistics reveal such cases it is difficult to investigate these in the field; in my own field experience I have no direct acquaintance with households where there has been any known violence against daughters or their mothers. However, my own field experience does show that there may be lesser forms of discrimination against daughters; these may not be unusual for there have been many such reports in China's media. In the early 1980s, the nation-wide survey conducted by the Women's Federation suggested that there might be a whole range of less tangible but nonetheless serious forms of physical discrimination against female infants and girls which would never be reflected in any statistics on mortality.[18] These largely had to do with lesser celebrations and care evident in patterns of ritual and practical behaviour surrounding the birth of the female child. In my own studies in two rural communes on the outskirts of Beijing in 1983, a series of local surveys undertaken by the Women's Federation there revealed that, although there had been no cases of female infanticide or untoward maternal deaths, a strong preference for sons still existed and was sometimes explicitly reflected in patterns of behaviour surrounding the birth of the first child. The birth of a son might be the occasion of much rejoicing by parents and their kin with the mother enjoying special foods and the son the focus of celebrations and feasting. In contrast, there were occasions when disappointed relatives had precipitately left the hospital on hearing that the infant was a girl, so that there were neither celebrations nor special foods. Grandparents were reported to be particularly likely to show their disappointment and there had been instances in one commune where the grandmother had taken a little time to be reconciled sufficiently to order milk for her baby granddaughter and special foods for the mother. There had followed a period of depression or deterioration in family relations, especially those between mother-in-law and daughter-in-law, once it was known that the first-born was a daughter.[19]

In one of Beijing's suburban communes I have visited, the worst case of prejudice against the mother of an infant girl uncovered by the Federation concerned a typist in the commune office. While she had been pregnant, a fortune teller had predicted the baby would be a boy and expectations surrounding the birth were high. However, once a girl was born, relations between the infant's mother and disappointed mother-in-law, who felt extremely let down, rapidly deteriorated. As the single-child family policy was stringently applied, it was not uncommon for the birth of a daughter to give rise to open tension within a family by setting husband against wife and mother-in-law against daughter-in-law. Disappointment and tension generated by the birth of a daughter were not confined to the countryside and were reported to exist also among city workers and cadres' families for whom the one-child rule was more rigidly applied. In the delivery room of a large city hospital in the north-east of China, there were instances reported where parents refused to accept that they had given birth to a daughter so convinced were they that the hospital had made a mistake; where husbands were said to have fainted with worry prior to the birth so anxious were they about the sex of their first-born; where voluntary abortions took place on the mistaken advice of the fortune-teller that the expected baby was a girl and where mothers were verbally abused on the birth of their daughters.[20] At another hospital, the degree of post-partum complications were found to be significantly higher among mothers of daughters and this was attributed to their fall in spirits immediately after a disappointing birth.[21] There have also been periodic newspaper reports of more extreme disappointment spilling over into rejection or abandonment of daughters and the mothers of daughters. In one case a new-born girl was left in a hospital by her family so convinced were they that the mother had given birth to a son and that the baby must have been stolen and replaced by a girl.[22] One young man who ardently desired a son reported his reactions to the birth of a daughter.

> The day my wife was to give birth I waited at the hospital, and did not eat a thing, looking forward to the good news. Finally a nurse came and told me: 'It's a girl.' At that moment my heart throbbed and I almost fainted. Finally I reeled out of hospital. From the time my wife gave birth to a daughter, I felt increasingly disgusted with her. I didn't return home after work. Either I would stay at the unit and play poker or checkers, or I would hang out on the street. I did not really want to see mother or daughter.[23]

There are numbers of similar stories where disappointment has turned into threats of abandonment or violence against wives. One young man in a large city in north-east China reported how he had told his pregnant wife that if she had a son she could stop working, but that if she had a daughter he did not want to continue with the marriage and would abandon her. The woman was beaten and encouraged to commit suicide by her husband, his brother and mother-in-law. When her appeals to various law enforcement authorities were of no avail, the wife did indeed kill herself and only then were the husband and brother arrested.[24] In another case reported in Shanghai suburbs, a woman threw her 9-day-old girl out of the hospital window. She had been convinced by a fortune-teller that she was going to have a boy. Although her husband's family had not said anything about a particular preference for a son, she had suffered greatly from the whispers of other people in the ward 'where she was the only one to bear a girl'.[25] In another case, a woman wrote to the news-papers to complain about her husband's domestic violence which had worsened following the birth of their daughter.

In the first month he cursed me, but this was still not enough to vent his feelings. Less than 50 days after I gave birth, he kicked my leg and injured it. His dog was more important to him than were either myself or our daughter.[26]

As in other societies in Asia, domestic violence is only now becoming a topic that is openly discussed in China, but in the case of violent responses to daughters and mothers of daughters it has been rare for the government not to intervene once violence is suspected. The press has repeatedly cited cases where cadres have helped husbands, brothers and mother-in-law to see the error of their discriminating ways.

Rural demands

Perhaps the most significant evidence suggesting that son preference remains extremely strong are the lengths to which rural parents are prepared to go to when the opportunity to have a son is threatened or denied by stringent birth control policies, including the one- or two-child rule. Even in suburban regions subjected to strict rules, my own field work in the 1980s suggested that the single-child policy was particularly difficult to implement where the single birth had been that of a daughter. Local birth control officials had to visit such couples many times before they could be persuaded to accept a one-child certificate; many refused despite considerable pressure and nearly all those who proceeded to a second birth were those who were determined to have a son because the first-born had been a girl. Many demanded the right to have a son and preferred to pay the consequent fines, which could be hefty, rather than forgo the opportunity to have a son. Perhaps there is no greater testimony to the strength of continuing son preference in China than the significant concessions modifying the national single-child policy in 1983 to permit rural couples who had a first-born daughter to proceed to have a second child after a suitable interval, so that by the 1990s there was a de facto two-child policy in China's countryside.[27]

From a southern Guangdong village, Jack and Sulamith Potter reported in some detail how birth control policies had been formally modified to take account of the demand for sons.[28] Here the ways in which local administrative officials modified national or provincial policy is instructive. In Guangdong province as a whole the rules permitted two children if the first was a girl and recommended sterilisation to ensure that the limit of two children was held. This meant that if a wife became pregnant for a third time then she was to have an abortion followed by the sterilisation of one member of the couple. However, within the province, county and commune, administrative officials allowed greater latitude by permitting couples to have two children, even if the first was a son, and thereafter policing the limits through sterilisation. At the village level the policy formulated made further concessions to son preference by permitting couples with two daughters, who would otherwise have fallen into the category to be sterilised, to have a third child in order to try once more for a son, although they had to pay a fine. Local birth control officials felt that their ability to implement any birth control policy depended upon their accommodating familial demands for a son. Despite these concessions, the villagers still opposed the policy of sterilisation because of their fears for the survival of a single son. Hence from 1985 the rules were again adjusted to permit couples with two children, at least one of whom was a son, to use contraception rather than undergo sterilisation. However, if the wife became pregnant again, the pregnancy would be ended and either the husband or wife would have to be sterilised. Couples with two daughters could try again for a son if they were willing to pay a fine; if the third child was a daughter, the couple could try once more, but the husband would have to agree to a vasectomy whatever the sex of the fourth child. Thus by the mid-1980s it was openly recognised at local levels that the one-child policy was only practicable if the demand for a son was accommodated. In another village located in central Shanxi, which was studied by one of my postgraduate students from Beijing, there was evidence of some demographic change in that fewer children had been born, but it was still the case that there were no couples who did not have a son, even if they had two or three children. Here again the villagers would only comply with the birth control policy if they had at least one son among their two to three children, so that only if the birth order of two-child families was female-male, male-male or male-female would they take birth control measures and have no additional children. Among the four couples under the age of 40 years who had three children, three had the same birth pattern of female-female-male.[29]

One recent study conducted in southern Jiangsu and northern Anhui provinces included a number of focus-group discussions which showed that villagers were not averse to fewer children, but that they still desired sons and discriminated against daughters.[30] Patterns of child gender composition here too indicate that couples still continue childbearing until they have a son. For those with one child, the sex of that child was more likely to be male than female and couples with two children were least likely to have two daughters. Parents with one son were demonstrably happier than those with one daughter, those with two daughters were the least satisfied while the most satisfied parents were those who had one son and one daughter. The attitudes expressed by young women who had yet to bear children shows that there is little likelihood of attitudes changing towards son preference in the near future. The response of one newly married 25-year-old woman with no children shows the ambivalence and ambiguity of contemporary statements about boys and girls.

If I don't get a son, I will consider that my fate is bad. After all, boys or girls are the same. I am a graduate of senior high school, but I still think boys are better. Of course, if I have a daughter, I will love her. At home, my mother and grandmother think it's bad to have a daughter. Most people think if you have no son, you will still want another. If you only have a daughter at home, you are considered incapable. That is stupid, but people in villages think that way.

Two young women who did not have children noted that a son is necessary for social status and that women with two daughters are particularly pitied in local communities.

If you have no son, you have missed something in your life. You didn't accomplish something.

To have a high status in the community, you need a son. Otherwise you are looked down upon in the family and community. Especially women with two daughters. There is very much discrimination against these kinds of women by the mother-in-law and the family. They live miserable lives, especially if they are sterilised. Then there is no more hope. You terminated your family line.

Some women anticipated that they would be treated badly by parents-in-law and husbands if they did not bear sons, even though they are protected by law. A woman aged 25 feared that 'without sons, your husband will dislike you and you will have low status'. She also feared that she might have a handicapped son, which would be bad enough, although the belief that even nine daughters were not equivalent to one crippled son was still prevalent in the village.

Again, a lengthy study of one small village in northern Guangdong province by my student in the 1990s shows the lengths and ingenuity of villagers in their 'often brave struggle' to have a son.[31] In common with most rural regions 'two but not three' children were now permitted in this small village of 45 households in which there were ten households without sons who were openly circumventing birth control policies. One woman with two daughters refused sterilisation and had to leave the village hurriedly to escape pressure to have an abortion when pregnant for the third time. She was rescued by a temple monk and helped to her father's home village where, along with three other women hiding from birth control officials, she awaited the birth of her third child. Fortunately, she gave birth to a son; she then returned to the village where she came under pressure to pay a hefty fine and had to distribute her belongings to other villagers to protect them from confiscation. Although she was subsequently sterilised and her son became the object of some discrimination, she was satisfied because she now had a son. Another woman, who had five daughters before she gave birth to a much desired son, repeatedly had to avoid a fine and pressure to have an abortion by hiding in other village homes. Despite the help of her fellow villagers she had lost most of her valuable household furnishings, including a clock, furniture and other properties. To bring up her son in peace she had 'given' three of her daughters to her own mother to raise in her household. Another woman in the village who had borne a son after two daughters had also hidden in her father's house and left a second daughter to live with her mother. A couple with two daughters had a son despite tremendous 'trouble' — their label for the pressure to have an abortion that she had endured during her third pregnancy. After the birth, a large fine had been paid with the help of overseas relatives, their television, furniture, bicycle and other property had been confiscated and their son had not been able to enter primary school easily. A woman with a daughter gave birth shortly afterwards to a son but not without previously hiding herself to avoid an enforced abortion. Afterwards they lost the family bed, furniture, stove and kitchen range because they were too poor to pay a fine and she had to submit herself to an enforced sterilisation. Although there was a de facto two-child policy in the village, most of those who had subsequently suffered fines and sterilisation were those who had embarked on a second or third pregnancy within the permitted four-year gap between births. They took enormous risks to satisfy their demand for a first or second son following the birth of daughters who now, in the minds of the parents, had come to symbolise 'a lost opportunity to have a son'.[32]

What is also interesting about this ethnographic account is the degree to which fellow villagers supported their quest, not just verbally by openly acknowledging the importance of sons, but by actively aiding in escapes, hiding pregnant women and looking after threatened property at times when such actions were extremely risky and could result in a heavy penalty. The villagers also aided and abetted in the hiding of couples or women from other villages who were in similar circumstances. One couple had come to stay with the pregnant wife's sister to give birth to a third child following two daughters. They had removed the IUD device themselves and had escaped from another province to this Guangdong village, where they had received much assistance, including a room and a piece of land from other sympathetic villagers, some of whom had been through a similar experience elsewhere. Despite strictures and periodic government check-ups nobody had reported their presence.[33] After an officious start and in the face of such opposition and determination, the village officials had felt that they had no choice but to modify their responses to the policy by becoming more tolerant of demands for a son. By the 1990s, local birth control officials were quite unwilling or unable to apply pressure in favour of abortion or sterilisation or openly implement the compulsory fines or confiscate property:

At ordinary times, it is impossible to employ coercive measures. How can we catch the people based on our own effort?[34]

In practice they only did so when there was a 'high tide' or birth control campaign marked by the presence of higher administrative officials or the police in the village and they felt they had no choice. Indeed, the local cadres were well aware of the tactics of the villagers to avoid detection and in practice or 'in ordinary times', the fine had become the only penalty. It was said in the village that local officials had learned to collude with their fellow villagers by keeping 'one eye open and one eye closed'.

> She [one local birth control official] had been damned to tears by the villagers. Having learned a lesson, she had become much cleverer and seldom carried out coercive practices on birth control. Now she has 'one eye open and one eye closed' in implementing the birth control policy.[35]

The village family planning officials, knowing that pregnant women hid themselves and their belongings, and in a bid to avoid clashes with the villagers and to escape punishment themselves, had adopted the strategies of under-reporting and mis-reporting numbers of births in their villages.

From my own observations, and the ethnographic accounts of others, these patterns are repeated throughout many of China's villages. I have been in some villages where there has been every sign of an active birth control policy and in others where there are young parents with two, three or four children in the interests of obtaining a son. The 'single-child policy' has effectively become 'a single-son policy'; although this transition has eased the pressure on first-born, daughters it has brought more pressure to bear on the outcome of second births where couples are likely to resort to more extreme practices such as sex-selective abortion or infanticide. In the face of such a response, the modification of the policy represents a tacit but open recognition by China's government that the demand for a son is still the main familial concern of villagers. It is one of the most visible cases where an important state policy in China has been modified in recognition of the wishes and demands of the rural population. At the same time these policy modifications do reinforce beliefs and assumptions about son preference and continue to designate the birth of a daughter as a 'lesser' or 'secondary' birth. If the government felt it had no choice but to subscribe to this demand for sons in the countryside, it has been less willing to make such modifications in the cities. In urban areas, where there has not been the same modifications to the one-child policy, the rules have been successively tightened to reduce the number of circumstances within which a couple might have a second birth. Although couples have had to be satisfied with an only daughter, and indeed many have done so with grace, there is still a legacy of son preference, even if it is not always articulated directly and openly.

Urban preference

In the cities parents speak of their ideal family as made up of two children including a girl and boy, but since only one child is permitted, some express a clear preference for a son while others show an increasing acceptance of a one-daughter family. In the largest cities the opportunities for having a son have been severely limited since 1980 and in the early years of the policy it was not easy to convince parents of a single daughter that they should not continue child-bearing in the hope of a son. In Beijing, for example, the single-child policy initially was introduced alongside a number of incentives and disincentives aimed at increasing the number of one-child families and reducing the number of third children. However, by the end of 1982 a new set of regulations had tightened the policy by permitting a second birth in certain specified sets of conditions: where the health of the first child was weak, the parents were themselves only children, the husband resided in the wife's household, only one brother was fertile, and in certain very poor mountainous regions of Beijing municipality. No other second or higher order pregnancies were permitted to proceed to term and, if they did, they were to be termed 'out-of-plan' births and the parents penalised.

When I carried out the field interviews with birth control officials in Beijing and its environs in 1983 there was no question that young couples still desired two children and preferably a boy and a girl. The most difficult households to persuade to sign a single-child family certificate were those where the one child was a daughter. Without exception birth control officials in the residential lanes, factories and suburbs of Beijing and its environs thought that the most difficult phase of their work had occurred in the first year (between 1979 and 1980), when couples who had only recently begun to accept the two-child limit were suddenly asked to be content with one child, whether it was a boy or a girl. More than a third of the population had refused to sign the certificate, mainly because they wanted a second child or more specifically a son. The birth of an only daughter caused anxiety and fears about the future of the family which were not easily allayed. Again the main problem facing birth control officials was how to persuade or convince those whose first child had been a girl to abide by the policy. The parents of daughters took longer to sign the certificate and accept contraceptives, while grandparents were often especially adamant in their desire for a second child and above all a boy.[36] Although birth control officials in one large state factory I visited thought that there was less son preference in Beijing, newspapers at the same time reported prejudice against daughters and cited a case in this very same factory.[37] There have been a number of legal cases in which male workers have beaten their wives, maltreated infant daughters, and subsequently deserted and refused to maintain them because of their fury at the birth of a daughter, but from the early 1980s onwards young couples have approached their first birth as if it was also their last. Some were accepting while others, as the figures of the previous chapter suggest, intervened and took action to ensure that they had a son.

Ten years later, in the early 1990s, Cecilia Milwertz undertook detailed field work and interviewed urban mothers and birth control officials in Beijing and a large city in northeast China. She concluded that in these cities it was now possible to speak of 'son preference' rather than 'son requirement', in that there was less urgency for a son but still some ambivalence surrounding the birth of a daughter.[38] In Beijing she found that upwards of 60 to 70% still preferred to have two children with the combination of a boy and a girl viewed as the ideal by a majority of women.[39] As to son preference she found there to be a range of opinions but was surprised at how many spoke openly of their preference for a son while others resorted to ambiguous expressions.

To give birth to a boy or girl is equal but to give birth to a boy is best.[40]

A girl is her mother's cotton padded winter overcoat, a boy is his mother's down jacket.[41]

Some stated their preference in terms of familial expectations of husbands or parents-in-law, thus expressing an opinion but attributing it to another. As one woman said: 'I hoped for a girl. My husband hoped for a boy. I think most men want a son.'[42] A young Beijing woman whose husband is an only child similarly ruminated: 'I have a good relationship with my husband, so I feel I ought to give birth to a son for him. My mother-in-law wants a grandson. To me it does not matter whether I give birth to a boy or a girl.'[43] Others referred to a distinction between their 'thoughts' (sixiang) in which the gender was of no consequence, and their feelings or literally 'in the heart' (xinli) desires for a son. Cecilia Milwertz concluded from her very nuanced field work that, while the number of single children is a measure of acceptance of the one-child policy, the politically-correct responses did not reflect or measure heart-felt preferences for two children including a son which urban couples quite self-consciously were determined to set aside in order to act politically and correctly. Despite these 'heart-felt' preferences there are now fewer overt problems in implementing a single-child policy in the cities and, according to one birth control official in Beijing, any resistance encountered in city districts is usually related to either the older generation insisting on having a grandson to carry on the family line or to second marriages when one partner already has a child. There is some indirect evidence that grandparents may refuse to accept a granddaughter and there were examples of grandsons being excessively pampered, but Milwertz found that about half of the women interviewed who gave birth to daughters did not feel undue pressure or that their status as wife or daughter-in-law in the family was compromised in any way.[44] Her impression was confirmed by my own field investigations in rich provincial cities in 1998 which also suggested that there was a growing acceptance of daughter-only families. They may not be so sanguine during or in anticipation of economic crises and it is not always the case outside the largest cities where urban and rural parents were not just more open about son preference but they may also act to disadvantage the daughters born.

Daughter neglect

There are no contemporary ethnographic observations documenting neonatal violence or infanticide, although reports and hearsay relate some disagreement between parents as to whether their daughter should be abandoned, adopted-out or neglected — a disagreement which has only been resolved by their subsequent decision to officially register the infant. Indeed, the act of birth registration is usually a signal that parents have arrived at a decision to accept and rear their daughter themselves, although the figures for rising female infant and child mortality suggest, alongside other evidence, that a daughter's survival and well-being cannot be assumed. For many years I have suspected that the well-documented disadvantaged access of rural girls to schools may well be reproduced in their differential access to health care and medical facilities. However, health workers in urban and rural health clinics and hospitals, when questioned over many years, have been very persuasive in arguing that there were few gender differences in nutritional intake, disease profiles, access to hospital treatment and general parental care. At the most they thought that there might be a slight but not significant difference between the care received by sons and daughters in that boys, sometimes referred to as 'big boys' or 'big happinesses', might be brought more often to the hospital. However, most were adamant that all children were valuable to their parents and there was no difference in their care, especially now that there were fewer children born in each household. They argued, quite rightly, that immunisation and routine child health checks had improved the health of all children by uncovering a significant number of cases of anaemia, rickets and malnutrition which were not gender-specific, but they were less justified in concluding that any remaining son preference was not translated into female neglect. For instance, more recent field investigations have cast doubt on the assumption that there is no gender difference in access to health services.

Several studies, published in the mid-1990s but based on data on child mortality a decade earlier, showed that there has been higher than expected female child mortality in China. Subsequent research in southwest Yunnan province also showed that girls were less likely to receive medical treatment and were more likely to die at home or on the way to hospital.[45] In my own field study of clinic and hospital admissions in Shandong province in 1998 there were noticeably more boys than girls in clinics and hospitals, sometimes higher by 40 to 60%. In one county-level hospital, where records were consulted for the previous 3 months, there had been 260 child in-patients made up of 157 boys and 103 girls (152:100), and 293 outpatients under 14 years of age of whom 169 were boys and 124 were girls (136:100). In interviews with the medical staff, such differences were explained away by gender differences in chromosome make-up and immune systems increasing health risks to boys. What was very interesting about such arguments was that they were entirely technical with no suggestion that these gender differences might be the result of familial bias. That such bias might be a significant factor has been confirmed by a very recent and more detailed field study on gender differences in child survival in one county in Shaanxi province, which shows excess female mortality rising sharply in the mid-1990s in line with national figures and trends.[46] This study revealed that infant mortality was 31.82 per 1000 births for males and 46.06 per 1000 for females, and that 28% of the deaths of girls between 1 and 4 years could be categorised as unexpected or excess deaths. They were not so much the result of lower food or nutrition, but rather took place 'following illness' either at birth or in infancy and childhood when they were less likely than their brothers to receive medical treatment. Both the amounts spent on medical treatment and the speed of hospital transfer were slightly higher for males than females, whose illnesses were less likely to be taken seriously by the parents and thus deemed to be less deserving of familial resources for better medical treatment and hospital care. Young girls with older sisters and/or brothers were particularly at risk and although excess deaths occurred in all kinds of households regardless of economic status, they were more likely to take place where girls had been born at home and in villages distant from or with no bus services to county and township clinics.

In the accompanying focus-group discussions, parents reported extreme behaviours, such as abandonment and infanticide and various forms of lesser discrimination against girls, including shorter periods of breastfeeding and smaller food allocations and less preventative, child health or daily family care. These discussions suggested two important trends. The first is that parents are likely to know the sex of their unborn child via either ultrasound or traditional Chinese medicine diagnosis, and are more likely to deliver female births at home at less cost in full knowledge of greater attendant risks. The second finding of focus-group discussions suggested that, although in households and villages, there were various forms of discriminatory behaviours that affected the health of girls, the most important factor leading to their excess deaths derived from discrimination in curative health care (see Figure 3.1). The attitudes reflected in this diagrammatic representation also point to the other types of discrimination which girls can expect to receive within their families. Overall then

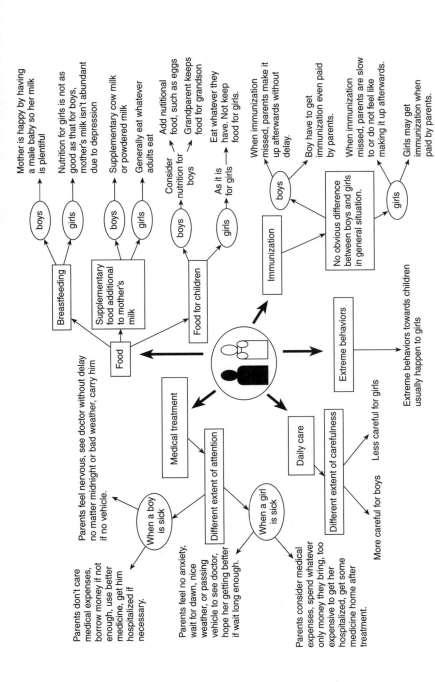

Figure 3.1 Illustration of gender difference in child survival in Jingyang

Source: Li Shuzhuo and Zhu Chuzhu, 'Gender differences in child survival in rural China: a county study'. Paper presented at the Annual Meeting of the Population Association of America, New York, 25–27 March 1999, p. 29.

there is an accumulated body of ethnographic research which suggests that in certain circumstances the birth of a daughter still remains a disappointment, although this is not the case now in all parts of China. While in the main cities there is a new and discernible acceptance of daughter-only families because parents have little or no choice open to them given the strictures of the one-child policy, outside of these cities and in the absence of a son, ethnographic voices suggest that parents may continue to be so disappointed that they take steps to defy the government, take radical steps before or during birth and take their daughters' illnesses less seriously in infancy and childhood. If the birth of a daughter in the absence of a son is still associated with some familial disappointment in much of China, so it is in India where, despite the absence of similar birth control policies limiting the number of children, girls are still spoken of in terms of disappointment in the absence of sons and suffer old and new forms of discrimination in the concurrent quest for sons and smaller families.

India

Numerous field studies and personal narratives for India have been published in the past few years with a common central feature: that it is a matter of importance before, during and after birth whether children are boys or girls. Differences between boys and girls were assumed and unquestioned in everyday conversations about family, livelihood and religion and at life-cycle events; the desire for sons was so central that it was emphasised time and again in men's and women's statements about the number and gender of their ideal family composition, the use of contraception, planning and responding to pregnancy and around child birth.[1] This preference for sons was not only a central theme in ethnographies of north Indian states for in south India too, everyday conversation time and again turned to the importance of sons, suggesting that while son preference in the south may be less intense than in the north, this is not so everywhere in the south and is increasingly less so. In sum, son preference and privilege with its correlative devaluation of daughters was still clearly and loudly articulated by ethnographic voices and recorded in some of the very interesting and informative field studies undertaken by a number of anthropologists in the last few decades of the twentieth century. As in China they commonly note that sons are listed and introduced before daughters and that the most common felicitations associate wishes and hopes for good fortune and well-being with numbers of sons. The old Sanskrit saying 'May you be the mother of a hundred sons'[2] was a time-honoured greeting, and at no time more so than at a wedding when the bride, groom and their families were reminded that marriage was primarily for procreation and birth of the next generation. 'May you give birth to eight sons' and other godly blessings are rained on the couple in the expectation that they will give birth to sons; it is only the number that varies while, in some regions, special ceremonies 'praying for a son' are additional to the usual supplications and held shortly after marriage. For example, the Garbhadhava ceremony consists of offerings and a prayer to the Sun by the husband and wife for the conception of a son.[3]

As in other East and South Asian societies, this period of watching and waiting between marriage and conception is an anxious time for bride and groom and again they have only to look around them to see the pity reserved for and the difficulties experienced by those unfortunate enough not to conceive. The term 'barren' parallels an unproductive and sterile field and is applied to a woman who fails to conceive or, according to some informants, fails to bear sons. Usually, however, wives become pregnant very soon after marriage and most brides would not wish it otherwise for they are likely to feel embarrassed, worried and under much family pressure if the signs of a first pregnancy appear tardy. In very recent focus-group discussions recorded in Gujrat, women took part in lively discussions about the interval between marriage and first birth.

> Maybe we would like to have the first child after one or two years of marriage, or perhaps after one-and-a-half years. However, in our area if a woman does not give birth to a child in about one year, she can even be beaten or insulted and humiliated. Even the husband starts asking or wondering why the woman has not become pregnant.

> In our area, if any woman has her child late, the other women in the village start saying that she is not able to produce children. She will not produce any children. We have to listen to such taunts.

> If we do not have a child one year after marriage, the in-laws would start saying that the woman is not likely to increase our welfare, so let us think of getting another wife for the son. In the villages here, bringing another wife if the first one has not produced a child is not uncommon. Therefore, even if the woman does not desire a child, she has to produce one.[4]

As in other societies it is noticeable that fear of childlessness sometimes seemed so great that it can become a self-fulfilling prophecy.[5] However, once conception takes place considerable efforts are turned to ensuring that it will result in the birth of a son.

The quest for a son

During pregnancy much discussion and conversation centres on parental and familial hopes for sons, especially if a couple's previous children have been daughters. The customary quest or search for a son is even more pronounced now that couples hope to have smaller families of between two and four children and at least one or two sons. The actual number of children which a couple proceed to have is still very much dependent on the early arrival of sons and the number born and surviving, and young pregnant women are most outspoken in their wish for a son, mostly in order to realise their objective within a minimum number of pregnancies. Almost all women categorically stated that they wanted sons first, even though they appreciated the help that subsequent daughters might provide. When one young pregnant woman first realised that she was pregnant, she was about 18 years old and she was delighted at the prospect.

> Some of the neighbouring women had begun to whisper that it was taking Rambai a long time to conceive, but at last her own baby would be born! Rambai hoped it would be a boy; after all it was best to have a boy first. She wanted to have several children, including girls, but it was most important to have a boy.[6]

Although the giving of children and the birth of sons was attributed to the will of God or Allah, and thus was very much seen to be a matter of destiny or fate and beyond parental control or responsibility, it is still a recurring hope and prayer that fate, God or Allah will grant sons and will accept a little worldly intervention to help in gendering the unborn and improving on fate or destiny. To this end pregnant women pray and participate in ceremonies 'in search of a son'. In one region a more formal Pamsavanen ceremony was held 3 months after conception, with the express intention and purpose of obtaining a son; while in the Atharva Veda, one of the four most sacred texts of Hinduism, mantras are prescribed for chanting so that if by chance the foetus is female it will be transformed into a male.[7] Again in the recent focus-group discussion in Gujurat the majority of women reported that they would like to have two or three children (two sons and one daughter), with younger women tending to prefer only two children with at least one son. For all women size of family and gender composition were inextricably linked, with most women still feeling very vulnerable until they had a son.

> One must have at least one son. Two may be better. Until we have one son, we keep waiting (i.e. keep having children). In the process, sometimes three or four daughters may be born. The older members of the family and the husband also keep wishing for a son.

> Without producing a son, we cannot stay here. We would be driven out. If we do not produce a son, our households would start looking for another wife. My mother's brother did not have a son at all. God did not give him one and they had to bear people's scorn all the time until they died.

Daughters are good to have. But we have to have sons. One may have four or five daughters but without a son a woman is labelled childless.[8]

Customarily the most common means of giving supernatural forces a helping hand to procure a son has been the imbibing of potions or medicines which were especially sought by women who had already given birth to a succession of daughters and who were under pressure from husbands and mothers-in-law to bear a son successfully. According to some local beliefs the sex of the foetus is not fixed until the end of the third month of pregnancy and there is much ethnographic evidence, particularly in north India, that the use and efficacy of countless locally obtainable medicines to ensure the birth of a boy are widely discussed and recommended. They are taken at the end of the second or third month of pregnancy alongside any number of dietary regimes. Women were often heard to say that, although it was a matter of fate or fortune in that 'what Allah gives Allah gives', they were resolved that after a succession of girls, they would intervene next time and attempt to overturn the pattern of their deliveries. In these circumstances female kin of the extended family are usually at hand with advice about medicines which were deemed successful elsewhere in procuring a son. For instance, one woman reported that after many daughters she got somebody to bring medicines from the town in order to obtain a son. They cost her a total of 31 rupees, but when they did not lead to the birth of a son, she blamed the fact that she had taken them in the third and not the recommended second month. When her sister heard about this, she asked her rather crossly: 'Why didn't you say anything to me? There is someone in a village near my in-laws' place where medicines are absolutely guaranteed. He doesn't take any money until your wishes have been fulfilled and then you give him whatever you want'.[9] It has to be said that there is also a certain degree of skepticism expressed about the efficacy of these treatments; Muslim women in particular are skeptical as to the efficacy of such medicines and are more adamant that God's will predominates in such matters, so that a child's sex is a matter of fate and fortune and exclusively in God's hands:

What, can a boy be made by taking medicines? No! It's a matter of destiny.[10]

I don't believe in them at all. There is no medicine that can overturn the *seh*. A boy comes from one's destiny.

As a result of her experiences one midwife concluded that if the medicines were truly effective then their would be no girls born at all!

There are no *seh palet* medicines. It is all a matter of what God gives. If it's going to be a boy or a girl, there's nothing human beings can do.

These so-called seh palet mediums are useless. Look, if boys really resulted from them, nobody would have girls, everyone would be having only boys![11]

It is certainly true that no treatments seemed to be available or requested to ensure the birth of a daughter, for girls are widely said to 'come without being invited'.

Most women do eventually bear a son with or without medicines; however increasingly they are unlikely to want to continue child-bearing endlessly in the hope of a son and now resort in greater numbers to more radical interventions made possible by new technologies. As one early advertisement in the newspaper *India Express* suggested, there are new ways of ensuring the preferred outcome of pregnancy.

Is it a boy or a girl? It is now possible to find the sex of your child in early pregnancy before it is born with the aid of latest sophisticated imported electronic equipment. What is the purpose of finding out the sex of a child which has already been conceived?

Most prospective couples, in quest of a male child as the social set up in India demands, keep on giving birth to a number of female children which . . . leads to a chain reaction of many social, economic and mental stresses on families. Amniocentosis and antenatal sex determination have come to our rescue and can help in keeping some check over the accelerating population as well as in giving relief to the couples requiring a male child.[12]

Although the prenatal procedures of amniocentosis or choronic villus sampling, referred to simply as the 'sex test', were first developed for the detection of genetic abnormalities, they were soon used primarily to determine the gender of the unborn child. Indeed most surveys showed that generally it is not known that these same tests could be used to diagnose birth defects. Perhaps this is not surprising given that a report cited by the writer Elisabeth Bulmiller showed that the majority or 84% of Bombay's private gynecologists conducted the 'sex test' solely to determine the sex of the child, and that these sex tests were most often followed by an abortion if the unborn child was female. A gynecologist in a busy middle-class practice told her that once a woman finds out that it is female, in 80% of the cases she is 'hell-bent' on abortion.[13]

Local studies and surveys reveal the wider distribution, privatisation and commercialisation of sex identification and abortion facilities, the greater awareness and use of relatively cheap facilities in villages, clinics and hospitals, and the absence or partial absence of regulation which have allowed sex identification facilities to mushroom. A number of local studies have shown the increasing availability and acceptability of such tests. A 1982 study in an urban educated and middle-class area in Punjab state revealed that, even at this early stage, all the respondents had heard of the amniocentosis test and that two-thirds thought its sole purpose was sex identification; three-quarters of the women and nearly two thirds of the men believed that a girl should be aborted if the parents already had two or more daughters and that the tests should not be banned.[14] A decade later in Maharashtra state a survey of six villages, three with ready access to and three more remote from health facilities, showed a similar awareness among 49 out of 67 women, with half of the 49 approving of abortion of females.[15] Investigations into the clientele of both private clinics and public hospitals offering 'sex tests' showed that it was not just the wealthy but also the middle classes and the poor who have taken advantage of such facilities. The cost of the test, ranging from Rs50 to Rs1000, does not seem to be a barrier to those with resources, and those without ready cash are apparently willing to take out loans. Although private doctors in Bombay charged high fees for the tests, hospital clinics in poorer areas offered amniocentosis at cut-rate prices well within the means of poorer families. In one of the first hospitals to offer low-cost tests, a study by a Bombay women's organisation between 1979 and 1982 found that of 8,000 women who came from all over India, 7,999 wanted an abortion if the test revealed a female child. Many advertisements set the costs of the sex tests and abortions against the future costs of a daughter, including that of her dowry, with slogans such as 'better 500 rupees now than 50,000 rupees later on'.[16]

Elisabeth Bulmiller sat for a week in the waiting room of one of the most expensive clinics in Bombay and interviewed its rich women clients who, although all aware of the costs of raising and marrying a daughter, were more motivated by avoiding the social embarrassment of having daughters and no sons. Most of the women interviewed expressed time and again the social status attached to sons and the need for a son in order 'to be a woman' and meet the expectations of their families and communities. One 36-year old mother of three daughters interviewed said that, although she could afford another daughter, it was the case in India that 'every parent must have a son'. Another 31-year old Bombay woman at the hospital who already had two daughters was quite clear that if the sex test showed a third daughter then she was determined to have an abortion. She simply wanted a boy even though she could have afforded financially to have another girl. 'Our society makes you feel so bad if you don't have a son. If you have to say that you have two daughters, the response is "Oh, too bad, no boy", and I feel very bad.' At this point even her more liberal husband, who was not so keen on the idea of the test, concurred and went on to say that 'You do feel bad, looked down upon if you have two to three girls'.[17]

Many thought that because the test is available and everyone is doing it, then 'why should we not have what we want?' It certainly suited the medical profession that they had such wants, for the tests have become extremely profitable for doctors, many of whom have argued that aborting a female was preferable to condemning an unwanted daughter to a lifetime of neglect and abuse. Indeed they saw themselves as performing a 'humane service'. Elisabeth Bulmiller also talked to the clinic's doctor who thought that 'until the attitude that a son is absolutely essential changes then all doctors as scientists do is help the poor mother who year after year produces a baby until a boy is born.' He performed 50 to 70 tests a year and aborted 20 to 30 female foetuses 'simply because they were female'. He rationalised that although he was not 'happy about it', he had to think 'that the child is not wanted'. He explained that the drive for male children was stronger among the business community who were the very people who could afford to have girls. He himself did not completely blame them for there were good reasons for not wanting girls: they marry out and cannot light funeral pyres. He admitted that he found himself in a very peculiar situation in that 'if you don't do it, you are creating an unhappy situation for the mother and child. And if you do it, you are discriminating on the basis of sex.'[18] An eminent female gynecologist also interviewed by Elisabeth Bulmiller spoke out in favour of sex selective abortion as 'the lesser of two evils' and better than the fate an unwanted daughter 'is going to face until the day she dies'.[19] The expansion of facilities for sex tests and abortion have proved to be a lucrative business for the medical profession; such was the ensuing and widening popularity of the sex test that the Indian government felt obliged to ban sex determination tests in most circumstances. Sex tests have been banned by a number of states since the late 1980s,[20] but these prohibitions are full of loopholes and have proved almost impossible to enforce, so that sex identification facilities continue to mushroom and reflect a growing societal acceptance of medical techniques in the name of reproductive choice if not son preference. Even today, as a recent BBC film showed, there are advertisements for sex tests outside clinics and on the roadside in both urban and rural venues in many of India's states. They will probably continue to be a familiar feature of the landscape until the birth of a daughter is not regarded as such a disappointment.

A lesser welcome

At birth, a recurrent ethnographic observation is the very different welcome which most daughters receive compared to sons. Nowhere is the secondariness of daughters more clearly expressed than at the time of birth, whether it be at that of an 'auspicious' son or a 'hapless' daughter. Conversations overheard and reported from the delivery room suggest that reactions to the birth of a daughter range from a vocal or muted welcome after several sons, to open indifference, disappointment or despair. The birth of a girl is most likely to be an unwelcome event in high parity births where there have been no previous sons; indeed there is a direct correlation between the absence of and desire for a son and the degree of disappointment at the birth of a daughter. The comparison can be summed up in a passage from the Atharva Veda which states a common wish: 'The birth of a girl grant it elsewhere, here grant a boy'.[21] While a daughter is said to arrive without an invitation, the birth of a son is likened to 'sunrise in the abode of the gods'. In one ethnography several women informants thought that the birth of their son was the happiest day of their lives while none mentioned the birth of their daughters in this way.[22] Indeed as the following accounts from the delivery room illustrate, young mothers without sons are more likely to greet the birth of their daughters with silence, disappointment and depression. Patricia Jefferey, who is one of the few ethnographers to have been present during labour and delivery, reported verbatim the following dialogue from the delivery room during the birth of a girl.

> All the women are crowding over her [the new mother, Muni] craving to see. One asks if the baby is a boy or a girl. Burhiya [her mother-in-law] stretches across the *dai* [midwife] and turns the baby over.' Another girl', she tells everyone.

Are you certain?
Can you see properly?
Yes indeed! It's a girl.
Aah!
Well, girls are all right you know.
Muni's fate is bad! That 'prostitute-widow' of a *dai* [midwife] has produced another girl.
What, is it my fault it's a girl? Is it in my hands to decide what will be born? Don't fight with me, but with God. Did I make the girl myself? Fie! That is God's will.
Why couldn't I have a son this time? asks Muni plaintively.
Burhiya looks sternly at her. God has given this girl. It's your job to accept her.
What's the matter? What children does she have now? asks the *dai*.
Two girls.[23]

Patricia Jeffrey watched most of the women drift away: they had seen the new baby, another girl, so that this birth was subdued, the midwife too is silent for she will be paid at a lesser rate for delivering a baby girl while the disappointed mother is left well aware that had the baby been a boy there would be celebrations, presents and jollity. She lies by her daughter in the full knowledge that not only has she produced a lesser being but she will have go through the same process and yet again suffer the same anxiety during another pregnancy and another birth.

The loneliness and plight of the exhausted and sorrowing new mother who, in 'searching for a boy', had given birth to yet another girl is a common figure in the ethnographic literature; sometimes the disappointment was palpable even at a first birth.

> Finally at dawn, when Rambai [the new mother] thought she could stand it [the labour pains] no longer, it was all over.
> 'Eh. It's a little girl', the midwife announced. Rambai's heart sank. A girl. Was it worth all the pain? Her mother-in-law was consoling. 'Never mind, all babies are made by God. You'll have a boy next time.' At the special blessing for the first child which followed, Rambai was directed to throw some small bits of fried pastry toward the sun. 'If you want another baby soon, don't throw them very far.' Rambai barely moved the pastry bits; maybe she would soon have a son.[24]

Elisabeth Bulmiller who witnessed the birth of a boy records how a semantic slip led to palpable disappointment in the delivery room which only turned into relief once the mistake was rectified. She reports how the health workers told the new mother that her baby was a boy, but her research assistant who came in a few minutes later smiled and congratulated the women on her new son, using a Tamil upper-caste term for 'boy' which in the local dialect meant 'girl'. The new mother then thought that she had given birth to a daughter and was shocked. 'You told me it's a boy', she said accusingly from the delivery table to the midwives, who were tying up the baby's umbilical cord.' Are you lying to me?' One of the midwives held up the baby for her to see. The mother smiled, relieved. 'No one is lying to you', the midwife said, and then explained the different meanings of the word. Afterwards the midwife said that they knew for certain that the birth of this mother's second daughter had resulted in infanticide and that, if the newborn had been a girl, she would have met the same fate.[25]

To their chagrin midwives often received the blame if a girl was born and, to add injury to insult, they customarily received less payment if the birth resulted in a girl. Since a midwife might receive 25 rupees and a 5 kilogram sack of grain for delivering a boy and only 10 rupees or so for delivering a girl, they had a vested interest in the birth of a boy.[26] Several ethnographers have interviewed midwives who are in a better position than most to appraise the differential welcome accorded to sons and daughters. Their testimonies suggest that among Hindus and Moslems alike, boys are greeted at birth with enthusiasm and joy while girls are born in silence and with subdued greetings.

> When a boy is born people shout very loudly, 'It's a boy', or they say in a dead voice, 'It's a girl'.

In their hearts no one wants a girl. If it were under anyone's control, no girls would ever be born!

Women often say that a dead widow co-wife has been born. Sometimes women swear, but I ask if they were not girls once and chide them for what they say.

If people complain when I deliver a girl. I say I did not make her and the girl was just in their fate.

Many people are sad when a girl is born, but never when a boy is born. Sometimes the mother gets no special food. There are no special customs when a girl is born.[27]

Much of the reaction to a daughter's birth is likely to be determined by her birth order, the sex configuration of siblings and the survival of previous children born to the mother; the ethnographic literature suggests that the degree of disappointment is directly linked to these three factors. There is less disappointment when a first girl is born, especially if there has been a previous history of still-births or miscarriages as her birth is proof that the couple are fertile and can 'lead in a boy'. Very often a first-born girl is celebrated to endorse the successful womanhood of the mother, enhance her position in her husband's family and offer hope of sons to come. Among Hindu populations, for instance, it is not uncommon for a lump of *gur* to be broken over the new-born girl's buttock to signify that even though her own birth was not a source of happiness, she may bring a brother in her wake.[28] Other circumstances in which the birth of a girl is less of a disappointment, and may even be welcomed and wanted, is when a daughter follows a line of sons. As one midwife said: 'If there are already several girls, people consider the birth of another a matter of sadness, though if a girl comes after several boys then people do not mind so much.'[29] In such circumstances a mother may less commonly although openly assert that she wants a daughter.[30] If the birth of a daughter after those of several sons provided the most auspicious circumstances for the birth of a girl, maximum disapprobation was reserved for daughters successively born in the quest for sons. While no one seriously objects to the birth of another son, there is little consolation for those who bear successive daughters and both they and their daughters are deemed increasingly burdensome. There was widespread and recurrent anxiety and fear that several girls might be born resulting in a large family of daughters while 'waiting' or 'trying' for a son. One mother who only had one surviving daughter following three births was pleased to be pregnant again, for two children had died and she still had no son. But when she had another girl, the birth was met with little enthusiasm from her in-laws and there were no special celebrations apart from a naming ceremony attended only by close family members. No news of the birth was sent to her own parents and no gifts were received from them, neither of the husband's sisters were called to help the new mother after the delivery or to receive gifts and she had an angry husband.

Now we have just two girls. There isn't a single boy. He [her husband]
was angry that I'd had another girl. He took his food from his
mother's hearth and didn't come to our house for three days, so how
could I ask him to call his sisters ... but if it had been a boy, my
husband's sisters would certainly come.'[31]

In part the negative response of a new mother to the birth of a daughter is occasioned by her realisation that she will have to continue childbearing in the hope of having the requisite son or sons. Most village
women report that a certain relief accompanies the early arrival of sons
for this reduces the need for additional child-bearing in order to reach
the desired number of sons and hastens their acceptance into their
husband's family. One mother who did not bear a son reiterated once
again that 'I myself would like one son. And I don't want many children.
But it isn't a question of what I want. Until I have a son I won't stop having
children'.[32] Only if the first or second birth was a boy could they relax a
little, although they also knew that the risk to a child's survival was such
that it was still desirable to have a second son.

Now we'll soon know what will happen. But even if I have a boy this
time, I won't be able to say anything about not having any more children. If one boy is born, the people in the house can also say, 'what is
one boy?' There can also be sadness and happiness, wasting and
illness. Call a second boy after the first.[33]

One woman who needed a hysterectomy after three births told Patricia
Jeffrey that her husband would not permit the operation because they had
just one son.

He wants another son. If two or three children had been boys he
would have been satisfied, but we have only one son. Many women say
that it is the women's fault if there are no sons — but it isn't. It's
God's will. The trouble is, how can we tell if another child will be a
boy or a girl? That's what I tell my husband when we discuss the
matter.[34]

It is not so surprising to find that women were reluctant to undergo sterilisation even if they had one son.

We can decide to accept sterilisation when we have only sons but not
when we have only daughters.'
　If we get daughters first, we do not consider the question at all. We
wait for the son to be born before we consider the question. In a situation like that, we do end up with more children than what we want.
But what can we do? Such things do happen in our lives.

> We would never go in for sterilisation after having one son only. No one from here would do that. We would be too scared. If something happens to that one child, what would we do? Supposing something does go wrong?[35]

If bearing a first-born son results in the resounding confirmation of the young mother's rise in domestic and social hierarchy, so that it is sometimes said she 'grows one fist in height', the corollary is that when she has a daughter, she 'shrinks one fist in height'. Many mothers who had no sons and several daughters felt the disapproval of their husband's family and feared that they might be set aside and abused for their seeming inability to bear sons. Occasionally there is evidence to suggest that the young mother herself may be punished or threatened because she has delivered a girl. One mother still trying for a son after three daughters watched her husband turn to alcohol and suffered incessant arguments and threats that he would take another wife on the grounds that 'your brothers all have sons and your sister has a son. But you don't and you won't ever have one.'[36] In another case a husband threatened to repudiate his wife if she had another girl, while another husband refused to enter his house for several days. The younger brother-in-law of one unfortunate wife even padlocked the grain store, saying that his sister-in-law could hardly expect food since he was meeting the expenses of the new-born girl's birth. For several days she lived on seeds and dried ginger washed down with hot water, in contrast to the delicacies she might have expected had she produced a son. Furthermore, the naming ceremony ended in uproar when the pandit realised that he was not going to be paid and he departed leaving the baby nameless and the defilement unremoved.[37] Sometimes so great was the determination not to have a line of daughters that disappointment turned to violence directed against the female infant herself.

What distinguishes several present-day field studies is that parents remain quite open about discussing female infanticide and the circumstances in which they resort to such practices. Elisabeth Bulmiller interviewed parents in a region in the southern state of Tamil Nadu where female infanticide was sufficiently widespread for health workers to fear for a newborn infant's life if it was unfortunate enough to be the third or fourth daughter.[38] She interviewed a number of poor farm labourers for whom the birth of another daughter had constituted a 'crisis' or 'a devastating blow' which the family believed could 'threaten its survival'. For each of the couples 'putting a child to sleep' had seemed to be their only choice. One couple, desperately poor, had fed a sticky white substance to their fourth daughter: 'We felt bad at the time but suppose she had lived? It was better to save her a lifetime of suffering.' Another couple of a slightly higher caste and not so poor had waited to put their second daughter 'to sleep' after birth rather than have a costly abortion. Instead of 'spending money and losing income', they had preferred to deliver the child and have it die, although the mother had waited 24 hours for her mother-in-law to give the lethal plant milk to the child.

> I was of half a mind to bring up the child. I could not decide. But because of the problems I would face at a later stage, I decided to do it. And everybody else was in favour of putting the child to sleep, so I decided to go along.

A third couple had allowed the mother-in-law to administer plant milk to their third daughter while the fourth couple, low-caste field labourers with an acre of land and not so desperately poor, had decided that if a second pregnancy had resulted in a girl they would put her to sleep because they wanted a son. When their second daughter was born they had given their daughter cow's milk and sleeping pills and the girl had not lived. The parents told Elisabeth Bulmiller that they had cried every day and 'felt bad', but after calculating very carefully the cost of raising a second daughter, they had decided that 'bringing up a girl is very difficult nowadays'. The husband's mother reiterated that 'it was not wantonly done' for 'we were not in a position to bring up the child'.[39] However despite such examples, which the statistics suggest are not uncommon in many regions of India, the majority of daughters in most regions do survive the rigours of birth, although the celebrations surrounding their arrival are likely to be muted in comparison to those marking the birth of their brothers.

The births of sons are auspicious occasions; they are celebrated elaborately with no expense spared and with generous feasting and exchanges of presents, all of which confirm the success and status of the fortunate mother, parents and family. The most elaborate celebrations are for first-born sons, whatever their birth order. Among Muslim populations goats may be sacrificed and presents given, with smaller celebrations and presents for second and subsequent boys. The mother's parents are also expected to send more gifts if the infant is a boy, and mothers and mothers-in-law may receive jewellery and presents from their husband's family if a son is born. Indeed the pressures to be generous can weigh heavily on their respective families.

> If I have a boy, I must give all my *susrai* women a *dhoti*, all the men a coconut each, and my brother-in-law (*hyb*) a suit as well. But if I have a girl, I might just give a suit to my brother in law (*hyb*) and money to my *nand*.[40]

The ceremonies and birth songs reserved for the birth of boys contrast with the lack of celebrations surrounding the birth of a girl,[41] a discrepancy which was commonly observed by midwives.

Village people don't like girls. Much more is done when a boy is born. The taking-outside and *jasthawn* are done with great expense, drums will be played and hearth tongs clattered against the griddle.[42]

Another midwife explained that there are no special customs when a girl is born because she will cost her parents all her life.

That is why people do not do *khushi* when a girl is born. That is why people do not give anything special when a girl is born. Yes, indeed some even swear at me.[43]

One mother, in describing how the birth of her second daughter had met with little enthusiasm by her in-laws, noted that there were no special celebrations apart from a naming ceremony attended only by close family members, no news of the birth was sent to her own parents and no gifts were received from them.[44] If the birth of a girl is welcomed with less enthusiasm or ceremony than that of her brothers, and may even be the cause for commiseration, recrimination and rejection, her negative start as 'not a boy' may also set her on a path of continuing disadvantage which, sliding into physical neglect, may threaten her chances of survival in later infancy and childhood.

Neglect and survival

Given the incidence of child death in villages it was not surprising that a sense of fragility surrounded a child's life, that fear of child death lay behind the wish for more than one son and that parents hesitated to use contraception until they were sure of their sons' survival. Although fewer children than before die before the age of 5 years, around a quarter of infants and children still die before that age from infectious diseases, inadequate nutrition and poor access to medical care when they are ill. In the late 1980s Patricia and Roger Jeffrey found that, although there had been some improvements since the 1950s when high proportions of girls did not survive to their fifth birthday, in two villages they studied in Uttar Pradesh, 3% of live born babies still died within the first week and another 3% before the end of the first month. If they added in still-births and babies who died at home, one in 11 babies born at full-term or three or four a year were dead within a month. In both villages the relatively poor had fewer living children than the relatively wealthy, with rich and middle peasant women having both more children and more who had survived. In the first week of life new-born boys, initially at high risk, were less likely to survive than were new-born girls, but thereafter boys were sufficiently more likely to survive to skew the rates substantially in their favour, with 79% of boys compared to 72% of girls reaching their fifth birthday. Before 1960, the differential survival had been greater (70% of boys and 57% of girls) while in the 1960s and 1970s, girls' chances of survival had equalled those of boys; but in the 1980s again girls were much more likely to die, with only 91 of the 117 girls (78%), born alive after January 1980 compared to 107 (93%) of the 115 boys surviving until September 1985. For their key informants, 15 of the 42 girls born to them after January 1980 were dead by September 1985, while only 3 of the 36 boys had died. These sex differentials in child mortality were greatest among Muslims and showed no sign of decreasing; indeed nearly half the girls born since 1980 in one of the villages had already died by September 1985. Again among key informants, 76% of the boys but only 58% of the girls born were still alive in 1985. Sex differentials in mortality were larger among the relatively wealthy for among rich and middle peasants in that 83% of the boys but only 73% of girls survived to the age of 5 years while among the poor peasants and landless, 75% of boys and 71% of girls survived. Additionally girls with one or more older sisters were most especially vulnerable and in some households several girls in succession had died.[45]

In these circumstances, parents did not expect all their children to survive into adulthood. Patricia and Roger Jeffrey heard many times that 'what Allah gives, Allah can also take', and this meant that parents, families and communities accepted that what was given might also be taken away so needed no further rationale or explanation. They observed that a stock response to a girl's illness was 'she just got a fever', whereas boys' illnesses were altogether a different matter.[46] In one village it was observed that two daughters died because they were not given water and another died because medical care had been deliberately withheld by her father. Exceptionally a woman with several daughters one of whom was sick was heard to comment that 'she does not even die'[47], but more commonly the response to the illness of daughters was more casual and left in the hands of fate, Gods and Allah.

> She got dryness but we didn't get medicine for her. We put her in the hands of God. If she was to live she would live, and if not she would die. What person can do anything if someone is going to die?[48]

Very few parents could give exact information as to cause of a girls' death for most had never reached a doctor for diagnosis. It was also evident to the researchers that parents expected higher female infant mortality and that daughters with several sisters were most at risk — not just among the rich. Ethnographers such as Barbara Miller had observed and documented in some detail the frequency with which female infants are breastfed less frequently and for a shorter duration than male infants, receive smaller amounts and less nutritious foods than a boy, with unequal distributions of food legitimated by taboos relating to meat, fish and eggs.[49] Her studies revealed that a girl's health was more likely to be neglected, with girls taken to doctors and hospitals less often than boys, so that hospital admissions in north India were heavily weighted in favour of boys in the proportion of two or more boys to one girl. In the south, too, there were still more boys than girls admitted but the discrepancy was less — 1.2 boys to 1 girl.[50] She also concluded that the way girls' illnesses were perceived and treated led to their lower survival rate, especially among the high-caste Brahmin property-holding families in the north, and were the result of favouritism towards boys in the allocation of food, medical supplies and love and care so that only the strongest females survived.

A later study also showed that 60% of female infants were born with low birth weight, female infants were breast fed for 6 months or less, while at older age groups girls were provided less nutritious food than their brothers.[51] A recent survey of infants, toddlers and pre-schoolers showed that 71% of the females suffered severe malnutrition, as against 28% of the males, and that boys were taken to hospital for the treatment of common diseases twice as often as girls.[52] Boys are believed to be sick more often as a result of their relative weakness, and when they are ill they are provided with more medicines and health care by parents.[53] Records in the Punjab in north India and Tamil Nadu in the south suggest that there are marked gender imbalance in expectations of duration and intensity of treatment.[54] When Patricia and Roger Jeffrey studied the familial behaviours responsible for such an outcome, they concluded that these mortality differences due to differential valuation and care were not so much overtly deliberate or specifically directed against girls, for parents frequently were devastated by the death of a daughter. Rather, boys were openly thought to have greater entitlements and needs for food and medicine, largely because they are seen to be more valuable to parents, more vulnerable than girls physically and at greater risk from superstitious influences of the 'evil or jealous eye'. Although the neglect of girls and their lesser chances of survival might not be openly perceived, their excess vulnerability is evident in the maternity histories of women, the majority of whom have lost more daughters than sons. As one activist has pointed out, daughter neglect was more the result of the belief in the greater entitlements of male infants: that they 'should want for nothing', that they 'should be fed when they howled, be dandled and coddled by everyone in sight and, when ill, 'be surrounded by acute feminine anxiety'.[55] Another field worker observed that usually a female child just does not receive the same attention and affection that is bestowed upon a male child in a Hindu family, and that this attitude may slide into 'indifference and coldness'.[56] In India it has been said that a girl may be born to be but 'a blossom in the dust'[57] and, as this chapter shows, ethnographic voices in both India and China over and again speak of a daughter with disappointment or ambivalence. This both reflects the lesser value attached to many daughters by their parents and contributes to the greater risks attached to the survival and well-being of many within their own families.

4 The generations
Expectations and entitlements

Ethnographic voices from India and China draw attention to the fact that it is parents, would-be parents and grandparents who express preferences, decide plans and rationalise the number, spacing and gender of children and that they do so in accordance with familial needs and interests. It is primarily inter-generational obligations which shape parental expectations, child entitlements and influence reproductive choices and behaviour. All these factors suggest that demographic and ethnographic enquiry should focus on the family rather than the nation and individual. Within demography there has been a recent interest in the ways in which household and family demography might fill the gap between the national- and individual-focused analyses that have customarily defined and limited the field of demography. Frances Goldscheider, in an article in *Demography* (1995), challenged the discipline's existing preoccupation with the 'two extremes' — of individual and nation — and instead advocated more attention to family decision-making.

> We will not answer any of the questions about the causes of demographic behaviour until we move beyond our focus on the individual decision-maker. We must increase our attention to the families and communities that shape individual decisions because these decisions make sense primarily in this context.[1]

Certainly the parental preferences, choices and rationales for favouring sons and penalising daughters revealed in ethnographies can only be understood if they are interpreted within the familial context and take account of familial needs and interests.

In the discipline of anthropology, the household and family have been at the centre of analysis largely because this discipline has placed primary importance on ethnographic participant observation in tribal, rural and urban communities in which informants are very much concerned with these institutions. Anthropologists have given considerable attention to the size and structure of households, the relations of family to state, class and other political and economic institutions, inter-generational and gender relations within the household and, in particular, notions of family and kinship. To embrace a diversity of structures and functions, a household is usually represented as a task-oriented unit and broadly defined as 'representing a multitude of roles and tasks encompassed within a relatively selective repertoire of shapes and sizes', while the family is defined as a kin-specified group.[2] There is a dichotomous view that refers to household and family as mutually exclusive categories, so that the household is concerned with activities, such as production, consumption and reproduction directed towards the satisfaction of human needs, while the family is seen as inhering symbols, values and meanings. However, this dichotomy misses the essential connections between the two. As Rapp has argued, 'it is through their commitment to the concept of the family that people are recruited to the material relations of the household'.[3] The household then is the primary arena for determining generational and gender roles, for forging kin solidarity, for socialisation, for economic co-operation and for reproduction of the family line, but it is because individuals accept a common notion or ideology of the family that they enter into the relations of production, reproduction and consumption within households, they plan and beget children, work to support dependents and accumulate, transmit or inherit material or cultural resources. Given that it is notions of the family which underlie reproductive choices and behaviour, the term family will be used in this study to embrace an instrumental view of the household. In East and South Asia it can be argued that the notion of the family is still especially important in determining reproductive choices and behaviour, for all generations remain intimately tied into family needs, collective activities and joint schedules.

In East and South Asia, the lives of individuals both old and young and their generational, gender and reproductive roles are deeply embedded in the affairs of the family and cannot be analysed outside of this primary reference point. Across the continent most economic, social and political activities take place within or via diverse family and kinship units which may vary in structure and relations across and within class, ethnic group, caste, culture and religion. However, a study of the varied family forms within the Asian region suggests that although there may be no undifferentiated Asian model, there is an underlying notion of 'the family' which, with a public face of unity and co-operation, has three core attributes: its centrality, collectivity and continuity.[4] The centrality of the family as the entity in which the production and reproduction of socio-economic and political life is carried out cannot be over-emphasised. Perhaps this should not be too surprising given that these societies are characterised by relatively fixed residence, the absence of government-sponsored social welfare and pervasive small and large family businesses. It is this central notion of the family, re-emphasised as a much-vaunted component of Asian values, which shapes collective ideas about the family line or continuity, ideal family composition, intra- and inter-household family and kin relations and resource entitlements. The identification of individuals with short- and long-term family interests is apparent in the motives for and rationales behind the reproductive choices and behaviours characteristic of family planning and building strategies.

Planning families

Ethnographic voices reveal that parents and grandparents had very clear ideas about their preferred numbers and gender of children as they planned their families. As has already been suggested in Chapter 1, the term 'family planning' is better reserved for the process of family building, with 'birth control' used to refer to the means by which family plans can be effected. This usage concurs with more recent research by demographers, which has concluded that the availability of contraception has not affected fertility decisions so much as made available the means to meet an existing demand to control the number and spacing of children. Indeed, long before the introduction of new birth control technologies, families deployed time-honoured methods to reduce the numbers and regulate the spacing of their children. Abstinence, abortion, infanticide or neglectful management of infant and child nutrition were no less effective in controlling family size, and families have for a long time been planned according to preconceived or preferred notions of ideal numbers, spacing and gender composition. Simultaneously, demographic understandings of family planning or building as an iterative and complex process have become more sophisticated. At first demographers were most interested in ascertaining initial fertility intentions and gender preferences of couples, and then in comparisons of plans or targets with completed family size and gender balance. Later more attention was given to planning as a sequential set of decisions each of which is determined or influenced by the number and gender of surviving children. The study of family planning thus became a study of sequential reproductive choices and behaviour in which intention is modified repeatedly as a result of successive birth outcomes. In 1983 Butatao and Fawcett argued that fertility decisions combine an initial family plan with a series of subsequent successive decisions which may change with each parity in order to reach ideal family size and gender composition.[5] Their conclusion that fertility decisions are continually variable is confirmed by the responses to the newborn child cited in the previous chapter which were not only influenced by gender and parity but also by the need for yet further childbearing to meet overall family preferences and plans centered on sons. The combination of initial and sequential fertility decisions has not only made the process of family planning more iterative than previously thought, but it has also led to a more complex understanding of the short- and long-term needs of families and how these may affect the value of children.

Central to an understanding of the motivations, attitudes and perception of parents in the process of family planning is a recognition of the value they attach to children or the costs and benefits associated with each successive child; these factors have been found to influence fertility intentions and sequential fertility decisions and interventions. Ethnographic studies show that the costs and benefits of children are considered at each parity level as current costs are weighed against the likely future gains of any additional child should it be of the preferred or non-preferred gender. Ethnographic studies also show that gender preference closely influences fertility intentions, especially at higher parity births, in that desire for another child is closely linked to the number of children already born and living, their gender composition and the strength of gender preference. In assessing the desire for and ways that the value of children is calculated, demographers early identified a number of measures to do with benefit, utility, reward and advantage or satisfaction. The first comprehensive project on this subject undertaken at the East-West Centre Hawaii defined the value of children as the 'hypothetical net worth of children, with positive values (satisfactions) balanced against negative values (costs)'.[6] The project identified five positive general values of children to their parents: emotional benefits; economic benefits and security; self-enrichment and development; identification with child; and family cohesiveness and continuity. There were also five negative general values: emotional costs, economic costs, restrictions or opportunity costs, physical demands and family costs. In the early micro-economic theories of fertility, primary attention was given to the economic value of children, with social and psychological aspects labelled as tastes, preferences or consumptive value often assumed to be constant or ignored. Mueller identified three categories of individual economic or opportunity costs to do with women's withdrawal from labour participation, reduced savings and consumption expenditures which might be foregone in order to be able to afford children.[7] Lebenstein, updating Becker's economic analysis of fertility based on parents' calculated costs and benefits of children, identified six different values attached to children: consumption value, work-economic value, economic risk, educational value, old-age security value, long-term family status maintenance and contribution to the extended family.[8] It is interesting that no demographic studies on the value of children divided them by gender and separately calculated their costs and benefits.

More recent analyses are less static and have focused on the changes in values attached to children by parents within the context of development, modernisation or urbanisation, although they also rarely introduce gender into their discussions. Demographers have assumed that development would bring a general reduction in the benefits and an increase in costs of children to their respective parents as child labour decreased, the costs of education and marriage rose, women's labour participation increased, opportunities for alternative economic and old-age support widened beyond the family and the consumption of goods and services other than children became alternative means and symbols of social mobility. In a path-breaking article, the Australian demographer John Caldwell hypothesised that the fertility transition from high to low fertility and the associated decline in demand for children and change in their relative values were all caused by a reversal of flows of inter-generational wealth, including money, goods, services and guarantees between parents and children.[9] He argued that the direction of wealth flows is from children (younger generation) to parents (older generation) in all traditional societies with high fertility levels, and it is reversed in all developed societies with low fertility (see Figure 4.1). He further argued that an increase in the costs of children and shift in the magnitude and direction of inter-generational resource flows can occur only when there is a transformation of familial relationships both economically and emotionally and an increase in nuclear households which in developing countries is not so much dependent on industrialisation as on 'a process of social westernisation'. He concluded that there were some exceptions to the validity of this latter observation. In China, for example, he suggested that systems of extended family obligations and flows of wealth from younger to older generations had been disrupted by political rather than economic means. However, he concluded that in all cases the effect was the same: a reversal in inter-generational wealth flows followed by fertility decline.

What is interesting several years after Caldwell's seminal article is that his hypothesis has not been further refined in two important ways. The first is that, even in the latest literature on value of children, there have been no comparable analyses of gender as a factor affecting differential costs and benefits of children.[10] The second is that the assumption that a reversal of inter-generational wealth flows is a necessary cause or accompaniment of fertility decline has not been refined in the light of Asian experience. Certainly, ethnographic studies in contemporary South and East Asia attest to the continuing importance of the parent-child contract and the maintenance or mutuality of obligations which still flow from son to parent, despite rapid and extended periods of economic growth and development. With few exceptions the dependence on sons for economic

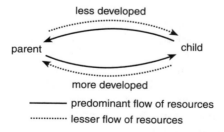

Figure 4.1 Caldwell's intergenerational contract

support has not lessened while simultaneously the costs of raising children have increased which, alongside political strictures in some countries, have caused a reduction in family size. There has thus been a fertility decline without Caldwell's reversal of inter-generational wealth flows so that the maintenance of parent-support and care within the smaller family has required an increase in the management and manipulation of inter-generational resource flows. It is this factor more than any other which has brought about a reassessment of the costs and benefits of raising daughters who largely remain excluded from the inter-generational contract.

The inter-generational contract

Whatever the household, family or kinship form in East and South Asia the central parent-child contract is still biased in favour of parent-support and care in their old age. The inter-generational flow of resources from child to parent in old age is time-honoured, sanctioned and enhanced as it is by the concept of filial piety which has been elaborated and reinforced by religious script or classic text. For centuries filial piety and the economic support of parents were extolled as the highest virtue and in contemporary South and East Asian societies, where there was little or no social welfare outside of family, the parent-child relationship constituted an essential prerequisite for old-age support. Indeed it can be argued that in East and South Asia today, child-care still is primarily practised and represented as a means of securing parent-care in old age. As ethnographers of both India and China have noted, there is a continuing and everyday assumption that it is the old rather than the young whose needs take precedence and that child rearing is still the main strategy for securing parent-care. For China, Sulasmith and Jack Potter and Charlotte Ikels have noted that, more than ever before, parents find it necessary to think and act strategically to nurture a sense of filial obligation in their children.[11] For India, Patricia Jeffrey has observed that family building is still very much perceived as ensuring parent care, while the costs of children compared to their returns are assessed almost exclusively in terms of future benefits to parents. Child care thus remains 'a means to an end' or 'a form of long-range self-interest'.[12] Despite economic development there is still little or no state support for the elderly among most socio-economic groups in most South and East Asian societies, where the costs of maintaining care and support for parents are increasing as life expectancy is lengthened and the costs of medical and other life-enhancing facilities rise. Even where there has been a recent history of some old-age support, as in urban China, this has been threatened by economic reforms which have reduced state-sponsored forms of social security. In other East Asian societies the importance of the family in providing social welfare and security has been acknowledged and exacerbated by the recent East Asian crisis. If economic development in East and South Asia has left child to parent flows of resources intact, it has altered the flow of resources from parent to child.

There has been an increase in the costs of children to parents largely because of the new availability and rising costs of education and an increase in the expenses associated with marriage. The result of these increasing child expenses in East and South Asia has made parents much more aware of the costs of child rearing with the increasing resources demanded of parents encouraging a desire for smaller numbers of children which, in turn, reduces the number of children available for parent care. Additionally, parents feel more vulnerable as the flow of resources to the older generation seem threatened by the educational, social and geographical mobility of the young, whose members tend to establish separate or distant households upon marriage. In the face of these new threats to the parent-care contract, parents have intensified their interest in family-building strategies and the management of resource flows to their children in order to ensure and maximise long-term returns. First, parents invest in their children's education and income-generating prospects in order to enhance their capacity for parent-care in later years. Second, they have sought to emphasise anew a sense of familial obligation towards older generations to counter new threats and risks to child-parent resource flows. Contemporary ethnographies alike reveal how a sense of children's indebtedness to their parents for raising them is instilled with investment in children commonly rationalised or even manipulated to encourage child indebtedness. This is evident in both city and countryside, and even among urban and privileged sectors; the returns expected from children are an acknowledged and important reimbursement for child rearing. Parents quite openly talk of their children's indebtedness and in one case children are even referred to as 'indebted ghosts'.[13] This new intensity attached to returns or indebtedness is directly related to the rising costs of child rearing and the desire for fewer children who will maintain the same support. The tension between maintaining the parent-child contract in the face of increased child costs and the bid for smaller families has been resolved by renewing efforts to ensure the birth of sons, for the inter-generational contract is primarily and almost exclusively a parent-son contract.

The most striking characteristic of the parent-child contract in South and East Asia is that customarily and still in recent years it remains largely a parent-son contract. One feature that is common to most but not all East and South Asian societies is the traditional patrilineal, patrilocal and exogamous marriage and kinship systems which, with their emphases on male kin lines, co-residence and long-term son support, diminish the presence and support of daughters. Although the southern parts of the India exceptionally had more endogamous and egalitarian marriage systems, with matrilineal family forms in many Southwestern coastal communities, social change in these regions has tended to move towards normatively patrilineal systems. Moreover, where kinship systems are more bilateral as in south India, they have neither prevented clusters of excessive female mortality nor served as an impediment to rising discrimination in these societies. Similarly, although one of the distinctive features of Asia's development programmes is an almost exclusive reliance on family support systems in old age, daughter discrimination also occurs in the few localities where there are alternative forms of social support in old age such as co-resident sons-in-law and occupational pensions.

In these circumstances it is surprising that neither the literature on the value of children nor the analyses of inter-generational resource flows initiated by Caldwell have taken sufficient cognisance of the ethnographic findings that show that the majority of resource flows between child and parent are between son and parent. This single factor alone counts for the continuing importance of son preference as the central pivot of parental strategies, although the rising costs of raising sons are such that parents now prefer to invest in fewer sons than previously.[14] As one woman in northern Anhui province said: 'I have two sons — that's too much burden. They have to go to school and get married. That's going to be expensive'.[15] Where the incidence of infant mortality is still a major factor threatening the survival of the single son then parents do continue to seek two sons as an additional insurance policy. Within the context of the smaller family size in East and South Asia not only has the pressure to ensure that one of the fewer numbers of births is a son increased in intensity, but the maintenance of the parent-son contract from which daughters are largely excluded lies at the basis of family building strategies.

> Family building is still very risky, but people's judgements about desirable family size and composition are increasingly influenced by the changing balance between the benefits of having children (especially sons) and the costs of bringing them up (especially daughters).[16]

As ethnographies in India and China continue to show, the inter-generational contract is still negotiated with sons rather than daughters so that the differential expectations and entitlements of sons and daughters continue to be reckoned quite vocally and openly.

Son–parent support

In China it is without doubt the importance of the family line and the permanent bonding of sons into chains of generations and networks of male kin which still underly the unique status of sons, positioned as they are between ancestors and descendants. It has long been and still is the expectation that sons will worship and care for the ancestors of previous generations as only they can do while, in turn, sons have been exhorted since ancient times to have many sons to fulfil their own obligations to their father and their father's lineage. Each new generation of sons is expected to continue the line of descent and, simply put, without sons signifying the unbroken continuity of the family line, there is said to be no bridge between family past and family future. It is sons, as sole performers of the ancestral rites, who are responsible for the welfare of their departed forebears in the spirit world, and in several recent field studies the importance of carrying on the family line is identified as still the most vociferous argument expressed against birth control policies. There has been a revised interest in genealogy and ancestral rituals and temples in recent years, and birth control officials in rural areas have found the wish to continue the family line to be the most difficult argument for them to counter in their work. Indeed they felt they had to pit their tireless and persuasive education against the weight of centuries-old beliefs and customs.

In the detailed and very recent study in northern Guangdong province, one of my students found that villagers remain very conscious of the fact that if they did not reproduce sons, the *zhong*, or the seed of their ancestors, would be extinguished and that this obligation to reproduce the family 'body and spirit' was one that they could not conceive of shirking.[17] They reiterated the need to keep 'the incense smoke burning at the ancestral shrine', stressing that without descendants, ancestors would have no support in the next life and become 'hungry ghosts without offerings'. No matter how harsh the birth control penalties, the villagers were determined that their house keys would be transferred to their sons. One man vehemently opposed the implementation of the stringent birth control policies in his village on three grounds.

> I oppose it! You must have a son to carry on the family name. If you don't have a son, you won't have anyone to worship the dead parent's soul. It will cut the generations, there will be no ancestors. You raise sons, sons support you in your old age. It is impossible for daughters to take care of the aged because they marry out.

In this respect villagers openly contrasted the roles of sons and daughters. 'The daughter is the outsider, like the water spilled out we have no reason to give the key to the outsider. All right?' Another said, 'The daughter is not ours. At last she has to follow her husband. So everyone wants to have a son.'[18] As temporary members of their parents' household, daughters are still in no position to compete with sons in perpetuating the family name or offering ancestral sacrifice.

It is still the case that before marriage a girl is both born within but distanced from her natal family by the practice of virilocal marriage, whereby daughters normally are destined to become daughters-in-law and wives in other families. An early term for marriage used exclusively for a daughter's marriage meant 'going out' for, after marriage, a daughter becomes the exclusive property of her husband's family and is said to be as beyond the control of her own parents as 'water which has burst its banks'. An old saying that 'a boy is born facing in and a girl is born facing out' reflected the transient nature of her life with her parents or the loss to her natal family on marriage, and numerous sayings still emphasise the very important gender difference that 'sons are your own people', while 'a daughter married is like water poured out the door', 'a daughter belongs to somebody else's family', 'investing in a girl is a loss', and 'a family with daughters is a dead-end family'. Marriage reaffirms both the permanence and continuity of sons and the transience of daughters who, even in their younger years, are taught that they are temporary and ultimately belong to another family. In other words, their future lies elsewhere and therefore parental expectations of daughters are quite different from those of sons. But it was not just beliefs about the family line or the ritual support of the dead that underlay son preference, for parents also remain almost entirely reliant on a son's support in old age, both in China's countryside and to a lesser but still important degree in the cities. Sons are not only for dreaming and descendants, for in very practical ways they represent prosperity, future security and even survival in old age. This had been so in ages past and is still so, despite a minimal safety net for the very poorest and the remnants of an urban pension system. The absence of a pension system in China's rural villages and the uneven distribution and declining pension support in the cities have meant that today sons are still perceived to be the most important source of support in old age by both men and women.

Research shows that sons are preferred by both mothers and fathers. Although many ethnographic studies have emphasised the importance of 'the family' as primarily a line of descent encompassing all male generations, including the dead and those not yet born, women-centered studies in China have shown that, although the unbroken line of descent may not have exerted so powerful an influence on wives to bear sons, sons were also preferred by women for their own purposes. Margery Wolf has cogently argued that the value women attached to the small truncated unit or 'uterine family', consisting of mother and children or rather sons, was such that she too had her own reasons for preferring sons.[19] As ethnographies show, sons are an important source of status and support for women who, using their sons as sources of long-term influence and protection, increase their bargaining position within the patrilineal household. Hence women continued to invest in their sons through weaving emotional ties that were not only personal, but also the most important if not exclusive source of security for their old age. Thus the absence of sons jeopardised the future for men and women alike and, despite differing perceptions of the family, sons as the permanent members of the household were invested in emotionally and structurally by both parents as a source of security and support in old age.

In villages sons are openly spoken of as the only important sources of permanent familial support and financial security. In a very recent study in rural Shaanxi, focus-group discussions showed the different contemporary expectations of boys and girls as perceived by parents, families and communities (see Figure 4.2).[20] In southern Guangdong villages, where there are no guaranteed salaries, no pensions and little welfare support, an increasing and recurring worry and topic of conversation was how the older generation could be supported or provided with 'happiness' in their old age. In this respect many villagers believed their worries to be greater than in the cities where before the reform of state-owned enterprises it seemed that they alone were entirely reliant on sons.

> Ai! The situation is quite different between the rural and urban areas. In the urban areas, workers can get salaries from the government, even after retirement. They have 'iron rice bowls' ... but the state does not provide any 'iron bowl' to the peasant, so how can you persuade them not to want a son?[21]

> In rural society we have no other choices. We have to get married and we have to have a son. Everyone has to repeat this cycle. When we become old, we have to rely on our son.[22]

A third very recent study in northern Anhui and Southern Jiangsu provinces suggests that parents with only daughters were the least sanguine about old-age security, for most respondents still expected daughters to marry out and therefore they constituted no match for sons.

> We are different from city people, a daughter married out, and there is no one left to get property and inheritance. We have to supply ourselves with housing and food. When we build a house and a daughter marries out, there is no one left. In rural areas we have to have sons to carry on the family line. I have one son and one daughter. Once my daughter leaves, who will be with me?[23]

Although it is sometimes said that daughters might provide better physical and emotional care in old age, parents tended to reckon more on the support of sons-in-law who would move into their households on marriage, rather than on their daughters, for there is still a certain shame attached to depending on daughters. Margery Wolf found that the main reason why only 4 to 5% of the 93 women interviewed would prefer to live with their daughters was because 'only women who had failed to produce sons' lived with their daughters. There was thus a certain loss of face involved in living with daughters: 'A daughter's house is someone else's house and a daughter belongs to someone else's family so there you must always be watching someone else's face'.[24] To this day I can still remember

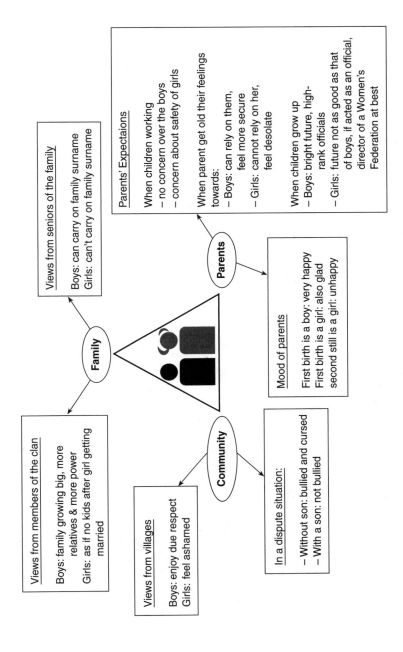

Views from seniors of the family

Boys: can carry on family surname
Girls: can't carry on family surname

Parents' Expectaions

When children working
– no concern over the boys
– concern about safety of girls

When parent get old their feelings
towards:
– Boys: can rely on them,
  feel more secure
– Girls: cannot rely on her,
  feel desolate

When children grow up
– Boys: bright future, high-
  rank officials
– Girls: future not as good as that
  of boys, if acted as an official,
  director of a Women's
  Federation at best

Family

Views from members of the clan

Boys: family growing big, more
relatives & more power
Girls: as if no kids after girl getting
married

Parents

Mood of parents

First birth is a boy: very happy
First birth is a girl: also glad
second still is a girl: unhappy

Community

Views from villages

Boys: enjoy due respect
Girls: feel ashamed

In a dispute situation:

– Without son: bullied and cursed
– With a son: not bullied

Figure 4.2 Difference between boys and girls in Jingyang

Source: Li Shuzhuo and Zhu Chuzhu, 'Gender difference in child survival in rural China: a county study'. Paper presented at an Annual Meeting of the Population Association of America, New York, 25–27 March 1999, p. 30.

one of the saddest encounters of my many years of field work which involved an elderly couple nearing their seventies with a mentally incapacitated son. They had moved villages to be near their daughter to enable her to take care of them and protect their son's welfare in the future. The reason that this memory has stayed with me for more than 15 years is that it is almost unheard of for this kind of movement to take place and, exiled from their own village and with no land, no roots or other kin ties in the village, they felt a certain shame, passivity or even sense of stunned disbelief at finding themselves in this position. To rely on any other source of support, whether of daughters, sons-in-law or the state, reflects an absence of able-bodied sons and is therefore second-best. Even the support of co-resident sons-in-law as a 'second-best' option is threatened now by the decline in fertility so that very few families in the future are likely to give up their only son to another household.

City workers too are beginning to think of extra-familial support in their old age as fragile and second-best as pensions, employment and other urban benefits are at risk for increasing proportions of their numbers.[25] Where local pension schemes have been instituted, as in Zhejiang province, sons are still perceived as the major form of security, for there is an apparent lack of confidence that any scheme mooted for providing family insurance for old age will mature. This is largely because past events have taught them that 'the future is far away' and are not insurance schemes at risk from inflation?[26] In sum, parents still expect old-age security to derive from sons rather than daughters or alternative extra-familial sources, so that socially and symbolically sons are still associated with securing the future. From the days of my very first field experiences in China the difference in familial expectations of sons and daughters has been observable. There is a great difference in degree of investment in and confidence about the future in households with several sons that is palpable and that is just not characteristic of households with only daughters. Households with sons build for a future; those without sons have no future to build for. Those with sons are full of hustle and bustle, building houses, storerooms and new kitchens in anticipation planning as they are for future expansion following marriage and the births of grandchildren. In those with only daughters there is no house building, no new storerooms and no new kitchen — all signifying an absence of plans and the demise or foreshortening of the future. This contrast directly reflects the continuing efficacy of the old adages associating the idiom of loss with daughters 'on which the future is always lost'.

In India, as in China, the disappointment associated with the birth of girls is closely followed by simple explanations of the difference in value of girls and boys to their parents. Most of these differences also had to do with the continuation of the family line, support in old age and, in particular, the costs of raising and marrying out a daughter who eventually becomes 'someone else's property'. As in China it is the continuing presence of sons and the movement of daughters in marriage which lies at the root of the differential perceptions of and values attached to sons and daughters. Here too sons are essential to the continuation of the family line; in ancestral rites, also a feature of the Hindu religion, only sons can continue the incense and keep the light of the house burning. It is of symbolic significance that a son should light the funeral pyre of his father just as he did for his own father and his son will do for him while, for grown women, the line of her husband is threatened until a son is born. As villagers were quick to remind Patricia Jeffrey:

> Family flows from the father to [the son] ... a daughter is merely a guest, someone whose dowry and proper marriage are constant worries to her parents during her childhood. Sons alone provide the hope that a line is not doomed to extinction.[27]

> Boys have always been preferred, like they are now. It's because the pleasure stays in the house, the light of the house keeps burning, and the name continues. Even when sons separate, the name continues. It's the same for the landless and those with land. Even if one son is no good, in your old age one at least will be of some use to you, will feed you, love you and fear God.[28]

Although villagers in India talk about the importance of sons in terms of 'name and mark' after their death, they emphasise more the need for sons to sustain them in their old age. As Patricia Jeffrey notes, the reasons why parents wanted sons was quite straightforward: they were acutely aware of the importance of having sons who would support them when they were old and infirm. Indeed the hazards of a lonely and impoverished old age in a society without pensions, life insurance or substantial personal savings and the importance of sons in providing 'comfort and shade' for their parents were subjects returned to time and again in conversation. She noted that such practical dependency was not considered demeaning, but was represented as a parental entitlement that enabled sons to repay parents for rearing them and settling them in marriage. In contrast, any practical dependence on a daughter was considered to offend all the local views of honour and prosperity and was resorted to with shame and only in the absence of sons.[29] In Gujarat too, focus-group discussions make it quite clear that the support of sons was preferred to that of daughters and sons-in-law. 'If there were no sons, one would have to depend on son-in-law. Who would want a son-in-law live with you? If we have a son we would not keep or depend on a son-in-law'.[30] This was the major contrast between sons and daughters: sons require early care just as daughters, but while daughters move to belong elsewhere, sons stay to provide for their parents in their old age so that both women's and men's security is bound up in their sons. This gendered difference in long-term support is emphasised time and again by informants in field studies.

> Boys look after their parents when they are old but people without sons would have to work until they drop. They will always be in difficulty. Besides, boys keep their names going and as soon as they are old enough they will do field work. Girls don't do fieldwork, and if they were to, it is never for their parents. The don't earn money for their fathers. When a girl goes away to her own house who will look after her parents if there is no son?[31]

> It's wrong to say that boys and girls are the same. Boys stay at home but girls go away. Boys fill your house but girls empty it. Without sons you lie on your bed and worry in your old age, but people with sons have their work done for them. And your name will live on. People say that's your son walking down the path when they see him![32]

> Parents love boys and girls the same — but a girl goes to her own family after she's married. Boys stay with their father. They do cultivation and animal husbandry, so their father can get some rest when he's old. Girls are fine, but the name of boys is greater. This is the reason: Boys make money for their father.[33]

> I'll tell you straight: boys and girls are not the same. You do need both, because other people will say you have only got sons or only got daughters. Girls are good because you can give a daughter away. But boys are better because they receive a bride, they bring people in and continue the family. Girls go away and do this work for someone else.[34]

> Boys and girls are good. But the girl's people stay down, they can never get their feet out of the mud, while the boy's people are racing up for the sky with their mouths open shouting all the way. Bringing up a boy is like eating food that is hot but it cools down quickly — you spend money on bringing him up but then he stays and pays you back. Bringing up a girl is like eating food that slowly-slowly makes your mouth hotter and hotter until it burns the skin off the roof of your mouth.[35]

What emerges as a recurrent theme in field research in both India and China is that any costs incurred in the raising of sons will be repaid in parent support while parents do not assume that daughters can or will be able to reimburse or provide for them at any time and especially in their old age (see Figure 4.3A). The raising of a daughter not only does not have the same degree of benefit, continuity and security that is associated with sons, but is also linked with the unrequited burden of the costs of her upbringing widely represented as a 'double-loss'.

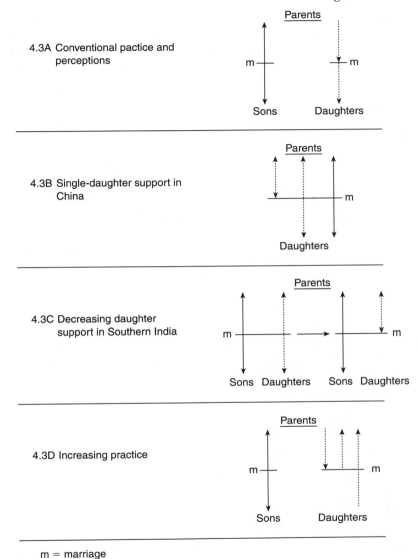

4.3A Conventional pactice and perceptions

4.3B Single-daughter support in China

4.3C Decreasing daughter support in Southern India

4.3D Increasing practice

m = marriage

Figure 4.3 Daughter familial support

Double-loss daughters

In both India and China daughters cannot compete with sons in their contributions to the collective family future, status or sustained support but, additionally, daughters are seen as a no-return cost to the family entailing a double loss. They consume rice, need clothes and their weddings are usually a drain on the family resources, for all of which there is little return. The expression 'a commodity on which money has been lost' is a paraphrase sometimes used for a girl; the reputation of daughters as a double loss or no-profit commodity is emphasised at marriage when she is then lost to her natal family and incorporated into her husband's family, whether or not the newly married couple co-reside with the groom's parents. In particular it is the passage of the dowry or the transfer of wealth in the form of money, consumer goods or other assets from the bride's parents to those of the groom which is identified as the chief burden. In this context farmers in south China refer to girls directly as 'money losers', and hence 'not worthwhile' to bear or raise.[36] In China as a whole, the recent increase in dowry expenses demanded by grooms' households during the recent and rising interest in consumerism has magnified the association of economic 'loss' with daughters. This is so even where daughters have increasingly entered the work force and contributed to their family's budget before marriage and thus to their own marriage costs. In India too it is the costs associated with dowries which have been influential in continuing daughter discrimination. The major reason why parents in India say that they do not want girls is because the costs of her upbringing, her dowry and the continuing expenses of a daughter, even after marriage into another household, all far outweigh the returns from a daughter to her own parents. Even at a daughter's birth, as midwives observe, parents begin to worry about how they first have to raise her and then collect money for her dowry.

> A girl is someone else's property and they will have to give to her all her life. That is why people do not do *khushi* when a girl is born. That is why people do not give me anything special when a girl is born. Yes, indeed, some even swear at me.[37]

There is the widespread feeling that, since her natal family does not get to 'keep' their daughter, they go to all the trouble of bringing her up just for another family's advantage. In China it is often said that raising a daughter is like 'watering a shade-giving tree in someone else's garden' and a Hindi metaphor likens a daughter to 'a bird of the courtyard who drops in only to scratch some grain and then disappears'.[38] She is then 'someone else's property' and a temporary resident in her parent's house destined to live elsewhere.

In India it is the continuing tension for parents between the pressures making for early marriage and the anticipated economic drain of a daughter's dowry on the family finances, budget or purse that is most widely feared and calculated. Even her very birth may have an immediate effect on household savings and consumption as the family starts a savings plan to stave off the crush of future costs. One family with one son and one daughter, who did not permit a second daughter to survive at birth, explained their action solely in terms of their family savings plan. When the first daughter was aged 1 year her father had deposited Rs.3000 (2000 of his own, 1000 borrowed); the bank had promised that when this daughter was 21 years of age and expected to be ready for marriage, it would give the family Rs.22,000 ($1700) which constituted an adequate dowry. The father explained that he would also ask the same amount in dowry at the time of his son's marriage in an exchange which constituted a common means by which people afforded acceptable dowries for their daughters. A second daughter would have ruined his financial plans and thus jeopardised the family's future, for to borrow another Rs.3000 deposit for a second daughter's marriage saving's scheme would have put them in debt for life. Yet without such a loan there would have been no dowry and therefore no marriage; hence he felt that they had no choice but to end her life at birth.[39] As Barbara Miller concluded: 'A baby girl is not just a person in her own right. She is also a member of her sex group and she places upon her parents many obligations and responsibilities.'[40]

Barbara Miller was one of the first researchers to cite detailed evidence in support of the connections between dowry costs, debts and high female mortality.[41] She hypothesised that the necessity of providing a dowry is a prime motivation for families wanting as few daughters as possible and that where the cost of marrying daughters out are prohibitive then the suffering of daughters is high and the survival rates of girls low. Miller compiled an impressive amount of ethnographic evidence in support of this hypothesis and concluded that, while the passage of dowry was widespread throughout the sub-continent in that no region was free of the passage of dowry, higher marriage payments between bride and groom's families in north India placed a heavy burden on the bride's family and could be correlated with higher death rates for girls among propertied groups in the northern states. She cited ethnographic examples contrasting the patterns of the north with those of the south, where the chain of marriage payments is spread more evenly and reciprocally between the bride and groom's families.

> The regional pattern of overall marriage costs is one of general North-South contrast. In the northern Gangetic plains region expenses are clearly greater on the bride's side. In the central region there is an indication of a transition to greater reciprocity between both sides, a situation found in many instances in the South.[42]

She found that in southern states where cross-cousin marriage commonly reduces the costs to both families, there is fairly close correspondence between lower marriage costs and lower death rates among girls. However, she also found that these north-south correlations of dowry costs and female infant mortality did not hold across all economic groups. In the unpropertied groups in northern states for example, marriage costs are lower yet sex ratios remain modestly high, and among propertied groups in the southern states higher marriage costs are not associated with excess female mortality.[43] These discrepancies suggested to Miller that marriage costs fail to account wholly for excess female mortality and that the patterns are as much due to the existence of two main cultural cores in India — the Brahmanical culture of the north and the Dravidian culture of the south. In the early 1980s she predicted that the spread of Brahmanism among unpropertied groups in the north and all social strata of the south may well adversely affect female survival rates in both northern and southern states in years to come, and her predictions have been confirmed by later ethnographic studies.

Richard and Patricia Jeffrey in their very fine ethnograhic study in the northern state of Uttar Pradesh concluded that providing a dowry was not only a major cause of rural indebtedness, but that the costs of dowries were increasing with the result that daughters are now regarded as more of a burden than in the past.[44] Many parents stated that more than ever before it could be said that 'a daughter takes all her life.'[45] In the 'old days', the Jeffreys were assured, parents simply gave what they could afford and it would be accepted without question.

> Parents used to give according to their wishes and capability: the poor give little, the rich gave more. But the giving was voluntary [and with good wishes — literally 'out of happiness']. These days people say, the parents of boys display greed and want to become rich with no effort, they want a good dowry more than a good bride, they 'demand from their mouth' [not hearts].[46]

Many lamented the escalating costs of dowries and lost no opportunity to assert that the government should ban it. One woman who had borne five daughters was very vocal in asserting that the worries facing parents of daughters in negotiating and jockeying over their engagement gifts and dowry should be ended.

> For us a girl seems burdensome. Her parents have to give her a dowry with jewelry, utensils, and so on. They have to give several parcels of silver and gold. And when the girl goes to her in-laws' house, her parents have to fill a whole trunk with clothes. It's a dreadful thing how much has to be given to get a girl married. Nowadays, people want to arrange their son's marriage only into a house from which they'll get a splendid dowry. Meanwhile, who knows how a girl's people will be able to marry her? They just have to get the dowry and the jewelry ready. There ought to be a law that dowry should neither be given nor taken.[47]

It is quite evident that families of grooms now make new and growing dowry demands as a result of the commercialisation of agriculture, the new consumerism and the rising costs of educating sons during the past decade.

> Parents felt themselves enmeshed in an increasingly competitive and materialistic marriage market where the stakes were continually shifting. A dowry which would have been acceptable just a few years ago now seemed inadequate. More utensils were expected; the bed and bedding should be of better quality; the items of clothing should be more numerous and of finer cloth; more jewelry should be given, and more of it should be gold rather than silver. In the rural areas, television sets and motorcycles would have been unheard of in the 1970s, but they were not uncommon among the wealthy by the 1990s. In real terms dowries have been increasing.[48]

In the southern province of Tamil Nadu, Karen Karpardia's detailed ethnographic study shows how in a southern area, the recent demand for a larger dowry has increased the costs associated with raising daughters and has been accompanied by greater devaluation of daughters.[49] She found a widespread rise in the passage of dowry at marriage among both upper and lower caste Tamil non-Brahmin women who are appropriating Brahmin practices as a means of legitimising upward mobility and new class status. Previously, non-Brahmin castes had engaged in agriculture, cross-cousin marriage with closely proximate affinal kin and a greater reciprocity in marriage payments in which the groom's family may well make the largest payments. However, with economic development there has been an increase in socio-economic differentiation between kin and in the appropriation of Brahmin practices which have both resulted in the greater incidence of hypergamous or upwardly mobile marriages, an increase in dowry and less proximity between a bride's and groom's kin. The increase in education of young males, the costs of this education and the entry of young men into new salaried occupations not available to young women has resulted in a new version of marriage payments with the parents of salaried sons now demanding a higher dowry from the parents of prospective brides. The groom's parents want to be reimbursed for the expenses of their son's education and this wish, plus increasing migration and a shortage of men, has escalated the costs of dowries for all but the poorest groups in middle and lower castes. As the passage of dowry has increasingly become the norm, daughters see their own position declining despite economic development.

Many of the young women Karpadia interviewed observed that their own parents had been humiliated by the parents of young men who had asked for more and more gold. They had no choice but to stand by and watch their own futures absorbed into this process. For instance one

young woman who had a high-school education and worked as a clerk in a
city post-office sorting-counter was the daughter of the most influential
man of the street and could expect to make a good marriage. However
she was determined not to get married after observing how her close
female friends had been rejected because of the value of their dowries.

> Today men no longer marry women, they marry money! Previously
> they asked about the girl — 'Is she well-behaved? Is she a good [sexu-
> ally moral] girl? How well is she educated?' That's all they're inter-
> ested in, because what they're really marrying is the gold. That's why I
> never want to get married, I'd rather have my job and stay with my
> parents.[50]

This young woman's vehement denunciation of the gold-digging parents
of eligible males of the community was echoed, but in more desolate
tones, by the parents of marriageable young women of other castes, for
while the wealthy already had been affected by the rise in dowry costs for
some 30 years and those of the middle castes for some 15 years or so, the
families of the poor or those with many daughters were the hardest hit, as
their daughters were rejected in favour of brides whose parents could give
more dowry.[51] The new perceptions of daughters as financial liabilities
rapidly spread as demands for dowries increasingly became the norm.
Judith Heyer, in her recent study of dowry-giving in a south Indian
community, has noted that as dowries had become widespread and larger
in an increasingly differentiated society, it was in the household's economic advantage to keep the ratio of surviving daughters to sons low. She
found that parents seemed really depressed when a daughter was born for
they viewed her as a 'lifelong obligation that would never end and a drain
on their resources'.[52]

   If daughters or parents of daughters in India need any reminder as to
the importance of making acceptable dowry payments they had only to
listen to neighbourhood gossip or read media reports of 'dowry murder'
or 'dowry suicide' which can result from the refusal of the bride's parents
to meet or satisfy the demands of the groom's family and therefore
protect daughters from mistreatment or even death. Suicide is most
common among educated unmarried girls who begin to feel that their
very existence is a grave disadvantage to their families.[53] Equally, after marriage, brides or young wives find that their dowry has been insufficient to
protect them from the ire of their in-laws or shame of their parents; in
some cases the death of the daughter-in-law has ensued. The line between
murder and suicide is often fudged; both are often referred to as 'dowry
deaths' as it is not always in the best interests of the husband's family to
have the exact cause of death identified. Second and higher-parity daughters may be especially disadvantaged in that their dowries may be smaller
than those for first daughters. For instance, one letter written by a young

wife who committed suicide expressly referred to the fact that, as 'the fourth daughter', her parents had not been able to give her a dowry as large as that of her favoured sister-in-law who was an only daughter.[54] The studies quoted here have all associated the widespread and increasing practice of dowry giving, which transforms daughters into financial liabilities, with greater discrimination against daughters and concluded that the advantages to parents of keeping the ratio of daughters low resulted in excess female mortality. Where women are objects of exchange along with other forms of wealth, excess female mortality is argued to be the inevitable outcome.[55] However, it is not only in these circumstances that excess female mortality occurs. In southern India and other parts of East and South Asia, where marriage costs are more evenly spread between the families of bride and groom, are more the responsibility of the groom's household or indeed of a newly independent young woman herself, dowry giving is less of a factor in encouraging discrimination against daughters and cannot entirely explain the excess female mortality or other forms of discrimination against girls in these societies. Nevertheless, the widespread increase in dowries and other costs has rebounded on daughters and had repercussions for their entitlement to familial resources in both north and southern states of India and in China.

Daughter entitlements

If parents expect virtually nothing from their daughters, who require resourcing but are reserved for another family, then it is hardly surprising that they are discriminated against in the allocation of familial resources. Taking Amartya Sen's analysis of entitlements and metaphors of bargaining as a frame and his elaborations on both objective and perceived contributions, it is hardly surprising that parents' expectations of their daughters will determine their entitlements.[56] As this study has shown, girls have less access to education than boys, may have a lower food and nutritional intake, and receive less familial attention and health care. That there is a direct link between expectations and entitlements is confirmed by the findings of two very contemporary field studies — one in urban China and the other in southern India. The field study in urban China shows that for the first time single-child daughters are being included in the parent-child contract and consequently the expectations and entitlements of these daughters have increased. Conversely, the field study in South Asia shows that where daughters once had contributed to the long-term care of parents but now no longer did so, then not only are expectations of daughters reduced but so also are their entitlements.

In China, one of the very interesting new areas of investigation of one-child families has been to observe how parents manage inter-generational resource flows in the enforced absence of sons or sons-in-law. As this study has shown, normally parents go to enormous lengths to give birth to or adopt sons or marry in sons-in-law where they have only daughters but, in the largest cities of China where only one child is permitted, there are increasing numbers of households with a single daughter who is likely to establish her own household on marriage and continue to have close relations with her parents. One of the very significant findings of Cecilia Milwertz's fieldwork in the capital city of Beijing was how mothers admitted that, in the absence of a son, they were raising their single daughters to assume the filial obligations of sons in order to ensure a future flow of resources from daughter to aged parent.[57] Her informants described how quite consciously they were cultivating a new reciprocal relationship with the daughter based on expected returns from her, so that investments in her education and recreation would secure support and care equal to that of sons in old age. Indeed, an important and explicit objective in bestowing new entitlements to family resources on single-child daughters is to cultivate the indebtedness of these daughters towards parents, thereby ensuring that in turn she will feel obligated to support them in old age (see Figure 4.3B). Cecilia Milwertz cites a very pertinent example in which a mother purchased a piano with the express purpose of ensuring lasting gratitude on the part of her daughter and therefore incurring her obligation to provide parent support at a later date. The mother was quite clear that the purpose of investing in the piano was to convey an explicit message to the child that her parents were saving their money specifically in order to please her so that she might support them in the future.[58] This field work provides interesting examples of parents who, once there is no possibility of a son, have no choice but to revise the inter-generational contract before and after marriage to include single daughters. In my own recent field work in smaller cities there is some evidence to suggest that this revision is widespread and that, while it is not necessarily a preferred option and is still presented as an unusual reversal of normal practice, it is increasingly acceptable as more parents who find themselves in this position observe others to be adopting this strategy.

In south India, Karen Karpardia's field study among women of Tamil non-Brahmin and lower-caste working women in Tamil Nadu suggest that one of the most noticeable changes there in recent years has been the gradual severance of economic ties between married daughters and their natal families, as they are now less likely to be employed in waged labour and therefore be in a position to offer support to their own parents.[59] Previously, non-Brahmin and low-caste working women were likely to marry a cousin, work locally, and thus maintain greater contact with their natal families after marriage; relations between married women and their own parents and kin remained important, despite the fact that they moved into their husband's families after marriage. As a result of economic development several changes have taken place. Now, with greater socio-economic differentiation within local populations and kinship groups, there is an increase in hypergamous or upwardly mobile marriages accompanied by the greater passage of dowry payments by the daughters' parents. Second, with increasing social mobility, married women tend to move out of the work force and become more secluded, with less economic independence and autonomy within their husband's households. As a consequence married daughters are less able to provide economic support for their own parents and families, their own parents have fewer expectations now that daughters are less likely to make any contributions to their support, and the daughters have fewer entitlements to family resources (see Figure 4.3C). Karpardia observed that the easy access of married non-Brahmin daughters to their parental homes, a right envied by Brahmin women, is being withdrawn steadily among upwardly mobile groups, and that the remarkable close and warm relationship of women with natal families has been partly a product of women's continuing ability to contribute to the incomes of their natal families even after marriage. However, when they no longer returned to their home to help their own parents with harvesting and transplanting, they became less of a direct familial asset to their natal parents and their visits after marriage were no longer so welcome. This trend together with the rising costs of the dowry meant that parents began to complain bitterly about the costs of marrying off their daughters though not, it is noticeable, about the increasing costs of their sons' education. In these circumstances daughters themselves have observed that, despite economic development, their own status has declined; increasingly they feel excluded from their natal families, even where as unmarried daughters they made substantial contributions to the family budget.

Familial exclusion

In the patrilineal kin-based societies of East and South Asia, the exclusion of daughters from the central parent-child contract is largely premised on their removal from the natal household and their incorporation into the household of their husband after marriage. Thus they are perceived to provide little or no return from the costs of their upbringing and marriage to their own parents; it is for this reason that a daughter's marginality or liminality is assumed and emphasised in discussions of the differential value of sons and daughters. However, such continuing assumptions also mask the existing and increasing contributions of daughters to their parental households. While daughters are not expected to have the same familial or filial obligation as sons, there is increasing evidence that there may be more contact and informal flows of resources between parents and daughters before and after marriage than previously recognised, assumed or reported by parents (see Figure 4.3D). Before marriage, it is sometimes admitted by parents that one of the reasons they would like to have a daughter was that she could care for siblings, undertake housework or use her waged labour to contribute to the household budget before marriage, but such contributions are rarely acknowledged in the specific cost-benefit analysis of sons and daughters. This might have been expected to change now that young women commonly enter the labour force and remit contributions to the family budget, but so far there has been little correlation between her entry into the labour force prior to marriage and parental assumptions about losses associated with daughters. There were few expectations that daughters would make any substantial or long-term cash contributions to the family budget and any contribution that was made was largely and merely perceived as a small and short-term return for the parental expenses incurred in raising a daughter or her rightful contribution to the much larger expenses of her coming marriage. After marriage, although much attention has been given to the break between daughters and their natal families and the transfer of their persons, property, labour, support and care to the families of their husbands, field research over the years in East and South Asia suggests that this break may be less radical than hitherto assumed and that continuing contact after marriage may involve her in making contributions to the support of her parents (see Figure 4.3D).

Although virilocal marriage, in which daughters move to their husbands' households, is rightly seen to be an important factor affecting the ability of daughters to support their parents, the degree to which daughters are physically and socially separated from their natal families and have an independent source of income after marriage may affect the degree to which a daughter can sustain close ties with and contribute support to her natal family. For instance, if married daughters are secluded within or entirely incorporated into the families of their husbands, they are unlikely to be in a position to provide support. However, if a married daughter is employed in income-generating activities and has access to individual inherited or acquired assets within the marital family then she may have access to resources which might be deployed for the support of her parents. As ethnographic studies already cited show, this was one of the major factors separating the ties of married daughters with their natal families in north and south India. In north India, for example, daughters-in-law in the richer propertied households were more likely to be incorporated into their husband's households and have no source of independent income or individual assets. Secluded, their contacts with their natal families were largely confined to a series of formal and periodic visits, each of which involved the transfer of gifts from her own family to the family of her husband, thus continuing the unidirectional flow of resources from parent to daughter after her marriage. In these circumstances married daughters were less likely to earn a wage or to have access to and control of marital assets which could be used to contribute to the support of their natal families. In south India, however, local and cross-cousin marriage was less likely to involve the physical or social separation of hypergamous marriages of the north, and thus married daughters continued to maintain formal and informal links with their natal families. Additionally, in the southern states married women were more likely to continue working in the fields or other occupations and have access to small but nevertheless controllable amounts of property which they could use to contribute to the material well-being of their own parents if they so wished.

In China, too, there are equivalent differences in the amount of contact and the number of contributions made by married daughters to their natal families, but this time the main difference is between city and countryside. In rural China where exogamous marriage is still a common practice, there is less sustained contact between married daughters and their natal families, as married daughters are more likely to live some distance from their parents. Daughters-in-law usually reside with and are expected to support primarily their husband's families with the most important exchanges of labour, services and other support between mother-in-law and daughter-in-law. It will be interesting to see if this changes as marriage partners increasingly are chosen from within the same rural neighbourhood, there is less co-residence of the generations and as women increasingly take up new and independent sources of employment in the countryside. In the cities the situation is somewhat different, as female and male members of the younger generation in employment and economically independent are more likely to establish a separate residence after marriage and maintain relations with both sets of parents. Daughters are as likely to continue informal day-to-day contact with their own parents as with the parents of their husbands, although how far this extends to include economic support is unclear. In terms of emotional support, parents often say that they prefer daughters because they are more likely to show greater care and affection and this preference rebounds on their attitudes towards daughters before marriage. Indeed throughout East and South Asia there is a growing belief that to acquire both material and emotional parent-care the ideal composition of the smaller family is now a son and a daughter, but that it is still a son who is central to the material inter-generational contract from which daughters are excluded. With the simultaneous desire for and/or strictures in favour of smaller families there is less space for daughters who remain outside this contract, despite their existing and increasing contributions to parental support. What field studies show is that with smaller families not only are daughters still not the equal of sons but, with the exception of the single-child daughter in urban China, they still cannot substitute for sons. That they cannot substitute for sons is a consequence of both gender bias that is familial in origins and of the ways in which gender difference and divisions of labour are constructed in East and South Asian societies. If entitlements are linked to expectations then the differing expectations of daughters and sons are rooted in interpretations or the reasoning of gender.

5 Interpreting gender
Hierarchy and difference

In ethnography, personal narrative, interview, ritual and everyday practice whether among the literate or non-literate, employed or secluded, or urban and rural populations in East and South Asia, two powerful messages emerge which are confirmed by the statistics. The first is that children are gendered; the second is that practically and cognitively daughters are reasoned to be secondary and a supplement, but rarely a substitute for sons. Notions of secondariness and unsubstitutability underlie son preference and are rooted in the culture of gender, so that an understanding of gender identity and the ways in which gender relations are defined and interpreted within everyday beliefs and behaviour is an important contributing factor in understanding daughter discrimination. It is one of the arguments of this book that daughters suffer by reason of gender and that this reasoning has been underplayed in previous analyses of son preference. Although daughters are the most junior and understudied members of the female gender, even the very term 'gender' is used universally as if there is an assumed uniform agreement about its meaning to which is ascribed powers of explanation as if gender identity and relations are pre-determined or beyond culture. Within demography, analysts may have given a great deal of attention to inter-generational relations, but they have given rather less to gender relations, although there is evidence that this is changing. Watkins in an important article in *Demography* in 1993 entitled 'If all we know about women was what we read in Demography what would we know?' argued that, with the exception of fertility studies, demographers have not been very sensitive to the importance of gender relationships in understanding demographic behaviour.[1] Although the intensity of son preference and daughter discrimination has been linked to gender roles, relations and degrees of inequality, few demographic studies analyse this linkage in any detail, although they often suggest that such studies should be undertaken. It has been left to anthropologist and feminist scholars to interrogate the notion of gender and analyse gender roles and relations in the context of the family, the community and society.

From the 1970s onwards much of the early feminist anthropological literature focused on the role and status of women in societies and aimed to make good the omission of women's voices from ethnography. These early studies were soon superseded by an emphasis on the broader analytic concept of gender which not only encompassed a concern with women but also highlighted women's roles, responsibilities and opportunities in relation to men. Researchers took up many of the hitherto unquestioned assumptions about sex and gender and drew attention to the way in which gender as socially constructed hierarchical relations between women and men shaped the lives and activities of women within households, communities and societies. Indeed the introduction of the more relational term 'gender' to complement the emphasis on 'women' was an important indication of a growing concern with sexual divisions of labour or the broader implications of differences between men's and women's biological and economic roles. In more recent years it is the notion of gender itself that has come under investigation, as studies differentiated notions of sex and gender by ascribing to sex biological or physical differences and to gender social or cultural constructions based upon or at least incorporating biological differences. However, more recently feminist theorists have challenged this sex-gender dichotomy that tends to essentialise sex as a pre-given entity by suggesting that both terms are socially constructed. Certainly ethnographic studies focusing on reproductive or birth culture confirm that conceptually no such differentiation between sex and gender can be made and that, in discussions about the value of children before and after conception and before and after birth, ideas about sexual identity and preference are as socially constructed as gender and reflect the gender culture of a society.

Cultures of gender

Throughout my many long years of research and study in Asia it has become clear to me that the culture of gender in China and India may be different in important ways from that of my own society and that the loose use of the term 'gender' camouflages such differences. In Europe and North America, cultures of gender emphasise the qualities common to males and females and variously embrace androgynous or overlapping gender categories or domains of activities, the achievement of equality at the very least in opportunity and oppositional or competitive relations between males and females. In Asia, on the other hand, there has been a traditional focus on gender difference or unique female qualities, divisions or separation of activities and an emphasis on complementarity rather than equality. In East and South Asia this emphasis on male–female difference has been re-asserted and pervades contemporary cultures of gender, be they those of governments, feminists, retailers, foreign and indigenous manufacturers or of populations in everyday practice. This coherent assertion of female difference derives from and has its origins in the ancient religious or philosophic texts of Asia which in common emphasise gender differences and complementarity as underlying and/or contributing to cosmic unity and harmony.

In China, gender differences and divisions are rooted in an elaborate Confucian code of beliefs and conduct which incorporated ancient cosmological notions that the universe was composed of two quite separate but interactive complementary elements: 'yin' the female and 'yang' the male. The 'yin' elements displayed dark, weak and passive attributes, in contrast to the 'yang' elements which were characterised by all that was bright, strong and active. The dichotomous rhythms of day and night, sun and moon, and summer and winter all reflected the balanced and harmonious roles of heaven and earth and male and female: while man was endowed with the 'firm nature of heaven', women partook of 'the yielding nature of the Earth'.[2] Originally conceived as interacting, equal and complementary, these divisions were soon arranged in a hierarchical relationship, with 'yin' elements in time coming to stand for all that was negative and inferior in the universe. These cosmological beliefs were incorporated into the teachings of Confucius and his disciples which became the established and ruling ideology from the second century BC. Confucius is purported to have said of women that 'they are as different from men as earth is from heaven' and that 'Women indeed are human beings, but they are of a lower state than men and can never attain to full equality with them'.[3] The ancient Book of Changes, an authoritative source of Confucian precepts, noted that 'Great Righteousness is shown in that men and women occupy their correct places: the relative positions of Heaven and Earth'.[4] According to another authoritative source, the Book of Rites compiled in the second century AD and later to become one of the venerated Confucian classics containing rules of correct conduct, 'to be a woman meant to submit', 'women were to take no part in public affairs' and 'a man does not talk about affairs inside [the household] and a woman does not talk about affairs outside [the household].[5] From these first principles establishing gender difference, segregated divisions of labour and hierarchy, a set of conceptual elaborations and practical rules were evolved which defined correct female behaviour and separate spaces in families, communities and society for daughters, wives and mothers.

In India the emphasis on gender difference has its origins in the most ancient of religious texts, the Ryveda, the Samaveda and the Artharvaveda all of which, dated no later than the second millennium BC, found their way into the classic Vedic ritual of a slightly later period and remain the primary sources of mythology, religious performance and social practice for ancient India. An examination of the sacred texts and rituals of the Vedas suggested that there was a mythic vision of celestrial and terrestrial worlds destined to be in a constant state of turmoil unless there was continual sacrifice by both gods and men to maintain a balance inclusive of male and female energies and making for cosmic unity and harmony.[6]

Although early texts and ritual incantations reveal that the wives of priests had a subsidiary role in these sacrificial rituals, religious educational opportunities and ritual sacrificial roles left open to women in Vedic times were repeatedly curtailed by later conventions and law books.[7] Their exclusion from the rituals of sacrifice undercut women's eligibility to participate in other aspects of Vedic and Brahmanical *dharma*, such as studying Vedic texts, officiating at religious ceremonies and even the right to drop out of the social order by becoming a wandering ascetic. Women were denied sacred and ascetic roles because of the impurity associated with the polluted and polluting sexually active woman. Women themselves were not only banished from the sacred arena and restricted in their paths to salvation, but the male ascetic had to renounce his sexuality and thus sexual relations with women in his bid for salvation. In the Orthodox tradition, too, the idea persists that a woman must be reborn a man before she can hope to attain salvation. Excluded by their physical impurity from Sanskritic ritual and religion from the late second millennium BC, women were confined to domestic religious devotions which aimed at increasing the welfare and extending the life-span of family members.[8] This ritual division between the sacrificial (*srauta*) and the domestic (*grhya*) represented and became the template for more extended male–female divisions in which women in India too became associated primarily with and confined to the domestic domain. With some exceptions such gender differences, divisions of labour and role allocations have been maintained in much of South Asia despite economic development and improvements in women's education and new employment opportunities. In China on the other hand, gender differences and divsions in labour were rhetorically cancelled out for some decades in the quest for revolutionary androgyny and then re-emphasised as a component of the new economic reforms and as a cultural-specific response to globalisation.

There are a number of socio-economic and political trends in contemporary East and South Asia today which emphasise the differences between male and female, or what is distinctive to and uniquely female, and these contemporary assertions of gender difference continue to underlie continuing gender divisions of labour evident in the region. In the economy, the establishment of the labour-intensive export-processing sector in industrial, free-trade or special manufacturing zones has been based both on the movement of foreign investment to and within Asia and on an abundance of cheap female labour. Indeed in these new economic and export zones of labour-intensive industries in East and South Asian societies, gender divisions of labour have been emphasised and gender differences exaggerated in the bid to sell a cheap, dexterous and docile young female labour force to foreign investors and trans-national corporations. The labourers in these new Asian economic, export and industrial zones are almost entirely made up of young unmarried daughters who are thought to be especially qualified for the mass assembly lines of the export-oriented light manufacturing industries. These young women have been introduced to new labour processes and labour controls based on deskilling and casualisation with resulting instability, low wages, poor working conditions and lack of labour protection. The cultural and gendered rationale for the feminisation of labour in these types of industries is that young Asian girls are small and nimble, have excellent eyesight and a finely boned dexterity ideal for the minute and detailed work of machine or craft. They are also deemed to be uniquely docile, accustomed as they are to the disciplines of patriarchal authority and thus especially tolerant of the demanding labour conditions, age or marital discriminations and exclusion from both supervisory, management or technical posts and protective organisations. They are much preferred to young men who, as one Chinese employer said, 'would not put up with having to work at the machines all day. They are more unruly and more difficult to handle and would surely rebel and cause trouble'.[9] One recent continent-wide study concluded that the young Asian women workers were the first contributors to as well as the first victims of the industrial restructuring in Asia.[10] If gender difference is a feature of new productive manufacturing and supplies of goods, it is also increasingly emphasised in the context of the new Asian consumer revolution.

In a world of near-saturated retail markets and recent consumer boom and crisis in Asia, the young urban Asian fashion 'miss' with her own disposable income and distinctive interest in brand and femininity has emerged as an important mainstay of the rapid consumer revolution which has characterised Asian societies in recent decades. As in Western Europe and North America this consumer revolution constituted new categories of goods, new times, places and patterns of purchase, new marketing techniques, new ideas about possessions and materialism, changes in reference groups and life-styles, diffusion patterns, product symbolism patterns of decision-making and the creation of demand. In Europe and North America, historians have recently argued that the profundity of the consumer revolution as a process is often ignored or at least underemphasised compared to the attention given to the industrial revolution, largely because of its gradual seeping nature over four centuries.[11] In Asia the onset of these processes was so fast, so highly visible that neither they nor the central role of young Asian women in these processes could pass unnoticed. *The Economist* has noted that it is to these young Asian women, who live at home without domestic responsibilities, watch television and read women's consumer magazines, that global markets increasingly look in their bid for economic recovery. It also concluded that no-one is spending except young women and that 'if the rest of Asia spends as young single females do most of Asia's economic woes would be over and the consumer boom revived.'[12]

At the centre of the new interest and boom in consumption in China and responsible for enticing young Asian women into a central role has been the novel profusion of new consumer goods in plate-glass department stores and shopping malls and an all pervasive interest in style, colour, material and above all 'brand'.[13] Together these have generated a 'new world of goods' increasingly evident in village and city, the coast and remote interior and in domestic and public spaces. The image of young women as consumers with curly hair, white smiling teeth and almond-shaped eyes who are both immaculately groomed and delicate of bone and demeanour, and forever in the company of washing machines, cooking pots, watches, televisions, toothpastes, cosmetics and fashion garments is a common but relatively recent feature of both television advertisement and consumer billboard lining city and county street or square. Anthropologists and sociologists have long recognised the importance of the language, signs and symbols of goods as a means of social communication,[14] but they have more recently turned their attention to shopping as an under-researched mass activity or everyday practice in which the consumer engages in an on-going process of self-creation as goods become agents of change and perception.[15] If it is via goods that individuals rethink themselves then young Asian female consumers have appropriated Western fashion, jewelry, cosmetics and other articles of attire and decoration in order to adopt or craft anew an identity which is gendered, feminine and modern. In the case of transitional economies, they have been encouraged by retailers to rehabilitate the feminine gender which had been lost during revolutionary years.

In China, the largest of the transitional economies, one of the most visible of recent changes has been the emergence of new female images and the rejection of the androgynous 'iron girls', 'masculinisation of the female', 'female man', 'superwoman's masculinisation' or 'man of a woman' of revolutionary years. To encourage male–female equality the revolutionary government had introduced new titles, dress and slogans aimed at reducing gender difference and establishing new androgynous categories inclusive of both male and female. Slogans such as 'let both men and women take part in our revolution', and 'women are the equal of men' or 'anything a man can do a woman can do also' were aimed at breaking down rigid gendered divisions of labour and changing the image, self-image and expectations of women to match those of their male peers in the revolution and in production or work. To reduce gender difference and hierarchy, an important role was assigned to the promotion of model women whose androgynous attitudes and behaviour were popularised via all forms of the media including bill-board, newspaper, magazine, broadcast, film, as well as in study and political campaign. What this novel denial of gender difference meant in both rhetorical and practical terms was that women were invited to cross gender boundaries, assume male qualities and enter male spaces on terms that were the same as or equal to men's with very few concessions to female-specific qualities.[16] Inviting women to shoulder 'half of heaven' or enter male spaces previously denied them became synonomous with the appropriation of public male roles in production and politics with few concessions to female roles in marriage, reproduction or in the family. The term 'female' was largely redefined to include male attributes, attire and measures of success which were acclaimed during the revolution as a 'reversal of heaven and earth' or the attainment of 'half of heaven'. However, in post-revolutionary years this androgyny has been re-appraised, with women retrospectively perceiving themselves to have entered the social and public domain of the urban enterprise or rural collective, but at the cost of their female selves with a consequent loss of image, demeanour and perceptions distinctive to women. Like so many other women, a noted female activist noted that in retrospect, 'they knew they were women, but they knew less the difference between themselves and men.'[17] It is the gendered differences between men and women encouraged by the new opportunities for employment and consumption, which now lie at the centre of the new cultural-specific discourses of both government and women's movements in contemporary Asia.

A prevalent theme within the much vaunted Asian values of recent years has been the virtues of family cohesion, inclusive of both gendered divisions of labour and the femininity of Asian women which are perceived to be in direct contrast to the androgyny of West or European and North American women. Asian governments alike have projected images of their societies which are to be distinguished from and stand outside of the process of globalisation, the spread and speed of which has provided a new opportunity to re-emphasise Asian difference. Recent works by anthropologists have drawn attention to Occidentialsm, or the construction of images of the West,[18] which, like its counterpart Orientalism, is at best a society imagined, often obscuring attributes which sit uneasily or conflict with a highly essentialised image or selected vision constructed for comparison. In the case of gender, the popular image of Western women emphasises their assumed androgyny or masculinity and their shoulder-padded stridency. As interesting as the range of images of the West constructed are the uses to which such images are put. In Asia, in the face of a perceived threat to cultural-specific identities, these contrasting images of the West have been used to bolster the specificity of local culture and values. The focus of this self-conscious culturalism has been a return to cultural roots as the most visible cultural markers collectively defining Asian ways or traditions. In the ensuing and strategic assertion of Asian values, an important component has been the emphasis on gender difference and the distinctive femininity of Asian women.

Many Asian women's movements too have emphasised their own distinctive gender cultures and the distinctive female qualities of their women as different from both the men of their own culture and from the women of Western cultures. In China my own interviews suggest a new interest in defining qualities that are distinctively 'female', with 'softness' the attribute most often thought to be uniquely female. Meanings are often borne of contrasts; in the case of gender, definitions often resort to age-old dichotomies with the search for what is different and distinctive starting with unquestioned assumptions about what is masculine and then proceeding to the identification of contrasting qualities unique to women. There have been a number of articles deriving from the birth of women's studies in China expressing an increasingly popular view that there is a distinctive female 'outlook' and 'world' which is inherently different from that of the males of their own cultures.[19] Indeed many platforms and writings of women's movements in Asia today attempt to combine both an international interest in women's rights and culturally specific elements of femininity which cannot be adequately summarised by the English-language term 'feminism'. For China, I have used an archaic English-language term 'feminalism' meaning 'womanly' and its Chinese translation of 'funuzhuyi' to best summarise the unique combination of elements of both femininity and feminism. Much as the term 'culturalism' is used to describe the strategic assertion of cultures, so the term 'feminalism' might be applied to the strategic assertion of the 'womanly' embracing both feminine qualities and women's rights that is common in Asia and perceived to be complementary to masculine qualities and male interests.

It is on this culturally distinctive and recursive notion of complementarity in Asian cosmologies, philosophies, movements and everyday practice that I want to focus, for it seems to me to be particularly relevant in interpreting gendered preference and bias in the values attached to children. In China now, the women's movement has taken great pains to stress that it has no wish to disadvantage or denigrate men or take men as a main adversary and, in doing so, it seeks to distinguish itself from Western feminism and what it perceives as its oppositional stance. As several feminist scholars in China have argued, the rhetoric of Chinese feminism speaks first and foremost for basic social justice, so that while its rhetoric might be feminine its concern is universal.[20] For India, Fruzetti has argued that it is complementarity which characterises the relations between men and women rather than the contradictory and oppositional relations between the sexes that may exist elsewhere.[21] Likewise, Menski has noted that role allocation on the basis of gender rather than equality between men and women is at issue in sub-continental societies.[22] Two activists in the women's movement in India have also emphasised the divisions between women's and men's separate but complementary spheres.

> It is really a mistake to see women as competing with and being restricted by men; rather male and female roles are clearly distinguished, and the sexes are seen as complementary to each other.[23]

It is this focus on gender difference and complementarity, derived from ancient text and time-honoured perception and re-emphasised by contemporary assertions of Asian values, that has led to the persistence of gendered divisions of labour and spheres of activities that are still difficult to traverse and underlie son preference.

Divisions of labour

In Asia gender segregated divisions of labour are assumed rather than questioned and are referred to time and again in the ethnographic studies of families and communities. One of the most prevalent themes in conversation and behaviour reported by ethnographers was parental emphasis on the roles and activities that are performed by sons and that cannot possibly be undertaken by daughters, which in turn reflect gender divisions of labour and the rigidity of the boundaries between separate but complementary sets of male and female activities. Ethnographies suggest that in urban and rural communities everyday notions or definitions of male and female identity are constructed around gendered sets of activities, so that gender itself is interpreted as more of a performative concept rooted in social practice rather than defined by any pre-given biological attributes. It is not what one is so much as what one does. Gender difference is thus less predicated on biological or physical attributes than on differentiated activities or divisions of labour within the family, the community and society. As one of my students conducting field work in a remote central Chinese village concluded from his observations, it was the divisions between activities and spaces which accounted for 'the sexual meanings and production of gender' in the village. For the villagers what makes a woman is not who she is (in the biological sense) but what she does (in the sociological sense). Therefore, he suggested, gender difference is located in social practice rather than biological difference and is thus something exercised rather than given.[24] In East and South Asia distinguished by rigid divisions of activities which are categorised as either male or female with few overlapping domains, ethnographic accounts suggest that men and women are clearly differentiated by the exercise of their occupational and ritual roles on daily and life-cycle occasions which reiterate and reproduce gender divisions of labour.

In my own studies of rural and urban households in China, I have been struck by the way in which activities are gender-typed within households and communities and that, although the content of the activities might change, divisions remain gendered with boundaries and taboos so rigid that activities, even those necessary for daily consumption, are left undone rather than be undertaken by the other or 'wrong' gender. Likewise in India's Gujarat State, Leela Visaria found that the women there were quite clear about the divisions of labour and that only sons could undertake agricultural labour or provide food for parents.

> We prefer more sons because sons help us in our work; they could help us in the agricultural work.

A son is needed because he alone can take care of parents later on. A son would feed you in your old age.

We prefer two sons because if one of them is bad or is not willing to take care of us, we can count on the second one for food.[25]

In South Asia, and to lesser extent in parts of rural East Asia, this division of labour was exaggerated by notions of sexual pollution or impurity and shame. For instance, as she reaches puberty a young unmarried girl's reputation requires parental protection which has direct implications for divisions of labour.

Whenever a girl reaches puberty — even if that's at a young age — she seems burdensome to both her parents. They can neither send her out to work in the fields nor leave her alone at home.[26]

... it's very hard to bring up girls these days and get them married. Because of girls, families get dishonoured.[27]

Before marriage the nagging worry for parents is that she will be involved in premature sexual relations and bear the child of a man without formal rights over her. There is a deep rooted cultural significance attached to purity and the defilement of an unmarried daughter, and the potential threat to the honour of her parents and brothers is best avoided. Hence from puberty onwards her person is closely guarded to prevent such a disgrace and it is perceived as an onerous chore given that she should not be left alone at home, at work in the fields or in very public places.[28]

Throughout East and South Asia it is quite clear that in parental discussions, expectations and calculations about family planning and building, the differential preference for and entitlements of boys and girls was largely rooted in anticipation that sons and daughters would follow customary divisions of labour. There is little cross-cultural evidence to suggest that separate divisions can ever be equal whether they be gender-, age- or ethnicity-based and this is so even where they are masked as interdependent, complementary or harmonious. So long as male qualities are assumed to be based on superior strength and authority and are the accepted yardsticks, it has been difficult for advocates of a distinctive female identity to do other than return to traditional stereotypes of Asian women based on secondary and submissive characteristics. If very rarely gender segregation and complementarity can be achieved without gender hierarchy so son preference is largely expressed and rationalised in terms of gendered labour. That is families assume conventional adult male and female roles that are separate, rarely interchangeable and arranged in work hierarchies with differential values attached to the content of these gendered divisions of activities. An ethnographic examination of the meanings and values attached to work confirm that, almost without exception, there is a gendered work hierarchy in which men's work is valued more highly than women's work. That is, the domestic and unskilled work of women which so often generates little in the way of a cash income is valued less than the public, productive and ritual, skilled and cash-earning work of the male members of the family. It is the ways in which 'work' is recognised and remunerated, and the dichotomy of inside domestic, light and unskilled as opposed to outside public, heavy and skilled work which underlie differential evaluations and hierarchies in work.[29] It is also the differential status accorded to men and women's work which reverberates on the status of sons and daughters.

If women's work is devalued by gender and work hierarchies, then the work of girls is all but rendered invisible, in that it is largely confined to the informal 'inside' or domestic or the casual and short-term of the informal sector and perceived to be a short-term or temporary asset to the family. The invisibility of girls' labour is reflected in the statistics and campaigns to improve the lot of child workers which rarely include either her domestic labour or care of siblings. Gender- and age-disaggregated data is not available routinely for child labour, but reports from South Asia reveal significant gaps between the statistics and actual rates of child labour with working girls rendered almost invisible. In 1996 the International Labour Office estimated that more than 150 million child workers are to be found in Asia, a significant proportion of whom are girls.[30] Among children gendered divisions are already apparent at young ages. According to one field survey of 15 to 20 villages in the Bihar state of India, very few tasks undertaken by children as young as 6 years of age are gender neutral, in that only 6 out of 58 activities are performed by both girls and boys.[31] The vast majority of young girls perform work that is hidden, non-renumerated and therefore under-enumerated, yet in all but the richest households in both South and East Asia it is not uncommon for unmarried daughters, often from their earliest childhood years, to contribute to the upkeep of their families. In China my own questioning of school pupils in both city and village suggests that girls undertake time-consuming duties in the household often to the detriment of their schooling and that their help is particularly welcome in households where all the adult members are employed in income-generating activities.

The schooling of daughters may be truncated as tens of millions of girls in East and South Asia perform domestic or farm chores for their own households, assist their families in home-based work for wages, work as maids in the homes of others, work in low-paid repetitive and unskilled factory jobs and in the sweat shops of the informal sector or, in some countries, are involved in slave, prostitution and other illicit activities. Routinely they are paid less than boys for the same work, are concentrated in sectors that are characterised by low pay and long hours, and are concentrated in industries which pose excessive dangers to their health, safety and welfare. As they reach their teens, it is more and more common for unmarried daughters in East and South Asia to be employed in farming or factories and in city services or professions, and to contribute to household budgets of their natal families. In many regions now they migrate long distances to cities or export processing zones where the factory work is so physically demanding and difficult that it is often observed that these same working conditions would not be tolerated by other categories of workers. Research, including that of one of my woman students who worked in a Shenzhen factory, shows that in some of these Asian factories, the young women who make up the work force have left home between the ages of 18 and 20 or even younger and that they work long hours, often 12 to 18 hours daily, at intricate and repetitive piece work in cramped, airless and noisy working conditions. They reside in crowded dormitories and intolerable living conditions, the standards of which are often worse than the poor conditions that they left behind to escape to the cities and remit a portion of their wages to families back home.[32] Despite these substantive and increasing contributions it is existing gender divisions of labour which render their work less visible than the potential contributions of sons. By reason of gender alone they are relegated to a secondary and supplementary position and girls soon learn that they cannot substitute for their brothers.

Gendered perceptions

Both daughters and mothers on behalf of daughters perceive this gendered secondariness and unsubstitutability to be a disadvantage for girls in their natal families from a young age. That daughters themselves experience the lesser expectations of their parents and fewer entitlements to family resources as factors contributing to their own unhappiness, their own lesser worth and an 'outsider' status is evident in a number of autobiographical narratives in which daughters, and particularly second or higher parity daughters, write of their own childhood experiences in terms of familial exclusion. Commonly they cite a number of remembered moments when they first became aware of the gender differences between themselves and their brothers which, constantly reaffirmed by the older generations, served as reminders of their lesser status and eventual removal from the family on marriage. For Republican China there are a number of autobiographies in which grown women remember how as small girls they observed it to be customary for boys to have a clan name, a generation name and an individual name which clearly defined their place and position in the family's ancestral records from which they were excluded. This difference was forcefully brought home to one 7-year-old girl in a way that she 'never forgot'.

> I was hurt, and could not understand why I could not share the name of my generation. It was the small beginning of a sense of injustice that was to continue and grow more and more sharp.[33]

If practices of incomplete naming made an early impression on small daughters, so also did familial ceremonies and ritual occasions, such as funerals, the worshipping of ancestors or tending the family graves in all of which girls were either marginalised, accorded spectator status or altogether excluded.

> This was my family and my home and yet I did not really belong. I felt unaccountably and unjustifiably shut out. I wanted to ask why my brothers could worship our ancestors and I could not. But I didn't dare.[34]

Many elder daughters could not help but notice that at the births of younger siblings, their sisters and brothers were welcomed into the family quite differently, and many second and third daughters felt themselves to be 'unwanted' or a 'disappointment from the start'.[35]

> When I was six I learned that Mother felt a wrenching personal shame at having failed to bear my father a male heir ... No one had paid more dearly than I for what she saw as her one failure. In the Chinese culture, it is no tragedy if the first-born is a female. There is time yet for a son to come. As the proverb states it, 'first the blossom, then the fruit' ... it was I, the Second Daughter, who bore the stigma.[36]

It is very noticeable that even as young girls, daughters formed images of themselves as secondary, 'less than a person' and as 'transient', 'detached' or 'outside of their families' in comparison to their brothers. One woman commented on the roundness and wholeness of the family with descent lines maintained by sons who alone fed the dead and the old. She remembered how as a young girl she had an image of herself as 'an observer who witnessed every nuance of an unchanging regime' from which she was excluded.[37] Another woman wrote that in the events and decisions of her household, she as a young girl had been ignored for 'she was only daughter to marry out' and only 'sons were people'.[38] Another woman duly surmised that as a young daughter, she was in the family but not of the family for her presence was merely temporary.

> In our household the women who had come in as wives from other clans, and the girl children who had been born to them and would be married out to other clans, constituted our women's world and had a psychology of its own. We were in the family but not of it.[39]

In contemporary China too a number of young girls have written shorter personal narratives that suggest that girls continue to be fully cognisant of lesser expectations and entitlements. In one short autobiographical account, a very young schoolgirl wrote of how her birth had not only been unwelcome but also seemed to be the cause of her parents' estrangement and her mother's subsequent death.

> I have a father, but I lost his love the day I was born. I experienced mother love for only a short time of six years. I was told that when I was born, Father came from another part of the country and asked loudly before he entered the delivery room, 'A boy or a girl?' 'A girl', my grandma answered unwillingly. He immediately turned away with a snort of contempt, banged the door and went out without even coming near the bed to have a look at me. My father's love ended then and there. My mother lived in tears and misery. Father never came to see us ... Mother got a serious illness and passed away when she was only 35 years old and looked so young ... That I am a girl is the only reason Father left home for a faraway place and Mother died.[40]

Another young girl in less extreme circumstances wrote of how unhappy she felt when she observed the privileged entitlements of her brother.

> My mom, no matter what happened, always considered my elder brother first and ignored me. At the table, she kept putting food into my brother's bowl and not mine, as if I were not her own child.[41]

In my own field work in Chinese villages I have been struck by how often elder sisters have been taken out of school to work because they were of lesser importance and deemed to be and indeed considered themselves to be 'stupid'. Simultaneously I have been impressed by how often these same young women find work and return home to visit their rural families, bringing welcome presents and cash sums for the school fees of their brothers and sisters. In Beijing I was recently in a room of 40 to 50 young migrant women who each in turn told their story. A predominant theme was the responsibility they felt to earn an income sufficient to support siblings in school back home and, indeed, many had dropped out of school in order that they might help in such a way. One young 21-year old graduate of junior middle school had come to Beijing to be a housemaid but she was studying in her own time to finish her high school education. She looked around the room and found it ironic that back home such migrant women were designated 'stupid elder sisters', yet here they were working in the city and supporting their siblings in school. Many thought that their contributions, although appreciated, were seen as merely reimbursing their parents for the expenses of their upkeep. In another Chinese society in Taiwan, several researchers have found that daughters compete to be thought filial and to pay back the debt they incurred to their parents for bringing them up, but they still 'believe that they themselves [are] worthless, and that literally everything they

[have] — their bodies, their upbringing, their schooling — belong[s] to their parents and has to be paid for'.[42] For the daughters though, even these efforts to recompense or repay the costs of their upbringing seem not to cancel out their debts to their families or permit them the family membership and acceptance that they sought. One of the songs still sung by daughters in a southern Chinese village in the 1980s testifies to this lack of familial acknowledgement.

> Your enemy goes out from your dragon door
> You will feel lucky when I am away
> I have worn hollows in your stone steps going about my work
> But however many names are engraved on your ancestral tablets
> Mine will not be among them.[43]

Jack and Sulamith Potter were impressed by the prodigious efforts of young unmarried daughters in these same villages to contribute to the familial budget in order to recompense their parents. They argue that the effort of daughters to repay such debts are rooted in the structurally liminal nature of the unmarried daughter's position in the family and her efforts to affirm the validity of her status as a family member.[44]

Although I have not had the opportunity to examine the same historical sequence of personal narratives for India, the voices of daughters in the ethnographic records or the casual identification of women friends in India with their daughter-order in conversation both suggest a similar awareness of differential family expectations and entitlements which shape their perceptions of their selves and their worth. Such is the 'invisibility' of daughters' contributions within families and communities that some ethnographers too have ignored this flow of resources and given credence to the stereotyped reputation of daughters as a loss or burden or commodities on which there is no return. In the diagrammatic age and gender pyramid produced by Frances Goldscheider in her article on gender and operational familial relationships, resource flows to and from daughters are omitted (see Figure 5.1).[45] However this omission is a faithful representation of parental perceptions and self-perceptions of daughters as secondary and unable to substitute for their brothers and enter any inter-generational contract. For daughters it may well be that it is familial exclusion rather than the broader notion of social exclusion commonly used in our own societies which, gendered in reasoning, precludes them from entering mainstream economic and social activities.

Mothers too, looking back over their lives, often expressed a wish to avoid having a daughter so as not to bequeathe to another generation a life of suffering and secondariness which they identified as the destiny of any daughters they might bear. In China women frequently referred to the 'superiority' of males and their own secondariness or suffering in explaining their own preference for sons. One Beijing mother of a 7-year

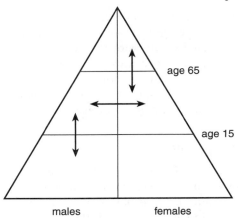

Figure 5.1 Generational and gender relationships in the age–sex pyramid

Source: Francis K. Goldscheider, 'Interpolating demography with families and households', *Demography*, Vol. 32, No. 3, August 1995, p. 473.

old son admitted that she was really glad to have a boy, 'not because I find it important to carry on the family line or because giving birth to a son is honourable, but because I feel that the suffering of women is too extensive. The lives of men are better than the lives of women'.[46] Others echoed the same sentiments but attributed them to their husbands. One woman thought that most men wanted a son. 'The reason', she supposed, 'is the tradition of exalting males and demeaning females which is still very prevalent in society.'[47] In India, too, many women have said that they still did not want daughters because of the secondariness and suffering experienced by women which was just not the same for men. Despite the fact that daughters would help them and share their problems, the prospect for daughters of repeating the suffering of their own lives 'makes them adverse to producing another sufferer like them'.[48] One ethnographer concluded that this 'perhaps tells us as much about these women's perceptions of their own lives as burdensome, as it does about the kind of discriminatory treatment that baby girls are likely to receive when their birth is so unwelcome'.[49]

Although gender relations rarely are examined in any detail in relation to son preference, it has long been assumed that if gender relations were less hierarchical and women more independent of the family, then there would be less son preference. Within demography it was early hypothesised that the degree of son preference in a society was directly linked to the status of women, which was usually measured by two indicators: access to education and entry into employment. Both of these steps, it was argued, would provide women with sources of economic support and social status independent of sons and reduce the suffering of women and their reluctance to have daughters. Thus it was assumed that female education and labour participation were the two most important means by which son preference and thus fertility could be reduced. Hence there has been both a demographic and development interest in integrating new educational and economic opportunities for female education and employment within women and gender development programmes.

Gender and development

During the past few decades there has been much research, policy and practical attention given to women's roles and gender relations within the context of development by international, bi-lateral and national agencies.[50] At first Women in Development (WID) focused on how to integrate women better into ongoing development initiatives which it was assumed would benefit women. WID projects tended to concentrate on income-generating activities whereby women were taught new skills or crafts and organised into marketing or credit co-operatives in which they were also taught aspects of hygiene, literacy and child care. This approach was based on the assumption that changes in gender relations would ensue as women become full economic partners in development — an assumption that was consequently challenged by a second approach. The Women and Development (WAD) approach took a more critical view and focused on the relationship between women and the development processes themselves, rather than purely on strategies to integrate women into development per se. This approach advocated that women have always been important economic actors in production and reproduction, both within and outside of the household but that, because of the way 'work' has been defined, women's contribution to economic development has largely been ignored. What was needed were carefully designed strategies to increase women's economic, political and social status in keeping with these productive roles. A weakness common to both WID and WAD approaches was a preoccupation with income generation and public status of women, so that the tasks performed and time invested by women in family maintenance, including child bearing and rearing, housework, care of the ill and elderly and other private, domestic or reproductive activities, continued to be assigned no economic value and thus lay outside the parameters of development projects. Additionally, women were segregated into their own programmes and projects which took no account of their relations to men which are important attributes and determinants of the development process.

In the 1980s an alternative Gender and Development (GAD) approach emerged which questioned the ways in which specific roles, responsibilities and expectations have been ascribed or assigned to women and to men in both production and reproduction across societies and rejected the public-private dichotomy which commonly had been used as a mechanism to undervalue family maintenance and domestic labour performed by women. Although the GAD approach went further than either WID or WAD in questioning assumptions underlying current processes of economic, social and political development, it has been difficult to integrate this holistic approach into new and on-going development strategies and programmes to redefine gender relations and ensure equality and empowerment for women. Nevertheless the sum of all these initiatives is that today, at least in principle, the inclusion of and separate focus on women has been accepted by a considerable number of international, government and non-government development agencies. It has become a necessary condition for funding that development research, policy and projects investigate women's perceptions and experiences and address their separate needs and interests within a gender and development context. Within this context too new opportunities for female education and employment have made for some improvements in women's educational and economic status which, although more substantial in East than South Asia, still have not had the anticipated effect of reducing daughter discrimination.

Research investigating the link between the status of women and girls has shown that in East and South Asia improvements in women's education and economic status may be associated with fertility decline but do not necessarily lead to reduced son preference. Demographers had long suggested that female employment offered a source of economic independence and status additional to, or instead of, that bestowed by the bearing and raising of children and would lead to subsequent declines in fertility. Researchers also surmised that son preference, the final impediment to reduced fertility, would also be lessened by increasing women's own access to education and income-generating activities. What recent research designed to test this hypothesis in East and South Asia has shown is that evidence for and against this argument is quite mixed. In the early 1980s, Dyson and Moore argued that female education and labour participation should lead to an increase in the value of daughters, although their own studies of the Punjab in India had showed that son preference persisted despite increased female education. Without the benefit of comparative research they assumed their own findings constituted an exception to the rule.[51] Monica Das Gupta researching in the rural Punjab a few years later found that son preference was especially marked among educated women, who by their late twenties wanted virtually no daughters even if they already had several sons.[52] As previous chapters have indicated, her research showed that female mortality for second and subsequent parity daughters was 32% higher than their siblings for uneducated mothers and 136% higher if the mothers were educated. She also argued that the juxtapositions of recent national increases in female education and labour participation with excess and rising infant and child female mortality suggested that there was no clear relationship between

women's status and daughter discrimination. A number of papers published in the 1990s have confirmed that the evidence for assuming such a
correlation is still far from conclusive.

In analysing a number of studies Muhuri and Preston came to the conclusion that the literature on the links between women's status and the
survival chances of daughters in India contains a number of contradictory
findings.[53] They cited several studies which found excess female mortality
to be greater in families with better educated mothers, while others suggested that gender differences were largely invariant regardless of the educational levels of mothers. Only one study claimed to find reduced
differences between female and male child mortality among better educated mothers. Muhuri and Preston concluded that since gender bias is
associated with both higher and lower rates of female literacy, perhaps the
only uncontested finding is that female labour participation tends to be
associated with lower levels of female child mortality, although even this
finding has been questioned by subsequent research. Basu's investigations
also confirmed that the links between maternal education or occupation
and fertility levels, child survival and sex preference were more complex
and less direct than usually supposed.[54] He found that maternal education
is linked to fertility decline and is a more important determinant of lower
levels of child mortality than virtually any other characteristic, but that
higher levels of education were also associated with greater son preference and gender difference in mortality. Basu concluded that 'the advantages of preventing mortality conferred by education are being used, at
least in the initial stages of the spread of education, to selectively favour
more boys than girls.' In contrast he argued that female labour participation, also associated with declining fertility, was positively correlated with
both higher levels of child mortality largely because of the physical incom-
patibility between work and child care but lower levels of female child
mortality. Like Das Gupta, Basu notes that juvenile sex ratios have scarcely
fallen over time even though female literacy rates have risen and, like
Muhuri and Preston, Basu identifies maternal occupation as the only
apparent variable which shows a clear fall in the gender differential in
child mortality, in that sons and daughters of working mothers face more
equal risks of death than do the children of non-working mothers. Finally
Murthi, Guio and Dreze also conclude that a wide range of empirical
investigations suggest contradictory findings. They note that although a
close relationship between education and demographic change has
already emerged and education is now considered to be one of the most
powerful influences on fertility and mortality, links between female literacy or education and child survival are far from clear. While maternal education leads to a general decline in child mortality, it has been found to
both intensify and diminish discrimination against female children and
gender bias in child survival. Female labour participation also seems to
reinforce the hypothesis that higher levels of female employment are

accompanied by increasing chances of female child survival, although they also note that some have argued that female labour participation is associated with decreasing chances of female child survival.[55]

For East Asia too there is no evidence of a direct correlation between female education or employment and reduced discrimination against daughters. In China such correlations have only recently been studied and again these are not as direct as they might be. Some researchers argue that increasing female education and female employment in non-agricultural occupations may be associated with lower son preference while others show evidence to the contrary. As previous chapters have shown there is evidence of greater discrimination against daughters with increasing levels of maternal education: in 1989 the sex ratio at birth was 112.5 for mothers below primary school education, 114.2 for those who had completed primary schooling, 116.2 for middle school graduates and a relatively lower 110.7 for the small proportion of women who had college education.[56] In China a very high proportion of women are engaged in the labour force and when women's occupation is correlated with sex ratios at birth, the 1990 census showed there to be a higher proportion of male births across all occupational sectors with the highest levels among women engaged in farming, forestry, animal husbandry and fishing and in service trades, where sex ratios reach a high 129.4 to 100 female births.[57] Another study in urban Harbin in 1996 also found that while son preference increases with higher levels of education it is also highest among those in less prestigious occupations.[58] Again as for South Asia, Monica Das Gupta and colleagues in East Asia conclude that although the correlations are not as clear as they might be, it has to be generally observed for East Asia as a whole that daughter discrimination, as reflected in sex ratios at birth and greater and/or rising female infant and child mortality rates, has risen despite increased female education and female labour participation.[59] There has been some debate about whether women in India have benefited from economic development or whether they have been further marginalised from agriculture and, less educated than their brothers, cannot compete for new employment opportunities in significant numbers. However as Sudha and Rajan point out even if economic development devalues women in India, in other countries similar trends do not lead to such familial discrimination against daughters.[60]

These simultaneous but cross-cutting trends suggest that, first, there is no neat correlation between the status of women and girls and, second, that where there are some improvements in the status of women these have led to fertility decline but not reduced son preference within smaller families, and thus do not necessarily affect values attached to girls. In China the lack of correlation between the status of women and girls is succinctly encapsulated in the following poem written recently which, already quoted in another chapter, aptly reminds us of this discrepancy.

Times have changed
Men and women are equal
Then why in a certain family
Do they respect boys and look down on girls?[61]

One of the reasons why an increase in the status of women may not lead to a correlative increase in the status of girls is that although girls and women have their female gender in common, they are also divided by generation and, as the last chapter illustrated, daughters are differentiated from daughters-in-law, wives, mothers and mothers-in-law in that they are the only category to reside in natal as opposed to marital households. In the families of their birth, daughters are transient and as temporary members thus have a quite different value to their parents than they do as wives and mothers in their husband's family or in a separate household following marriage. When gender hierarchies are added to those of generation, then daughters are not only devalued in comparison to sons but additionally are devalued in relation to grown women, be they daughters-in-law, wives or mothers. Adult women may be secondary to men but they are less excluded from the inter-generational contracts of their husband's families than are daughters in the families of their birth.

If divisions between gender and generation as outlined in this and the previous chapter are taken into account then it cannot be assumed that there will be neat correlations between the status of boys and girls or between women and girls. Just as it cannot be assumed that benefits accruing to men or boys deriving from development will advantage women or girls in the same way, so improvements in the role and status of women deriving from development cannot be assumed to result in more positive expectations of and improved or equal entitlements for daughters. This is not to suggest that programmes on women, gender or children and development should be discontinued, but rather that they might be said to be a necessary but not sufficient step to increase the demand for daughters or raise their status. Instead programmes which are designed to reduce daughter discrimination will have to take cognisance of the meanings attached to gender, of gender differences or divisions of activities and the rigidity of the boundaries emphasising complementarity and unsubstitutability. They will also have to take account of the specific needs and interests of girls in their natal families as the 'last' or most junior members of the generations *and* of the female gender if they are to succeed in reducing daughter discrimination.

6 The girl child
Agendas and campaigns

Given the pervasiveness of son preference it is surprising to find that despite decades of demographic research revealing the degree and extent of excessive female mortality, it is not until the 1990s that there has been any concerted or sustained attempt internationally, regionally or nationally to reduce or end such daughter discrimination.[1] During the past decade however there have been a number of policy and practical interventions in which the needs and interests of young girls have begun to receive the attention that they surely deserve. Much of this new interest in girls has taken place either within a rights framework or in campaigns focusing on the girl child.

Girls' rights

The rights' framework of the 1990s has proved to be an important tool in directing attention to discrimination and violence against girls. The new emphasis on the rights of girls is an extension of two main sets of rights: those of women and those of children. The International Convention on the Elimination of all Forms of Discrimination against Women (CEDAW) was adopted by the United National General Assembly in 1979 and came into force 2 years later to provide a legally binding basis for the implementation of measures to guarantee the recognition and protection of rights of women. Since that time most of the work of the United Nations Development Fund for Women (UNIFEM) in support of CEDAW has emphasised the rights of adult women but, in the past decade, it has also drawn attention to its support for girls' rights.

> Because discrimination against female children is so pervasive and so destructive to the social order, strengthening girls' rights offers a critical opportunity to enhance not only individual lives, but also the lives of nations. Girls' rights are inseparable from women's rights. Raising the needs of girls high on the international human rights agenda represents an important step towards carrying out one of CEDAW's most powerful and urgent mandates: To modify the social and cultural

patterns of conduct of men and women, with a view to achieving the elimination of prejudices and customary and all other practices which are based on the idea of the inferiority or the superiority of either of the sexes or on stereotyped roles of men and women.[2]

The extension of this mandate to protect the rights of women *and girls* is rooted in the conviction that *girls' rights* and women's rights are inseparable in that the rights of girls today are the rights of tomorrow's women.[3]

There has also been a new international interest in children's rights. Historically the rights and status of children have depended solely on the laws and customs of the countries in which they live, but in 1989 the Convention on the Rights of the Child (CRC) drafted by an international team was adopted by the UN Assembly and ratified by most member states to become the most widely endorsed human rights treaty in the history of the United Nations. The CRC sought to guarantee the rights of all children in every conceivable circumstance and it identified four key principles on which all actions for children should be based: the best interests of the child, non-discrimination, parental guidance and children's participation. It also aimed at specifically eradicating discrimination against girls and the establishment of equal rights and opportunities for both male and female children. A year later, the 1990 World Summit for Children singled out the 'urgent situation of the girl child' by declaring that 'girls must be given equal treatment and opportunities from the very beginning'.[4] The Summit's 27 Worldwide Goals included targets to advance girls' health, nutrition and education, on the premise that the focus on the girl child is critical for a country's efforts to achieve children's rights and development. Within the context of children's rights, UNICEF (the United Nations agency for Children) has worked to publicise the importance of girls' rights as an essential framework for a forward-looking strategy to promote and protect the fundamental rights of girls and women and decisively eradicate inequality and discrimination. Both the CRC and CEDAW have been jointly supported by UNIFEM and UNICEF to guarantee human rights for girls and the two conventions have been very much seen as complementary instruments to ensure the protection of girls' rights.[5] During the 1990s the most important steps placing the rights of today's girls on the international agenda have been taken under the auspices of the United Nations. First, UNICEF has taken up the broader cause of the girl child which embraces her rights and, second, the Platform for Action resulting from the United Nations Fourth World Conference for Women in September 1995 incorporated a total of nine strategic objectives in support of the girl child.

The girl child

In 1990, UNICEF's Executive Board endorsed the focus on the girl child and recommended that the organisation's strategy and programmes in the coming decade explicitly address the status of girls and their needs.[6] In retrospect this decision was to mark a significant step, in that an important international agency began to campaign on behalf of women *and girls* in the development field and draw international, regional and national attention to the scale and types of discrimination experienced by girls. UNICEF, since its founding in 1946 and as its name suggests, has taken children as its primary focus of interest, but it has also long recognised that the well-being of children and women are invariably interlinked and hence expanded its programmes to include an interest in first mothers, then women and later gender equality. Its annual publication, *The Situation of the World's Children*, includes data and analyses on key socio-economic and demographic indicators and trends affecting and reflecting the status of children and women.[7] UNICEF's interest in women and gender as well as children in development has led to some focus on girls.

> In discussing some of the most pressing global problems concerning population, women and social development, UNICEF has resolved that girls not be left behind or left out again.[8]

In addition to designating discrimination against females of all ages as one of the fundamental obstacles to development UNICEF has highlighted the importance of girlhood in preparing for womanhood.

> Today's girls are tomorrow's women, her future clearly mapped out in the stages of her life-cycle. To ensure that life-cycle doesn't become a vicious circle, we must work together to stop disadvantage and discrimination at its roots in the lives of girls.[9]

Gradually the needs of today's girls have become the focus of an important campaign in their own right, centring on the girl child and on the factors that impede her normal growth and development. Subsequent publications sponsored by UNICEF have emphasised how many societies continue to place girls in peril and how this discrimination is so routine that it is both pandemic and virtually invisible. As one of its recent pamphlets stated:

> To be born female is not a crime but you would never know it by looking at the deplorable conditions of girls in many parts of the world.[10]

UNICEF, taking a life-cycle approach, has spent some considerable effort investigating and documenting the ways in which girls are restricted or denied rights to nutrition, health care and education in infancy and childhood.

Beginning from birth, girls in many parts of the world experience the 'apartheid of gender', with her lesser claims 'decided at the moment her biological sex is known.[11]

Indeed, UNICEF has identified the period from conception to birth, infancy and childhood as the most vulnerable points in the female life-cycle as she sets out on 'a perilous path' to and from a girlhood beset by a wide range of discriminating and violent practices that owe nothing to random violence and everything to 'being female' (see Table 6.1). As UNICEF's own pamphlets point out, not only does this perilous path for girls often result in physical disadvantage or even death but also, for those who survive, this path to girlhood is a time of harsh lessons when girls 'begin to deny themselves', to expect little and to think less of themselves than of their brothers, husbands and sons; a lesson which they too 'will pass on to their own daughters unless this vicious circle is broken'.[12]

At an operational level within country offices, UNICEF has prioritised girls' education as the key to development. 'If countries want to achieve sustainable development, they must turn their attention to girls' education.'[13] Although the proportion of children entering school has grown dramatically in the past 20 years, boys have fared much better than girls.

Table 6.1 Girlhood: a perilous path (a UNICEF approach)

Prebirth	Tests that tell the gender of the foetus may be used to de-select girls and abort them.
Birth	An unwanted girl baby may be killed at birth in parts of Asia, or allowed to die when she falls ill.
Infancy	Girls are more resilient than boys but shorter breast-feeding and less nurture reduce their chances.
Early childhood (ages 1–5)	Less food and fewer visits to the health clinic make a girl more susceptible to sickness and stunted growth.
Childhood (ages 6–12)	A heavy load of domestic duties — sibling care, cleaning, cooking, water-carrying, minding the house — robs girls of childhood and education.
Adolescence	Girls who are unschooled and an economic burden are married at an early age by arrangement and sometimes for cash.
Teenage motherhood	Babies born to girls under 18 are often born too early and are too small. A quarter of the 500,000 women who die annually from maternity are teenage girls.

Source: Adapted from UNICEF, *Girls and Women*, A UNICEF Development Printing, New York, 1993, p. 8.

UNICEF has reported that two-thirds of the estimated 960 million illiterate persons in the world are women, over 81 of the 130 million children in developing countries with no access to primary schools are girls and that by age 18 girls have received an average of 4.4 years less education than boys.[14] Millions of girls in developing countries face a host of obstacles that keep them from enrolling and staying in school and girls' education has attracted a great many donor resources and government attention. There is a wide recognition that education changes a girl's own self-perception and thus it is not only her right but society's gain and an impressive amount of documentation and research has been generated on girls' access to schooling, strategies to close gender gaps and innovative approaches to making schools 'girl friendly'. However, despite the considerable effort directed by both governments and international agencies towards identifying the basic obstacles to girls' education and sustaining a girl-friendly educational environment, the gender gap in educating boys and girls remains large despite some progress. It is not only a question of access, for the work of feminist scholars has shown that there are several mechanisms in both official and 'hidden' curriculums through which schooling itself contributes to traditional gender role stereotyping and stratification. There is a growing recognition that gender-aware analyses are necessary to move from 'girl friendly' to 'gender progressive' or 'gender pro-active' schooling and require some rethinking and restructuring of schooling, rather than making it merely more 'responsive to the special needs of girls'.[15] Although girls' education has become the main objective of almost all the girl child campaigns of UNICEF,[16] the agency has also recommended that country programmes promote broader policies and programmes in favour of girls to strengthen family and community support for the girl child, develop a database and disaggregate statistics in order to visibilise discrimination, reduce gender disparities in access to services and foster new and positive attitudes towards girls.

Internationally UNICEF has aimed much of its campaign towards raising the awareness of other multi- and bi-lateral and non-government development agencies and encouraging them to include discrimination against girls within their respective agendas.

> If you are working for human rights and equal rights, human development, women's health, literacy, education, population control, economic development, foreign labour laws, AIDS prevention, in fact almost any of today's pressing issues, then girls are your concern — and need your support.[17]

This international concern and support for the girl child was an important contribution to and deciding factor in the preparations for and events of the Fourth UN Conference for Women held in Beijing in 1995. Here for the first time in the history of human, women's and children's rights girls won an important place on an international agenda. The Beijing Platform for Action is the latest international document for women requiring signatory support and so far 189 governments have committed themselves to taking concrete steps to 'end all discrimination against girls and to prepare girls to participate actively and equally with boys at all levels of social, political, economic and cultural leadership'. Section L of this Platform identified an international agenda made up of nine strategic objectives for the girl child.

1   Eliminate all forms of discrimination against the girl child.
2   Eliminate negative cultural attitudes and practices against the girl child.
3   Promote and protect the rights of the girl-child and increase awareness of her needs and potential.
4   Eliminate discrimination against girls in education, skills development and training.
5   Eliminate discrimination against girls in health.
6   Eliminate the economic exploitation of child labour and protect young girls at work.
7   Eradicate violence against the girl-child.
8   Promote the girl-child's awareness of and participation in social, economic and political life.
9   Strengthen the role of the family in improving the status of girls.[18]

As a result of this international Platform for Action there have been new country programmes and national initiatives to examine and redress the debilitating effects of gender-based discrimination in childhood. It also contributed to the recognition of violence as a rights issue for girls as well as women. Despite the fact that girls as both female and minors are especially subject to direct and indirect violence, ranging from physical and sexual abuse within the family to physical and sexual exploitation for profit outside of the family, it was many years before girls were included on the agendas of movements aiming to reduce violence against women. Indeed their inclusion still is not routine or widespread. In East and South Asia infant abuse may result in foeticide, infanticide and infant death, while much of the childhood violence and exploitation is associated with physical neglect and trafficking involving forcible or deceptive recruitment and transportation into prostitution, marriage and labour. With respect to violence and trafficking, South, East and Southeast Asia have attracted donor attention since 1995 with policy and legislative reform, increased funding and working groups sponsored by UNDP, UNAIDS, UNICEF, UNIFEM, UNESCO, bi-lateral agencies and non-government organisations. However, although the Platform for Action prescribed specific actions to further the nine objectives on the girl child to be undertaken by governments, international bodies and non-government organisations, the chapters on implementation and on institutional mechanisms to review and monitor the Platform were silent on the subject of the girl child. This may mean that the National Plans of Action set up by many governments in South Asia, East Asia and elsewhere to continuously monitor the implementation of the Platform will not pay as much attention to the girl child as they might. It is one of the aims of UNICEF to get the 5-year review of the Beijing Platform (Beijing + 5) and the National Plans of Action for Children in each country changed to make good this omission. India and China are two countries in which there have been new national and international agency-led programmes to promote the rights of and educate the girl child; in both cases these built on a longer-standing national concern for the needs and interests of girls.

India's girl child

In India in the past two decades attention has been drawn to the perils besetting girls, first by women's organisations as part of an expanding campaign to eradicate all forms of violence against women and, second, by a government campaign to investigate and draw attention to many forms of discrimination against the girl child. For many years now a number of very articulate women's organisations and campaigners have drawn attention to violence against women. Much of their attention has focused on dowry-related deaths of young brides which have become more common as the practice of dowry-giving has extended both geographically and socially to different regions and castes. This single issue has united urban-based women's groups across the country, who have taken up the cause by investigating so-called dowry-suicides and publicising instances of maltreatment or even the murder of young wives by the bride's parents because their dowry was insufficient.[19] There has been much media publicity given to their investigations, to reports of helpless and wounded daughters calling on their parents for help that is not always forthcoming, and to dowry and dowry-related deaths, so that this cause has acquired a legitimacy rarely achieved by other such issues. Gradually, though less conspicuously, campaigns against infanticide and 'foeticide' often referred to as a 'silent violence which shadows young female lives' have been added to this cause.[20]

A number of women's organisations have opposed the spread of sex determination tests and the subsequent abortions of unwanted female lives. As activists have argued, violence against women begins before birth if the foetus is female and the dangers haunting young female lives within the womb or at birth are such that it is not surprising that a girl is said to be born 'but a blossom in the dust'. They complain that in poor rural areas the bias of development has been such that, although there is still no drinking water, there are new technological procedures available to 'turn gender into a disease', encouraging 'cultural and social prejudice valuing one sex over another'.[21] There has been some attention given to the linkages between violence against daughters and the 'obsession' or 'mania' for sons. Thus women's organisations have attempted to document and understand the circumstances of son preference, to reduce the son as icon or chief measure of women's status and to increase the worth or value placed on daughters by encouraging girls' education and a female pride in womanhood which rejects the lower or lesser value attached to and felt by girls. Before the 1990s such campaigns on behalf of young daughters were somewhat sporadic and less co-ordinated than those focusing on dowry-related violence, but in the past decade there has been a concerted effort by the Indian government to investigate and reduce violence against girls.

The increasing awareness of discrimination against girls was largely the result of new statistical analyses revealing the high masculinity rates among younger age groups in the population and the higher rates of young females who are illiterate, school drop-outs and child labourers. In 1986, the South Asian Association for Regional Cooperation (SAARC) held a conference on children and, working in close collaboration with UNICEF, called for an improvement in the situation of the girl child. Two years later in 1988 there was a state-level workshop on the girl child at which there were discussions of the origins of discrimination, gender bias in nutritional status, child labour, girls' education, sexual exploitation, child marriage, prostitution and passive stereotypes of girls in children's literature.[22] This SAARC Workshop called for a new and holistic approach by governments and other organisations which would stimulate investigation and research into the problems of young female children and provide positive media images for girls. At that time the problems of girls were sufficiently well-recognised for SAARC to designate 1990 'The Year of the Girl Child', and this was subsequently extended to become the 'Decade of the Girl Child' in order to maintain momentum through to the year 2000.

With UNICEF assistance, Bangladesh, India, Nepal, Pakistan and Sri Lanka have begun to compile gender-disaggregated data and develop a profile of the girl child which, with the exception of Sri Lanka, shows that in each country there is a consistent pattern of gender discrimination in health, education and parental care. Some of the significant outcomes of this activity have been intensive advocacy for and wide acknowledgement of gender discrimination in childhood, a profusion of information and educational materials and high profile events, as well as pilot interventions by governments and non-government organisations in the health, education and legal sectors. All these added up to a significant regional programme which constituted an important precedent encouraging the substantive inclusions on the girl child at the Fourth United National Conference for Women and its Platform for Action in 1995. So far in India there have been two separate but linked areas of activities designed to effect a common strategy of awareness-raising: academic-based research aimed at understanding daughter discrimination and popular education aimed at parents and others to reduce daughter discrimination.

In the 1990s one of the largest national projects on the girl child in India has been that sponsored by the Department of Women and Child Development and several other government ministries and undertaken by 22 women's studies centres located in different regions throughout the country.[23] The aim of the project was to observe and document the special problems of girls in each separate region and at the same time identify the common features so as to provide an overall picture of the condition of girls throughout the country. This collaborative survey-based research project aimed at generating comparative data relevant to the condition of the girl child that would help to improve planning and implementation of programmes. In the regional West Bengal study, for example, the School of Women's Studies at Jadavpur University surveyed a total of 600 households in several selected areas of the state and targeted girls aged between 7 and 18 years. Using a national questionnaire formulated by the Central Co-ordination Committee for all the 21 regional centres involved in the project, information was collected about the girls themselves, their attitudes towards their mothers and about the households in which they lived, for family backgrounds and environments were considered to be important factors in shaping young female lives, their ideas and their perceptions. The results of the study in West Bengal were incorporated into a very interesting book entitled *Loved and Unloved: The Girl Child in the Family*, the preface of which reiterated the project's clear objective.

> Our purpose is to focus on the precarious existence of the girl child in the family. She remains a drudge, is kept illiterate, fed inadequately and married off early in order to maintain the family's status as well as to provide for its future. Fifty years of independence have not been enough to guarantee the natural claim to childhood for most of our girl children. The girl child is caught in a complex social process which, in a sense, 'naturalizes' her deprivation. This book attempts to study her situation within her family and is published with the hope that she will cease to be the endangered sex and that her future will become secure.[24]

The main finding of the study was that the neglect of the girl child mainly derives from and is located within the family.

> Traditionally the family has been viewed as a supportive and protective institution, especially for girls. We have critically examined such a deeply entrenched but grievously mistaken view. Questions of gender-based discrimination within the family have been addressed, and possible areas requiring intervention have been discussed, revealing the

retrogressive forces that operate within and outside the family, in restricting the opportunities and choices available to the girl child (and hence to the woman). We find that very little is known about these matters.[25]

The authors concluded that the profile that emerged from their survey suggested that girls felt themselves to be excluded from the family.

> We get a picture of the girl child pre-conditioned to see herself as a 'sojourner' in her parent's home. She is told from childhood that her husband's house is her true home and that she will be married as soon as she grows up. As a result, she is never given a chance to consider herself a member of her parental home and in turn regarded as a liability by her parents. Denied a sense of belonging to the family in which she is born and reared, she is treated, and learns to think of herself as the lesser child. Her needs are dispensable and in a scarcity situation she is the first to be sacrificed.[26]

As part of the project the researchers and their assistants conducted meetings and classes to encourage parents to recognise the hard-working contribution daughters made to their households, to value their daughters and thus question the conventional idioms of 'loss' and 'burden' customarily associated with daughters. At one all-male farmer's meeting in West Bengal the visiting women researchers asked the farmers why they thought girls were perceived to be inferior to boys and why men with only daughters were considered to be childless and their wives sterile? The men, most of them fathers and grandfathers, were taken aback by the very question.

> 'Of course daughters are inferior'. They bring nothing to the family but additional expenditure. Not only in the form of their food and clothing but also in the form of the dowry that had to be provided when they reached marriageable age. After all, a daughter would never look after her parents in their old age. But a son? Why, a son was the only asset that they had![27]

When the researchers pointed out that girls too did a lot of important work and in fact looked after their parents as much as the boys did, the men were at first slow to recognise the contradiction.

> They had never so far considered women's work to be important at all. What would they do without wives and daughters to run the household? Who would cook their meals? Who would fetch water? Whom would they call upon when they needed additional help in their fields? Who, indeed, would give them their sons? These were questions that they had never asked themselves.[28]

The researchers found that without the articulation of these questions the work of daughters was rarely recognised and that because it did not directly guarantee a cash income it was rendered invisible and 'quietly forgotten'. When it was recognised it was quickly anticipated that any benefit would be lost to her parents on marriage.

This large national research and action project sponsored by the government generated a number of academic papers on discrimination against the girl child and popular articles published in the media. Some of these included short stories and poems about and by girls. One anthology of short stories derived from this project and translated from the various regional languages was entitled *The Childhood That Never Was.*[29] It was compiled by a women's study centre in Bombay, with the express purpose of 'touching the hearts of people' and thus deploying literature to bridge the gap between academic research and social action in a society where 'deeply entrenched ideas about the innate qualities of masculinity and femininity pervade the cultural ethos defining and depicting female roles' and by implication 'deny the girl child cultural space to grow'.

> Literature has the intrinsic potential to create sensitivity as it explores the images created of the tender girlhood years and depict the world through the eyes of the girl child growing up female within the Indian sub-continent, unveiling in the process the various dimensions of gender injustice experienced by the girl child.[30]

To achieve these aims the stories included ranged from the pleas of the unborn to live, the anxieties, responses and responsibilities of unwanted girls, and the defeat of girlhood dreams in the face of discriminatory socio-economic structures. Several short stories in the volume feature both the desperate longing for sons, the isolation and ceaseless praying of mothers who feel they have been denied fulfilment, meaning or even motherhood as they continue to give birth to daughters and the deep-seated feelings of rejection fed by a familial atmosphere of indifference felt by later-born daughters who wonder why they are unwanted and why it should be such a crime to be born a girl.

Although there has been a quantum leap in the newspaper coverage of the girl child in the contexts of child trafficking, sexual abuse and female infanticide, and excess female child mortality, in practice both government and non-government girl-child campaigns mainly focused on girls' schooling. In India a high proportion of girls are never enrolled in or attend school or, if they do, the likelihood of their dropping out is so high that large numbers of females remain illiterate. Parents are still reluctant to finance their daughters' education, particularly where familial resources are scarce. Furthermore, though child domestic and waged labour may be an important contribution to familial budgets, this burden is likely to fall heaviest on girl children as the education of sons is perceived to be of greater value given their obligation to support parents in their old age. Recognising that the problem of girls' schooling is rooted in differential parental perceptions of sons and daughters, the media, television and radio have been mobilised to influence the perceptions of both parents and girls. Periodically, too, women's rights and public education movements have turned their attention to wider causes. Some of the most conspicuous events of the 1980s included a rally led by daughters on 22 November 1986, a children's fair challenging the sex stereotyping and degradation of daughters, the picketing of clinics conducting sex determination tests, and the promotion of positive images of daughters with slogans such as: 'Daughters can also be supportive of parents in their old age', 'Eliminate inequality, not women', and 'Make your daughter self-sufficient, educate her, let her take a job [and] she will no longer be a burden on the parents'.[31] Again in 1986, a 'Women's Struggle to Survive' mobile fair was organised in different suburbs of Bombay to convey similar messages via songs, skits, slide shows, videotapes, exhibitions, booklets, debates and discussions.[32]

As a result of worsening sex ratios and some public disquiet, the Indian government has attempted to legislate against sex identification and sex selective abortion. The state and government of Maharashtra passed an act regulating the use of prenatal diagnostic techniques in 1988, the states of Punjab, Gujarat and Harayana followed suit, and the central government passed the Prenatal Diagnostic Technique (Regulation and Prevention of Misuse) Act in 1994. The Act states that determining and communicating the sex of a foetus is illegal and that genetic tests can be carried out only in registered facilities and then only in certain circumstances.[33] In July 1996, the Indian government furthered the legislative drive against discriminatory practices by announcing a ban on abortions of healthy female foetuses identified during permissible genetic tests with ensuing fines and prison terms for parents and doctors.[34] Given the loopholes and partial regulations there is some pessimism that these measures will be effective. Other government plans to tackle the problem range from adoption schemes for unwanted girl children to economic-incentive packages for women who only have daughters and who agree to undergo sterilisation.[35] Like many other proposed practical measures, a central government scheme advocated in 1997 to provide cash subsidies to girl children in all families identified as poor has not so far been implemented.[36]

More recently in the 1990s one of the most successful communications project aimed at school-age girls and their parents has been a joint initiative developed with the active involvement of the governments of Bangladesh, India, Nepal and Pakistan, the UNICEF regional office for South Asia and the Norwegian government. Media specialists, artists and animators have worked together to produce a 13–episode animated film series about a young girl, Meena, with music, sound effects and dialogue translated into Bengali, Hindi, Nepali, Urdu and English.[37] The issues covered in the MEENA series include son preference, girls' unfair treatment within the family, their lesser access to health and education services, sexual harrassment and harmful traditional practices such as early marriage and dowry-giving. The entertaining stories featuring the young heroine Meena are full of colourful adventure and comedy, but at their heart lies a concern with the real-life problems faced by young girls and insights into how these might be overcome. The first episode tells the story of how Meena goes to school. 'Please can I go to school?' asks Meena, looking appealingly at her parents. ' "Girls don't need to go to school", her father replies.' But Meena is a resourceful girl and sends her pet parrot off to school to learn what the teacher says. Using the knowledge her parrot brings home, Meena catches a thief and wins the gratitude of the village. With the help of other villagers, she convinces her parents that, like her brother, she should also go to school. It is anticipated that by publicising this characterful little girl who has an infectious vitality, humour and determination to fulfil her aspirations for the future, Meena will become a positive dynamic role model for young girls throughout South Asia, as well as a catalyst for reflection and discussion on gender discrimination in childhood. To promote the new image of Meena, the film series has become part of a multi-media communication, advocacy and mobilisation package consisting of a variety of items including facilitators' guides, story books, audio cassettes, local theatre roadshows and children's education materials developed for use in community groups and schools in Nepal, Bangladesh and India. In India it is reported that MEENA clubs are being planned to build on and extend the influence of this media package. In China too there have been extensive efforts over the past two decades to improve the status and revise the image of the girl child.

China's girl child

In China it was the introduction of the single-child family policy in 1979 and the subsequent rise in female infanticide in the early 1980s which was responsible for new government-sponsored campaigns to reduce son preference and increase the status of daughters. Probably the single most immediate and public consequence of the single-child family policy was the increase in violence against daughters and mothers of daughters. Many women could hardly believe that, after all the reforms of the 30-year revolution, female infants should be so discriminated against as to lose their lives. As several mortified and perplexed mothers of daughters from Anhui province wrote to a national newspaper in March 1983:

> We simply cannot understand why 32 years after China's liberation, we women are still weighed down by such backward feudal concepts

... We long for a second liberation.[38]

In the early 1980s the government-sponsored Women's Federation was charged with not only investigating the scale of the problem, but also with persuading parents that, just as women were the equal of men, so daughters were as valuable as sons. In one pamphlet, entitled *It's as Good to have a Girl as a Boy*, the Beijing Women's Federation explained that it was the current wave of violence against mothers and female infants which had made it necessary for them to emphasise that boys and girls were equal.

> The question of how to regard having a boy or a girl is an important part of socialist morality and not to be ignored. These materials on the sameness of boys and girls and on protecting women and female infants should be widely studied to promote anti-feudal education and to teach people about the legal system. They set out to convince people that boys and girls are equal and that we should oppose actions which harm women and which lead to loss of life.[39]

The Women's Federation initiated an educational campaign to convince the population that daughters could also participate in economic and political activities on an equal basis with sons and to their family's advantage. Daughters too could care for their parents, especially if sons-in-law married into their households and provided long-term support for a daughter's ageing parents. Stories published at this time featured reluctant grandparents and disappointed husbands who eventually came to accept and appreciate a new-born daughter and support the mother.[40] Posters on village and urban walls began to uniformly depict the single child as an infant girl alongside her smiling mother or parents. Cartoons appeared in the newspapers which featured forms of inequality between boys and girls. As one girl wrote:

> One day when I got home from school, I opened a newspaper and saw a cartoon. It showed a balance scale with a boy sitting high up on the left side, holding various fruits and foods in his arms, while a little girl was sitting listlessly on the other side being beaten and scolded by her parents. Under the cartoon the words said: 'Don't regard men as superior to women'. As I looked at it, I thought of myself and felt I was just like that little girl. I cut the cartoon out of the newspaper and put it on the wall so Mom would see it.[41]

Cartoons also illustrated the long-range problems which would result if boys outnumbered girls on any scale. In one, ten fond mothers watched proudly as ten sons played in the park while, years later, ten fond mothers are seen searching far and wide for ten daughters-in-law. Much of this literature and visual material aimed at improving the images of daughters, but some also had special messages for mothers who had given birth to daughters.

> We also hope that young women who give birth to girls will not feel a loss of self-esteem, will value their own rights and life, will rely on various organisations and will struggle resolutely against backward, ignorant ideas, and stand up for their own rights.[42]

The new campaigning focus of the Women's Federation was apparent in the reports of its Fifth National Congress in 1983 which, in contrast to the Fourth National Congress 5 years earlier, made specific references to violence against the girl infant.

> What demands attention is that remnant feudal ideas of regarding men as superior to women and traditional prejudices against women have re-emerged in recent years ... What is intolerable is the fact that some ugly phenomena that had been wiped out long ago in new China have begun to recur. Criminal acts of drowning female infants, insulting women, persecuting mothers who give birth to girls, and selling and harming women and children have occurred frequently. In some areas these have reached serious proportions. We women must unite with others in society and resolutely struggle against all acts harming women and children and vigorously help the public security and judicial organs crack down on these criminal activities and firmly protect the legitimate rights and interests of women and children ... Only in this way can the Women's Federation hope to deal effective blows at crimes cruelly injuring and murdering women and children, stop the drowning and abandoning of infant girls and eliminate all those ugly phenomena that should never exist in a socialist China.[43]

In addition to drawing attention to discrimination and violence against daughters, the Women's Federation also set out to protect and popularise the legal rights of girls and women. One of the causes of female infanticide, according to the Women's Federation's own investigation, was a lack of understanding of the criminal nature of the offence and ignorance of the legislation banning infanticide and others forms of violence against female infants. During the 1980s the new Marriage Law, the new Constitution and the new Criminal Law all prohibited violence against girls and women and in 1992 the government took the unprecedented step of promulgating a special law solely concerned with the Protection of Rights and Interests of Women. It protected the general rights of women in education, in employment and of her person and property, but Article 35 made special reference to violence against daughters.

> Women's rights of life and health shall be inviolable. Drowning, aban-
> doning or cruel infanticide in any manner of female babies shall be
> prohibited; discrimination against or maltreatment of women who
> give birth to female babies or women who are sterile shall be prohib-
> ited; cruel treatment causing injury or even death of a woman by
> superstition or violence shall be prohibited.[44]

Much of the recent work on women's rights has taken place within a legal
framework and the experience of local women cadres has suggested to
them that this is a relevant and productive framework for advancing
women's rights.

> The rights and interests of women and children are best protected by
> enforcing the laws and regulations designed to help abused women
> and by acting as their legal advocates and helping them exercise these
> rights.[45]

However, although in theory a number of laws might offer protection to
women and children, it is quite another matter, in a country the size of
China and where legal institutions are themselves underdeveloped, to
implement them and provide protection for women and children in practice. As one cadre of the Women's Federation said to me recently, 'we are
good at making but not implementing laws'. Nevertheless what has constantly impressed me over the years have been the serious attempts by the
Women's Federation and the government both to popularise the laws and
provide support for individual women in their attempts to exercise these
rights.

Compared to legal and popular education, the amount of attention
given to the socialisation of young girls and the messages of secondariness
they receive from their families and kin has been small. There were the
beginnings of an interest with the publication of an article in the official
women's magazine in the mid-1980s which was unusual in that it drew
attention to familial responsiblities for young female socialisation and for
the importance of this socialisation for adult female self-esteem. Because,
unusually, it elaborates this linkage in some detail it is quoted here in its
entirety.

> People often sigh at the feelings of inferiority of some grown women,
> and blame them for lacking self-confidence. It never occurs to them
> that much of this sense of inferiority is formed in childhood. This is
> mainly because parents do not understand how to cultivate a girl's
> self-confidence. So in order to train strong self-confident women
> appropriate to a new era, it is necessary to begin in childhood.
>
> If parents pay attention to educating their girl children in self-confi-
> dence, giving them more encouragement, more support, more help,

more opportunities to temper themselves, and help them to form a strong, brave character, then after they grow up they will be able to fully develop their own abilities and shoulder the heavy task of constructing the 'Four Modernisation's'. Conversely, if parents impose on their girl children the concept that 'males are worthy of respect and females are inferior', this will cause them to form a sense of inferiority and a weak and timid character. It will limit them in giving full reign to their intelligence, ability, and wisdom, constrain their creativity, strangle their enterprising spirit and cause them to become weak people.

At present, many parents have not yet become conscious of the importance of fostering the self-confidence of girl children. Some even unconsciously undermine their self-confidence. For example, some girls are bright, like to study and have high aspirations, but their parents don't encourage them and even say that girls have low intelligence, that no matter how hard they work it will be a futile effort, and that they are better off doing more housework instead. Aside from doing housework, girls very seldom have the chance to temper themselves in other ways. Thus a difference is created in the abilities of boys and girls, which in turn becomes a reason for deprecating girls. Then there are some parents who often say in front of their girl children that girls are not as good as boys, causing the girls to feel they are second-class citizens from birth. The result is that in all respects they become careful and cautious, and are always shrinking back. With all of this, how could a girl's newly sprouted self-confidence not come under attack?

People often praise boys for their spirit of striving hard, seeking to outdo others, and swearing not to stop until they reach their goal. But this spirit, this self-confidence, this self-strengthening and courage, are by no means innate in their minds. They are the result of social education, and more important parental education. When a boy is easily upset and cries, his parents often say 'Why are you crying? Men don't cry'. When boys retreat in the face of difficulties, parents often say, 'Be brave — it's not like a boy to shrink back'. This talk, these exclamations, are a form of education and encouragement. They bolster the courage and confidence of boys. If girls were given the same treatment, I firmly believe that a spirit of confidence and steadfast bravery would take root and sprout in the virgin soil of their pure souls.[46]

In the context of the single-child policy, the State Family Planning Commission has also introduced measures to reduce discrimination against girls before, during and immediately after birth, largely because of its concern at the increasing imbalance in sex ratios at birth. After the 1990 Census, a number of Chinese demographers called on the government and international agencies to take immediate steps to reduce the imbalance in sex ratios at birth and violence against girls. A Seminar on Population Issues conducted by the State Family Planning Commission in early 1993 drew attention to its 'serious concern' at the high sex ratio at birth and recommended the vigorous promotion of sex equality.[47] Subsequently the State Family Planning Commission began to add daughter–son equality to its campaigns popularising fewer and healthier births. Beginning in June 1993, the head of the State Family Planning Commission stressed in a number of her speeches that 'publicity and education on gender equality and a balanced sex preference at childbearing' should be included in its programmes.[48] For example, in July 1993 Peng Peiyun stated at the National Conference on Policies, Laws and Regulations concerning Family Planning Programmes that 'family planning programmes can in no way be regarded as being effectively implemented if an imbalanced sex ratio at birth of population appears'.[49] Although it is not clear how this objective has been incorporated into policy at local levels, at the national level there has been new legislation outlawing pre-birth sex identification, new economic incentives to encourage satisfaction with only daughters and debates initiated about the exclusion of daughters from lineage geneaologies and family contracts.

China's government, like its Indian counterpart, has attempted to restrict the use of ultrasound technology to medical purposes, such as the diagnosis of certain sex-linked genetic diseases and the detection of congenital malformations. The use of any prenatal sex identification technique for the purpose of sex-selective abortion was first discouraged and then banned. Article 32 of the Law on Maternal and Infant Health Care stated that 'identification of the gender of the foetus through technological means is strictly forbidden unless it is necessary on health grounds'.[50] How far this prohibition can and will be implemented is quite unclear, given the shortfalls in local health service funding and the fact that medical personnel, clinics and hospitals are expected to generate incomes and be self-supporting. With both salaries and infrastructure dependent on fees, it is not surprising to find that the use of ultrasound for sex identification, albeit it indirect and masked, is one of the easiest and most lucrative sources of funding. In one Anhui county, about half the township hospitals I visited had an ultrasound, although I was specifically told that it was not now normal to give a pregnant women an ultrasound unless special circumstances invited such an examination. In Anhui too, there was mention of increasing the number of hospital or fixed-site births to 'effectively prevent female infanticide and protect girls' and thus eliminate old style deliveries at home in which it was more likely that some mishap might occur. This may be a significant step given that for China as a whole, some 70% of rural births still take place at home.[51]

There has been a consistent effort to emphasise that girls too can support parents in their old age. One of the means recommended by family planning workers to increase a girl's value to her family was the introduction of a number of economic measures contributing to the short- and long-term welfare and security of daughter-only households. At the national level there has been persistent talk of combining birth control and development strategies while, at local levels, family planning workers have suggested that only by practically helping farmers with no sons to increase their incomes, solve their labour shortages and lighten their prospects for old age could they begin to convince them of the benefits of family planning. In several villages, co-operatives were established and popularised as models to illustrate how couples with only daughters could become 'well off quickly'. Measures usually included the privileged allocation of or access to resources in agriculture for livestock raising and processing, or in initiating and developing handicraft or industrial enterprises. In these ventures, farmers with daughters and no strong son labourers were shown not only to receive immediate economic advantages but also to benefit in the longer term in old age.[52] In addition to these innovatory schemes which are still very rare and limited, there have been more widespread measures to provide old age insurance for all parents regardless of whether they have sons or daughters. *Nongmin Ribao* (Farmers' Daily) pointed out that the only way to correct the growing imbalance between births of boys and girls was to provide proper social provision for farmers in their old age so that they need not fear an impoverished and insecure future [53]. Various national programmes in the 1990s have advocated the introduction of new forms of insurance which will ease the anxieties and enhance the long-term prospects of the single-child family and especially the family with single- or only-daughters.[54] Not surprisingly, one of the most popular new forms of insurance is old-age insurance, which potentially relieves the fears and anxieties of those with only daughters and guarantees an alternative pension to that of son support.

> Now the money a son gives his parents every month is 30 odd yuan at most but after we joined an insurance company we got more than 200 yuan for an elderly pension. This is much more than a son's 30 yuan. So it is more reliable than relying on a son for old age.[55]

Another younger 31-year old mother of an only daughter was reported to have asked, after she had arranged for a retirement payment or a monthly pension of 80 yuan per month, 'so why do I have to rely on a son when I am old?'[56] Such examples have been publicised to encourage families to purchase insurance as an alternative to dependence on sons, but the lack of information and confidence in long-term schemes, perhaps understandable given the twists and turns in government policy and the vagaries of the market, have not inspired sufficient popular confidence in the efficacy of such schemes to become widespread.

Finally, there has been some attempt to debate the importance of the family lineage and the exclusion of daughters from the family line. A discussion of the issue was launched by the editorial board of *China Population News* beginning in April 1992.[57] More than 130 views were published over a 6-month period, with contributions from urban and rural scholars and researchers, government and family planning officials, workers, farmers, shop assistants, students and soldiers of various age groups, as well as couples of child-bearing age who had only daughters. The questions posed by the periodical were: 'Can a daughter carry on the family line?' and 'Can she play the same role as a son in supporting her elders?' The views reported expressed very mixed attitudes towards the idea that daughters could equal sons in maintaining the practical work on the farm and provide support in old age. Some correspondents thought that something 'is lost from the bottom of their hearts' if the male descent line is not continued, while others were more concerned with the opinions of others. 'If any couple doesn't want to be *juehu* [an offensive word meaning a person or household which has no son to continue his family line], doesn't want to be blamed by his parents and doesn't want to be spoken ill of by others, they will always long for a son.'[58]

It was only a minority who thought that if there is no son, then why could not a daughter support them and continue the lineage by bringing in a son-in-law to live with their parents? Many thought that this was the only realistic solution for families without sons and combined the long-term economic support of a son-in-law and the superior care and affection of a daughter. In the words of one father, 'my daughter also supports me in my remaining years of life as a son and does even better than those familes with sons'.[59] However there was more agreement that a son-in-law was a poor substitute for a son.

> Such familes are often held in contempt among their fellow villagers. Besides that, farmers have a strong sense of the patriarchal clan system. They believe that the bigger the family is, the more power the family has. Therefore families without male offspring are usually at a disadvantage compared with their fellow villagers who have sons. This further stimulates farmers to a greater desire for sons to continue the lineage.[60]

It is also a fact that reliance on a son-in-law, as currently advocated by the government and parents, is not likely to continue in future years as families with an only son are much less likely to give him up to another family. This is probably why no government has made a serious attempt to alter marriage patterns in ways that would end the transience or passage of young girls from her parents' to her husband's household. However, economic reforms in the countryside which have led to the establishment of larger numbers of nuclear households after marriage may well have the same effect, although young persons are still more likely to retain close ties with the husband's parents given existing patterns of close residential proximity and customs of filial piety.

One way in which the government has worked to benefit daughters directly is by campaigning to equalise the access of girls and boys to education. During the past two decades there have been a number of policy initiatives to implement compulsory primary education, improve the standards of schooling and sponsor initiatives to help children in poverty-stricken regions attend school. Simultaneously, there have been a number of initiatives to increase popular awareness within families and communities of the importance of girls' education, to encourage girls to enter and stay in education, to investigate the reasons for girls dropping out of school, and to implement a number of remedial programmes for these girls. As a result of these initiatives, the proportions of girls in primary education have risen dramatically, so that upwards of 90–95% of girls are enrolled in primary school. However these figures, impressive as they are, mask the fact that attendance is not the same as enrolment, that fewer girls than boys graduate from primary school and proceed to middle and higher education, and that girls are more likely to be taken out of school at an earlier age in order that the education of sons take priority. Nevertheless, the campaigns of both the government and the Women's Federation to popularise education for girls have reinforced the principles that girls should go to school and that girls are more likely to contribute to their families if they have the benefit of schooling.

On one of my own field trips to central Anhui and northwestern Ningxia provinces in 1995, it was evident in interviews at both provincial and local township and county levels that the Women's Federation had placed a high priority on popularising and emphasising the importance of education for girls. Women's Federation cadres had visited villages and individual households to encourage parents to send or keep their girls in school and to persuade mothers that their daughters might be better educated than they were themselves. They had drawn attention to some of the new opportunities for girls as a result of the economic reforms once they had the ability to read, write and calculate; they helped girl graduates from middle school find employment commensurate with their qualifications and they publicised the examples of girls whose incomes and lives had been improved as a result of their schooling. Parents had been encouraged to establish their own links with the school via open days and special classes or 'schools for parents', so that they were both encouraged to and commended for sending their girls to school. In each county visited in Anhui and Ningxia provinces, Women's Federation leaders had conducted house-to-house investigations searching for girls who had dropped out of school and compiling records of their names, dates, grades, ages and reasons for dropping out which had aided them in undertaking a number of practical initiatives to help girl drop-outs. The Spring Bud programme for girls' schooling was established nation-wide in

1994 to raise funds within and outside of China to help drop-outs return to school in the poorer and remote regions of northwest and southwest China. It specifically focuses on girl drop-outs in poor and remote regions and from ethnic minorities; by mid-1995 it was reported to have already achieved its initial objective of establishing 1000 classes, each of 50 girls who had been persuaded to return to school. The programme is managed by the Women's Federation which raises the funds, investigates local need and persuades girls to return to school. It aims to provide Y300 per year for each girl for 3 years which is allocated as follows: Y160 food subsidy, Y40 textbooks, Y10 health, Y30 clothes and bedding, Y20 for stationary and Y40 for miscellaneous expenses. Generally separate girls' classes, called Spring Bud classes, are established for the drop-outs largely because by the time they return to school they are older than normal. I have visited several of these programmes over the years and been impressed by the work of the justly proud students and their teachers and parents.

A second practical initiative taken at national and local levels specifically to provide female role models for girls has been to increase the number of female teachers. Despite the fact that primary school teaching is a profession which nationally attracts female recruits, in the village schools I have visited a minority of teachers have been women and almost all have been recently recruited as a result of new initiatives. The most notable example of female-teacher influence I have encountered was in a girls-only Muslim school where the majority of the teachers were young women and recently recruited. Here there seemed to be a noticeable correlation between the incidence of female teachers and the numbers of girls who said that they wanted to proceed to higher education and themselves become teachers when they left school. Certainly, the girls in the higher grades had more confidence in expressing their support for their school motto: 'Be clever in mind, skilful in hand and depend on your own resources and abilities'. They had more decided opinions on a number of topics and showed a greater awareness of their secondary position within their families and community than did girls in comparable grades in the many schools I have visited elsewhere.

A third initiative taken by the Women's Federation has been to make the school curriculum more relevant to the vocational needs of rural pupils and to equip girls with skills which will be of practical value to them in increasing their incomes and those of their families. The expansion of the curriculum to include practical skills of potential and greater relevance to the working lives of peasant girls is thought to be an important factor in persuading parents to send and keep girls in school. In a few rural schools in Anhui and Ningxia, skill training on a small scale was provided for girls in the higher grades, but more schools hoped to provide such training when they acquired the necessary funds. As elsewhere, most of the skills provided were thought to be particularly suitable for girls and these included sewing, embroidering, tailoring and some agricultural activities, such as raising animals and planting fruit trees. The selection of these activities was entirely appropriate given the present gender divisions of labour in poor and remote rural regions, but do not make for change. It was difficult not to observe that, as in urban schools, girls continue to be encouraged to take 'soft' rather than 'hard 'subjects or manual activities suited to 'their nimble fingers'. In all my visits to urban and suburban schools over the years, teachers and pupils have seemed quite oblivious to the assumptions underlying such categorisations and gender divisions of labour. There have also been a number of national projects to promote the education of girl children in poor and remote rural regions facing special difficulties. One was the 3-year Research and Action Project on Current Problems and Policies for the Girl Child co-sponsored by the Education Department at Beijing University. As for so many programmes to do with women and children in China, it was the UN Women's Conference held in Beijing in 1995 which not only provided an impetus to extend many of its existing programmes but also specifically introduced the cause of the girl child.

The preparations for the Fourth UN Conference for Women in Beijing marked an important milestone not only in the development of women's studies, policies and organisations in China, but also in drawing attention to the world-wide cause of the girl child fostered by UNICEF. Influenced by the international agenda and its own past experience, a few specific references to the girl child have been incorporated into China's National Plans for Action among women and children. In the Programme for Development of Chinese Women, promulgated by the People's Republic of China in July 1995, which stipulated the major objects and measures for improving the position of women between 1995 and 2000, there were a number of specific references to the girl child.[61] In addition to protecting the special interests of under-age girls in education and employment, the plan specifically advocated a reduction in discrimination against infant girls by recommending serious investigation and punishment of such criminal acts as infanticide, trafficking and persecution of new-born female infants, and strictly forbidding the use of modern medical equipment for foetus sex identification. Simultaneously the National Plan of Action for Children also addressed these very same issues.[62] Through legislation and law enforcement efforts, the government has also been stepping up its protection of the legal rights of girls, including the enforcement of the Maternal and Infant Health Care Law and the 10–Point Guideline for Strengthening Girl Child Education Work in Poverty-stricken Areas and Ethnic Minority Regions by the State Education Commission's Elementary Education Department.

The establishment of a National Working Group on the Girl Child in 1997 was one of two important initiatives of that year. In order to further consolidate and monitor its work on the girl child, the National Working Committee for Children and Women of the State Council (NWCCW) set

up a special Working Group on Girl-Child Development to take responsibility for conducting policy research, establishing guidelines and co-
ordinating the implementation of the National Programme for Action on
Women specifically dedicated to girl-child development. The NWCCW
anticipated that this group would set up an organisation for 'Girl-Child
Development Studies' to collect information, conduct research and
encourage the disaggregated data collection by the State Statistical Bureau
and others in order to monitor girl-child issues, provide a situation analysis and make policy recommendations. Its practical aims were to incorporate girl-child issues into on-going government programmes, such as those
to do with poverty alleviation and education, and to strengthen legislative
protection of the rights and interests of girl children. Finally this special
Working Group has been charged with encouraging the national and
local media to promote the significance of 'girl-child development' alongside the issue of equality for men and women. Interviews with members of
this new working group made up of representatives from the Women's
Federation and a number of researchers on children and gender issues
and specialists in health, nutrition and education suggest that they have a
serious agenda, although still more devoted to research and investigation
of the problems than to identifying policy solutions or advocating change.

The second important event focusing on the girl child in 1997 was the
organisation of a national symposium on 'The Girl-Child Development
Strategy in Poverty-stricken Areas' which was co-sponsored by UNICEF
and the Women's Federation.[63] It drew together representatives from
various government ministries, non-government organisations and
workers responsible for girl-child issues at local levels to debate development issues relevant to the health, education, poverty and legal protection
of girls. Participants from provincial, prefectural and municipal education, public health departments and the Women's Federation presented
some very interesting papers based on their efforts to further the cause of
the girl child. In examining contemporary problems, they identified key
areas for further in-depth study on girl-child development strategies and
measures, and made a number of proposals for promoting girl-child development in poverty-stricken areas.

> The focus for current girl child work should be the promotion of girl
> child development in poverty-stricken areas and solving the problems
> of all girls living under difficult circumstances with special reference
> to improving their physical growth and development, education and
> employment. Sustainable girl child development should rely on
> strengthened policy-making and legislative work, improved institu-
> tional infrastructure and administrative efficiency, increased
> community support, consolidated law-enforcement, deepened theo-
> retical research and heightened public awareness.

A new understanding based on giving research priority to every facet of young girls' physical development should offer new guidance for future efforts. It will also help make related law- and policy-making more consistent and systematic, call for closer co-ordination among various social sectors in executing projects and direct research attention to girl-child development. All these results will eventually promote and mainstream gender awareness and equality of the whole of society.[64]

In the concluding speeches the national organisation for women also committed itself anew to furthering interest in the girl child.

> The Women's Federation has a historic responsibility to undertake and bring forward the women and girl-child development cause. We will strive to push the government and administrative departments to adopt our feasible proposals. On our own part, we will prepare to work as soon as possible on what are considered to be more easily achievable objectives: more focused and co-ordinated efforts by researchers nation-wide, more information exchanges, special symposiums on specific research topics and the compilation of a list of priority research topics so as to more readily collect, evaluate and submit the data needed for the formulation and implementation of policies pertaining to the state of the girl-child in poverty-stricken areas. We will also promote the publicity and extension of both research findings and work experience. We understand that attaching higher importance to the girl child is a manifestation of a society's progress, and that achieving the girl child development will push for further progress.[65]

As part of their new commitment to the cause of the girl child, the Women's Federation itself subsequently set up a small consultative group made up of representatives from the Women's Federation, UNICEF and myself as the foreign consultant to develop a public education strategy to identify and protect the needs and further the interests of girls in China. The new project was to be primarily action-oriented and its aims were to identify:

(a) issues underlying continuing types of discriminatory attitudes and behaviour towards the girl child within the family, the community and society;
(b) key interventions, messages and measures appropriate to countering discriminatory attitudes and behaviour towards the girl child within the family, community and society;
(c) channels of communication and appropriate sources for the popularisation of the concept of equality between boys and girls;
(d) measures and appropriate testing mechanisms for trial implementation in a number of pilot projects; and

(e) comprehensive guidelines for the introduction and implementation of a nation-wide public education effort to popularise legal rights and procedures for the protection of the girl child.[66]

At the beginning of this 3-year investigation into the needs for and means of conducting public education, short field studies were undertaken in Shandong province and the rural environs of Beijing and interviews conducted in Beijing ministries. The field visits focused on investigating the types of education and interventions that were identified locally as important in countering continuing forms of discrimination against girls in both poorer and richer regions. As a result of the field visits, the group made a number of general recommendations which were to become the basis of further phases of the project. First, it was observed that, in developed regions, government policies to improve the 'quality' of children had resulted in a number of general national and local programmes which, alongside rapid economic development, have encouraged immense improvements in the education, health and general standards of children's lives in China. However, it was evident that there had been less attention devoted to the specific needs and interests of girls who, because of a set of surviving beliefs and practices, remain disadvantaged. Second, it was observed that although government programmes to improve the overall status and quality of women's lives have resulted in some general improvements in the position of Chinese women, these programmes have extended less attention to the specific needs and interests of girls. Where there have been a number of initiatives to do with the girl child these are almost exclusively centred on improvements in girls' education with little equivalent awareness or attention given to the survival and health of girls.

One of the main conclusions at the end of the first year of this project was that there was little government or popular awareness of the scale and dimensions of discrimination against girls. There was also little understanding of the underlying factors which affect the survival, health status and education of girl children and this was so among leaders with direct responsibility for relevant policies and projects in national ministries and at local administrative levels, among professional staff in schools or hospitals and within families. This ignorance was largely the result of both lack of gendered data and disbelief that boys and girls could be anything but equal. Although there were high levels of government, professional and popular awareness about the importance of improving the position of children and women, there was still less attention explicitly given to the position of girl children. There was little interest in gendered statistics at hand, such as sex ratios at birth, which were reputed to be unknown and there were few gendered statistics to do with health and nutrition which meant that the educational value of such statistics was often lost. There were several assumptions that constrained or inhibited the establishment of special campaigns in support of girls. There was a general assumption that because men and women were now more equal so by implication girls were as good as or equal to boys. Second, it was assumed widely that, although in the past and in poorer regions there might have been discrimination against girls, this inequality no longer existed in the richer regions of present-day post-reform China. This was largely because there was a third general assumption that rapid economic development and high incomes were the new panacea for all ills, including any remaining discrimination against girl children. Finally, it was assumed that since the work to improve the quality of children's lives was wide-ranging and successful, there was no need to separate out boys and girls. This last assumption was responsible for the low level of attention and lack of effort to collect gendered statistics which might have suggested otherwise. In contrast there had been much effort expended to increase awareness of the laws which protected the interests of girls and which have been incorporated into laws to do with the Protection of Minors, Compulsory Education, the Convention of Children's Rights and the Law for Women's Protection and Rights. The Civil Affairs and Justice bureaux at local administrative levels were concerned with popularising these laws and explaining both their content and their importance in effecting changes in the social attitudes of communities, households and in schools. However, the laws specifically applicable to girls were generally subsumed within general laws affecting women and children and in only one instance were the sections of these laws which are relevant to girl children compiled separately into a special booklet.

Overall the field study suggested that there was a general lack of popular awareness in communities, institutions and families of the dimensions of discrimination experienced by girls. Moreover, any explanation for existing discrimination was almost always interpreted as a biological, economic or technical matter which would probably be solved or at least reduced by economic development. Given the lack of knowledge by both government and professional bodies, the two major goals for Phase 2 of the project in 1999 included getting the National Plans of Action to take greater account of the girl child, and educating government and professional personnel. The field team had been very impressed with the levels of acquaintance of officials at all administrative levels and in all institutions with the general goals of the National Programme for Child Development in China and the Programme for the Development of Chinese women. Unfortunately, although there are a few references to the girl child in these programmes, there is no one section in which there is a sustained or detailed focus on the protection of needs and furthering of the multi-faceted interests of girls. This is partly an accident of timing in that the programme documents were drafted prior to the new international importance attached to the topic. Given that there are plans or steps about to be taken by all administrative levels to monitor and evaluate these programmes, the revision of these documents offers an ideal opportunity to update the programmes by including and focusing attention on the girl child during the forthcoming phase of monitoring and evaluation. In addition this would achieve the establishment of a local and national statistical base on the situation of girls in relation to boys, highlight areas for further investigation or research and raise awareness of the scale or potential scale of discrimination against girls resulting in their lesser survival, health status and education.

The project organisers came to the conclusion that the focus for pilot education on the girl child should first and foremost be among those who are responsible for the relevant policies and programmes affecting children and women at the national level. The constant reference to central policies at local levels suggested that local administrations would be less likely to introduce new initiatives at community levels if these had not first emanated from the centre. To this effect the team recommended that a major goal of Phase 2 should be educating those in Beijing who are responsible for national policies and programmes in order to focus attention on and mainstream separate girl child policies and programmes. The centrepiece of Phase 2 was thus a Symposium for representatives from relevant ministries and official bodies in Beijing to acquaint them with the dimensions of discrimination experienced by the girl child in both China and East and South Asia and to solicit their advice as to the best means of countering this discrimination. A record of the Symposium and the results of its deliberations are being compiled into a training manual to be used at other administrative levels. Given the lack of any substantial written or visual materials alluding to or illustrating the specific needs and interests of girl children which might increase levels of popular awareness and understanding, the Third Phase in the year 2000 is to be devoted to the provision and communication of popular written and visual materials. The project team has not so far found any one publication devoted to the subject of girls or daughters, although there are short sections on the equality of girls and boys in a few existing general publications on family planning, family education or child rearing. It is planned that these should be compiled and expanded into a separate publication which incorporates a considered understanding of the causes of inequality and is presented in various forms to attract the attention of a wide audience. In the longer-term it is planned to produce an array of visual materials, including videos, which will stimulate further concern about the continuing discrimination against daughters.

In China then as well as in India, there have been a number of serious attempts by governments, women's movements and international agencies to draw attention to discrimination against girls. Yet at the same time, as this study has shown, demographic statistics and ethnographic evidence suggest that, despite these efforts, this discrimination, so far from being reduced is increasing and resulting in extreme cases in new imbalances in sex ratios at birth and in infancy and childhood resulting in rising numbers of missing girls. This increase in gender discrimination, reflected in ethnographic records, makes it imperative that there are transformative, more effective and sustained agendas or campaigns in support of daughters in the future.

7 Daughter empowerment

A new destiny?

If at the end of the twentieth century, there is evidence of a new international and national focus on girls deriving from an increased interest in women's, children's and human rights and the advocacy of UNICEF, government's and women's movements, there is also evidence of new and rising discrimination against girls. One of the reasons why this book has been written is that despite these efforts, the scale and forms of daughter discrimination still remain invisible in development circles and have yet to be incorporated into women, gender, children and development dialogues, frameworks and projects. If it is to girls as daughters that this study has directed attention, it has done so within a development context, largely because of a number of major assumptions in development circles which prolong daughter discrimination, relegating them to the lowest status or Ghandi's 'last persons of the last houses'. It is still widely assumed that the many interventions aimed at including women and children in the development process will advantage and empower girls automatically. This study has shown that the very considerable attention given to the contributions of and benefits to women of development processes has not reduced discrimination against girls. This study also shows that the very welcome interventions to improve the well-being of children have not taken sufficient account of gender disparities in childhood experiences of the family and of differential resource allocations. Where son preference is acknowledged, it is still widely assumed that son preference and daughter discrimination are associated with under-development or a lag in social attitudes and will disappear with greater economic and social development. What the study of South and East Asia confirms is that daughter discrimination has not declined alongside development and that a number of factors have combined to contribute to its exacerbation.

Economic development in South and East Asia has embraced various states of steady growth, lesser growth, miracle and crisis, but whatever the pace of economic and technological progress there lies one common denominator throughout the region and that is an absence of a social security or welfare system which might supplement or substitute for the family. The inter-generational contract, albeit with new and more reciprocal flows of resources between family members, thus remains intact and essential to parent-support and in the longer-term to the welfare and the security of all. So long as it does so and remains grounded in the notion of filial piety which, sanctioned by the patrilineal cultures of the region, is largely son-centred, it will continue outside of exceptional circumstances to exclude daughters. Simultaneously the rapid voluntary and involuntary decline in fertility and increase in the costs of raising children in Asia has meant that, despite smaller numbers of children, there is a continuing need or preference for a son or sons which has resulted in fewer spaces for unwanted daughters. In these circumstances daughters have become less wanted or tolerated than before when larger-sized families accommodated both daughters and sons. In East and South Asia recent trends combining smaller families with gender preference have been facilitated by the introduction of new technologies for sex identification which, followed by abortion, has meant an exacerbation of discrimination against daughters in family planning and building. It is ironic that new and improved technological advances to improve prenatal care and an acceptance of abortion have had such negative repercussions for daughters. In addition, and very importantly, gender divisions of labour frozen by cultural-specific notions of gender difference and complementarity have made it difficult for daughters to substitute for sons in the performance of certain roles and as indicators of status. As this study has shown, all the above factors contribute to discrimination against daughters that is sometimes extreme and results in rising numbers of 'missing girls'. How far other societies in Southeast Asia and elsewhere duplicate similar trends and reflect similar characteristics will have to await a further study. Meanwhile, in countries of every economic and social profile in East and South Asia, the gender inequality of the female child is so routine and pervasive from birth, or even earlier, that a wide range of discriminating and violent practices compromise her health and her chances of survival, well-being and education. Yet daughter discrimination remains largely hidden and invisible.

The lack of attention to daughter discrimination, the lack of acknowledgement of the consequences of differential parental expectations of daughters and sons, and biased entitlements against daughters in infancy and childhood have all been masked largely by the use of such terms as son preference, gender preference and sex ratios. Such approaches, with one or two major exceptions, have rarely encouraged due recognition of their logical corollary, namely daughter discrimination. So far it is primarily demographers who have endeavoured to draw the attention of governments and agencies to the dimensions of discrimination as reflected in the statistics on sex ratios at birth and excessive female mortality during infancy and childhood. Their concern has not yet permeated into other sectors, where broader and extended statistical analyses disaggregating children according to gender would immediately draw attention to important differences not only in mortality and morbidity, but also to the importance of differential access to and receipt of family and community resources. Together both demographic and other statistics would build a profile of the girl child which would act as a powerful educational tool for governments, professional and other personnel and provide a foundation for identifying new policy and practical interventions that would benefit girls. The collating of gender-disaggregated statistics is no easy task as it has been difficult to persuade governments, statisticians and health professionals that the disaggregation of child-related statistics by gender might be important in establishing routine indicators which would provide valuable data and information on the vulnerabilities of girl children. However, a concerted movement to disaggregate statistics is beginning to gain ground, largely because of the impetus and funding offered by the Swedish International Development Agency (SIDA), the United Nations Development Programme (UNDP) and other international agencies. My own experience in China suggests that the absence of gender-disaggregated statistics on sex ratios and gendered indicators of infancy and childhood discrimination is a major factor limiting both national and community awareness, and that further advocacy and sensitisation is contingent upon reliable data showing the scale, dimensions and trends in discrimination against daughters. Having advocated the benefits of the qualitative approach of the anthropologist for development over many decades, I now find myself in the unexpected position of emphasising the importance of a quantitative approach to provide a context for ethnographic observations which, in sensitive areas, are in danger of being dismissed as exceptional or unrepresentative. Ultimately it seems as if it is the power of statistical data which is gender disaggregated that gives credence to ethnographic voices and is persuasive in convincing national, community and familial decision-makers that it is important and necessary to allocate attention and resources to girls' development.

Discrimination against daughters is also camouflaged by the familial sources of much of this discrimination. As this study has argued, ethnographic studies show that it is not so much a matter of availability of services for education or health but parental attitudes, behaviour and choices which affect differential familial resource allocation to sons and daughters and ultimately the livelihood and lives of their daughters. Within the development context, it has long been assumed that the household or family was a unitary body with indivisible needs and interests which benefited all its members on a more or less equitable basis. It has only been in recent decades that feminist scholars have argued that there may exist multiple voices and interests within a household and an unequal distribution of resources among family members, divided as they are by generation and gender. In East and South Asia, family planning or building strategies primarily aim at collective well-being and continuity, with the importance accorded to joint family needs and schedules paramount in shaping reproductive choices and behaviour and in taking precedence over any individual needs and interests. Only rarely is there any hint that family and individual needs and interests may differ or clash. Yet parental attitudes and behaviour differentiating the roles and status of sons and daughters show, more than any other set of intra-household relations, the degree to which concern with the collective and continuous good of the family may deny the needs and interests of individual members. While this is so, the primordial contest for familial attention and resources between sons and daughters remains with the family deciding life or death, growth or stunting and education or illiteracy for its sons and daughters. It is this familial discrimination, grounded in inter-generational contracts and gendered divisions of labour which prioritise sons and exclude daughters, that is left unchallenged by current campaigns in support of the girl child.

The focus on girls' rights and the girl child by development agencies, governments and women's movements constitutes a valuable and welcome step, but so far these agendas and campaigns do not yet provide the attention necessary to translate policy and intervention into widespread and sustained practice or add up to a comprehensive and systematic endeavour to address the needs of daughters. Moreover, many of the present policies and interventions are themselves limited in scope and less than effective. The emphasis on the girl child not only masks the familial derivations of her discrimination but also leads to an emphasis on girls' schooling to the exclusion of other factors such as health, violence and even survival. In most countries and campaigns any reference to the girl child immediately turns attention to girls' education which, sometimes referred to as the gender jewel in the policy crown, is represented currently as the panacea not only for discrimination but also for poverty eradication if not underdevelopment itself. Indeed, the two are seen to be synonomous and it has been an uphill struggle to broaden any agenda to embrace the survival and health of girls which surely are important prerequisites to education. There has been a very noticeable government and agency reluctance to recognise the existence of any disparities in the distribution of familial resources between sons and daughters, or that such disparities might affect sex ratios at birth or discrepancies in male and female infant and child mortality or morbidity. Indeed it seems to me that the current emphasis on the girl child and her schooling is reminiscent of and analogous with a former phase in women's or gender studies which emphasised women's entry into social production and other public roles and services to the exclusion of their less visible domestic and reproductive roles as if these did not affect their contributions to and benefits from the development strategies of governments and agencies. One of the reasons this study has emphasised survival and health at a very early age has been to draw attention to factors other than education, such as family planning, inter-generational contracts and gender divisions of labour which structurally and specifically marginalise and invisibilise daughters in ways that do not similarly affect adult women be they daughters-in-law, wives or mothers.

If this study has suggested that the very welcome interest in improving women's status is a necessary but not sufficient component of girl development strategies and does not directly embrace the special needs and interests or improve the lives of young girls, it also suggests that there is a reverse correlation. Cross-cultural studies suggest that one of the single most important determinants of women's empowerment and therefore gender equality is the degree of female self-esteem and that one of the single most important factors underpinning or making for female self-esteem is the value placed on daughters by parents, families and by a culture. The corollary of these findings is that any strategy to improve the position of women and redefine gender relations should also begin with changing attitudes towards and of daughters, so contributing to female self-respect and empowerment at all ages. Yet there have been few attempts to examine critically the processes of socialisation whereby daughters acquire a measure of their own self esteem or worth. What is still less considered or even defined as a problem are the repercussions which rising sex ratios and new prenatal and postnatal initiatives may have for the self-image of the young girls who survive and read or hear about the fate of their less fortunate peers. The direct linkage between the self-esteem of women and of daughters makes it all the more surprising that the widespread interest in women's empowerment has not extended, either analytically or practically, to include the socialisation of young daughters as an important route to women's empowerment. Thus on two counts the empowerment of daughters is important: for daughters in their own right and for 'tomorrow's women'. Sole attention on the latter however dilutes and directs attention away from the specific needs of today's girls and denies them a participatory voice in their own empowerment and development processes.

If agendas and campaigns are to go beyond the public roles of daughters and identify policies and interventions within the family that are both transformative and sustainable, then it has to be said that there are no immediately identifiable and simple solutions. However, there are a number of first steps which might be taken in order to move beyond cosmetic and compensatory or palliative and sporadic gestures. The first is that there is a case for taking a comparative approach which embraces societies outside of South and East Asia and, in particular, Southeast Asia where it seems that there may not be the same type or degree of discrimination against very young girls before, during or following birth. However there is evidence that daughter discrimination kicks in at a later age with a low educational and nutritional status among adolescent girls in Southeast Asia and with much trafficking and employment of young girls for sexual exploitation. This lag in daughter discrimination may be due in part to differences in kinship structures, and the reckoning of kinship lines which are more bilateral and involve a greater reliance on daughters for parental support. Second, a synthesis collating the various types of interventions which have been advocated or implemented to reduce daughter discrimination and their evaluation might aid in identifying those interventions which can reduce daughter discrimination. A preliminary inventory of policy and practical interventions in South and East Asia so far includes new messages and vehicles for popular education, economic incentives to do with community resource allocation and new forms of old-age support, but it also shows that few of these practical interventions have been implemented on any scale and all stop short of marriage, family and kinship reform.

It is certainly timely for the adoption of new indicators and new policy interventions which embrace both the familial and public status of girls to be incorporated into the current revisions of National Plans of Action for Children and Women which are taking place in the individual countries of East and South Asia and because of the Beijing and other global platforms of action at the international level. They should aim both to specify the platforms necessary to meet the special needs and interests of girls and to integrate these platforms into wider debates and policies to do with women, gender and children within the development context. So far, however, daughters have remained marginal to most national and international debates and policies. Instead of being assigned to their rightful place in the design of practical interventions that recognise both the old and new contributions of daughters to their natal families and their own rights to survival, development and empowerment, this rightful place continues to be ignored and denied by daughters, families, analysts and policy-makers. In East and South Asia, despite some new and important moves to counter such invisibility and discrimination, there continues to be, continent-wide, some denial of her birthrights, of her life-threatening suffering in infancy and childhood and of her existing and potential contributions to her parents, family and community. Indeed, it is this continuing continent-wide invisibility, exacerbated by the pace and type of development, that this book aims to counter as it has been an important factor in prolonging the culture of silence that collectively denies and belies daughter discrimination and endangers or disempowers daughters throughout the most populous societies of East and South Asia and into the new millennium.

Notes

1 A weaker destiny

1 Amartya Sen 'More than 100 million women are missing', *New York Review of Books*, 20 December 1990, pp. 61–5.
2 Ansley J. Coale, 'Excess female mortality and the balance of sexes in the population: An estimated number of missing females', *Population and Development Review* Vol. 17, No. 3, December 1991, pp. 517–23.
3 Ibid. p. 522.
4 John C. Caldwell, 'The Asian fertility revolution: It's implications for transition theories', in Richard Leete and Iqbal Alam, *The Revolution in Asian Fertility*, Clarendon Press, Oxford, 1993, p. 300.
5 Ibid. p. 299.
6 Geoffrey McNicoll, *Changing Patterns and Fertility Policies in the Third World*, Working Papers in Demography, No. 32, Australian National University, Canberra, Australia, 1991, p. 1.
7 J. R. Rele and Iqbal Alam, 'Fertility transition in Asia: The statistical evidence', in Leete and Alam, op. cit. pp. 23–4.
8 Ibid. p. 18.
9 McNicholl, op. cit. p. 34.
10 Rele and Alam, op. cit. pp. 20–1; UNICEF, *The State of the World's Children*, New York, 1999, pp. 124–7.
11 Amartya Sen, Africa and India: What do we have to learn from each other? United Nations University, WIDER Discussion Paper No. 19, 1987, in S. B. Agnihotri, 'Missing females: A disaggregated analysis', *Economic and Political Weekly* 19 August 1995, p. 2074.
12 Ansley Coale, op. cit. p. 517.
13 Ibid. p. 519.
14 Nancy E. Williamson, *Sons or Daughters: A Cross-Cultural Survey of Parental Preferences*, Sage Publications, London, 1976, pp. 67–102.
15 Mead T. Cain 'Patriarchal structure and demographic change', in N. Federici, K. Oppenheim Mason and S. Sogner, *Women's Position and Demographic Change*, Clarendon Press, Oxford, 1993, p. 56.
16 For selection of papers see *Asia-Pacific Population Journal.* Economic and Social Commission for Asia and the Pacific, UN, Vol. 10, No. 3, September 1995.
17 Barbara D. Miller, *The Endangered Sex*, Cornell University Press, Ithaca, 1981, p. 25.
18 Ibid. Elisabeth Croll, *Feminism and Socialism in China*, Routledge and Kegan Paul, London, 1978, pp. 23–5.

19 Susan C. M. Scrimshaw, 'Infanticide in human populations: Societal and individual concerns', in G. Hausfater and S. Blaffer Hrdy, *Infanticide: Comparative and Evolutionary Perspectives*, Aldine Press, New York, 1984, pp. 450–1.
20 Simone de Beauvoir, The Second Sex, New English Library Edition, London, 1969, p. 9.
21 Monica Das Gupta, 'Selective discrimination against female children in rural Punjab, India', in *Population and Development Review*, Vol. 13 No. 1, March 1987, pp. 77–100.
22 Frances K. Goldscheider, 'Interpolating demography within families and households', *Demography*, Vol. 32, No. 3, August 1995, pp. 471–80.
23 Ansley Coale, 'The demographic transition', in International Population Conference Vol. 1, Liège International Union for the Scientific Study of Population (IUSSP), 1973, pp. 53–72.

2 Demographic narratives

China

1 *UN World Population Prospects*, 1990, New York 1991; quoted in Rele and Alam, op. cit. p. 15.
2 Ibid.
3 Judith Banister, personal communication, p. 54.
4 *Dual Effects of Family Planning Programme on Chinese Women* (Jiaotong Report), Research Report of Institute of Population and Economy in Xi'an Jiaotong University, 15 December 1995, p. 51; UNICEF, *State of the World's Children*, op. cit. p. 124.
5 Peng Xizhe, 'Recent trends in China's population and their implications', Paper presented at Seminar on Development Implications of Population Trends in Asia, 29 September–1 October 1993, Canberra, Australia, p. 3.
6 Editor's Note in *Gongren Ribao* (Workers' Daily), 4 August 1982.
7 Central Document No. 7 1984; for themes see *Survey of the World Broadcasts* (SWB), British Broadcasting Corporation (BBC), Caversham, England (SWB) 24 July 1984.
8 Zeng Yi, 'Is the Chinese family planning programme "tightening up"?' *Population and Development Review*, Vol. 7, No. 3 pp. 255–76.
9 Peng Xizhe, op. cit. p. 9.
10 'Analysis of Reproduction of Rural Population', *Jingji Yanjiu* (Economic Research), 20 June 1982.
11 E. Croll, 'The single-child family in Beijing: a first-hand report', in E. Croll, D. Davin and P. Kane *The Single Child Family in China*, Macmillan, London, 1985.
12 Zeng Yi, Tu Ping, Gu Baochang, Xu Yi, Li Bohua, Li Yongping, 'An analysis of the causes and implications of the recent increases in the sex ratio at birth in China', Paper presented at International Seminar on China's 1990 Population Census, Beijing, 19–23 October 1992.
13 This section is based on: J. Banister, 'Implications of sex ratio data from China's 1982 Census', Paper presented at the Workshop on China's 1982 Population Census, Honolulu, December 1984; Terence Hull, 'Recent trends in sex ratios at birth in China', *Population and Development Research*, March 1990; Li Yongping, 'Sex ratios of infants and relations with some socio-economic variables: results of China's 1990 Census and Implications', Paper presented at International Seminar on China's 1990 Population Census, Beijing, 19–23 October 1992; T. Hull and Wen Xingyan, 'Rising sex ratios at birth in China: evidence for the 1990 Population Census', ibid. Tu Ping, 'The sex ratios at birth in China: results from the 1990 Census', ibid. Tu Ping and Liang Zhiwu, 'An evaluation of the

quality of enumeration of infant deaths and births in China's 1990 Census', ibid. Zeng Yi et al. op. cit.; Gu Baochang and Li Yongping, 'Sex ratio at birth and son preference in China', Paper presented at UNFPA Symposium on 'Issues related to sex preference for children in the rapidly changing demographic dynamics in Asia', Seoul, Korea, 21–24 November 1994.

14 Hull and Wen, op. cit. Monica Das Gupta and Li Shuzhuo, 'Gender bias in China, South Korea and India 1920–1990: effects of war and famine', *Development and Change*, Vol. 30, No. 3, July 1999. pp. 619–52.

15 Jiaotong Report, op. cit. p. 51.

16 Banister, Loose pages, p. 54.

17 *China Statistical Yearbook*, State Statistical Bureau, Beijing, 1991, pp. 427–9.

18 Tu Ping, 'Woguo chusheng yinger xingbiebi wenti tantao' (An Explanation of sex ratio at birth in China), Renkou Yanjiu Population Research, Vol. 1, 1993, pp. 6–13.

19 *China Daily*, 15 March 1990.

20 *The Guardian*, 14 April 1994.

21 *China Statistical Yearbook, State Statistical Bureau*, 1991, pp. 45, 427–9.

22 Susan Greenhalgh and Jiali Li, 'Engendering reproductive policy and practice in peasant China: for a feminist demography of reproduction', SIGNS, 20 No. 3, Spring 1995, pp. 601–41.

23 Gu Baochang and Xu Yi, 'Zhongguo yinger chusheng zingbiebi zonglun' (A General Review of China's Sex Ratio at Birth) *Zhongguo Renkou Kexue* (Chinese Population Science), Vol. 3, 1994.

24 Gu Baochang and Li Yongping, op. cit.

25 Peng Xizhe & Huang Juan, 'Abnormal Sex Ratios at Birth in China: Trends and Causes', mss, p. 30; Calculated from original data set of the National 0.2% Sample Fertility and Contraception Survey conducted in 1988 by China's State Family Planning Commission.

26 Ibid.

27 Gu Baochang and Li Yongping, op. cit.

28 See especially Tu Ping; Zeng Yi et al.; Li Yongping; Hull and Wen, op. cit. for discussions of under-reporting.

29 Gao Ling 'An analysis of the sex ratio at birth of the Chinese population', *Population Research*, No. 1, 1993.

30 Tu Ping, Zeng Yi et al., op. cit.

31 Zeng Yi, Tu Ping, Gu Baochang et al., 'Causes and implications of the recent increase in the reported sex ratios at birth in China', *Population and Development Review*, Vol. 19, No. 2, 1993, pp. 283–302.

32 Peng Xizhe, op. cit. p. 26.

33 S. Johansson and O. Nygren, 'The missing girls of China: a new demographic account', *Population and Development Review*, Vol. 17, No. 1, 1991.

34 'A programme upholding rights of women and children of China', *Women of China*, April 1984.

35 For discussion of abandonment and adoption see Kay Johnson, 'Chinese orphanages: saving China's abandoned girls', *The Australian Journal of Chinese Affairs*, No. 3, July 1993; Kay Johnson, 'The politics of the revival of infant abandonment in China with special reference to Hunan', *Population and Development Review*, Vol. 22, No. 1, March 1996, pp. 77–98.

36 Ibid.

37 Johnson 1993, op. cit.

38 Gu Baochang and Li Yongping, op. cit.

39 Peng Xizhe and Huang Juan op. cit. p. 31.

40 Ibid.

41 Johnson 1996, op. cit. p. 90.
42 Ibid. p. 77.
43 'Report from three Counties in Zhejiang Province', *Renkou Yanjiu* (Population Research), No. 3, 1981.
44 Yong Fan, 'Save Our Baby Girls', *Zhongguo Qingnian* (China Youth), November 1982.
45 *Renmin Ribao* (People's Daily), 7 April 1993.
46 Hull and Wen, op. cit.
47 Ansley Coale and J. Banister, 'Five decades of missing females in Asia', *Demography*, Vol. 31, No. 3, August 1994, pp. 473–7.
48 See especially Tu Ping; Zeng Yi et al.; and Li Yongping, op. cit. for discussion of pre-natal sex identification techniques.
49 Gu Baochang and Li Yongping, op. cit.
50 Li Yongping, op. cit.
51 Ibid.
52 Gu Baochang and Li Yongping, op cit.
53 Ibid.
54 Ibid.
55 Banister, personal communication, p. 54.
56 *China Population Today*, June 1993.
57 Sun Fubin, Li Shuahuo and Li Nan, 'A study of the under-reporting of deaths in the 1990 Census', *Population Science of China*, No. 2, 1993, pp. 20–5.
58 Gu Baochang and Li Yongping, op. cit.
59 Jiaotong Report, op. cit. pp. 51, 53.
60 Ibid. p. 53.
61 For data on all these factors see State Statistical Bureau, 1992 *National Sample Survey on the Situation of Children*, Beijing 1993; see also Wang Shaoxian and Li Ninghai, *Women's Voices from Rural Yunnan Needs Assessment of Reproductive Health*, Beijing, 1994, pp. 483–5.
62 Judith Banister 1992, p. 30; Judith Banister, personal communication, p. 53; Coale and Banister, op. cit. 1994.
63 Ibid.
64 Ibid. p. 53.
65 *Nongmin Ribao*, 5 December 1992.
66 Banister, personal communication, p. 54.

Republic of Korea

1 Fred Arnold, 'Measuring the effect of son preference on fertility: the case of Korea', *Demography*, Vol. 22, No. 2, May 1985, p. 280.
2 Chai Bin Park, 'Preference for sons, family size and sex ratio: an empirical study in Korea, *Demography*, Vol. 20, No. 3, August 1983, p. 334.
3 Gu Baochang and Krishna Roy, 'Sex ratios at Birth in China, with reference to other areas in East Asia: what we know', *Asia Pacific Population Journal*, ESCAP, UN, Vol. 10, No. 3, September 1995, p. 19.
4 Kwon Tai-Hwan, 'Exploratory socio-cultural explanations of transition in South Korea', in Leete and Alam, op. cit. pp. 43–5.
5 Williamson, op. cit. pp. 95–9.
6 Chai Bin Park and Nam-Hoon Cho, 'Consequences of son preference in a low fertility society: imabalance of the sex ratio at birth in Korea', *Population and Development Review*, Vol. 21, No. 1, March 1995, p. 64.
7 Arnold, op. cit. pp. 284–5; Park, op. cit. p. 333.
8 Minja Kim Choe, 'Sex differentials in infant and child mortality in Korea', *Social Biology*, Vol. 34, Nos. 1–2, 1987, p. 12.

9 Ibid. p. 19.
10 Ibid. p. 17.
11 Park, op. cit.; Choe, op. cit. p. 19.
12 Choe, op. cit. p. 22.
13 Ibid. p. 23.
14 Park, op. cit. p. 349.
15 Park and Cho, op. cit. p. 60.
16 Gu and Roy, op. cit. p. 20.
17 Park and Cho op. cit. p. 60.
18 Ibid. p. 61.
19 Ibid. p. 63.
20 Gu and Roy, op. cit. p. 24.
21 Park and Cho, op. cit. p. 67.
22 Ibid. p. 68.
23 Ibid. p. 69.
24 Ibid. p. 67.
25 Ibid.
26 Ibid. p. 68.
27 Ibid. p. 70.
28 Ibid. p. 71.
29 Ibid. p. 64.
30 Gu and Roy, op. cit. pp. 29–30.
31 Ibid.
32 Ibid.
33 Park and Cho, op. cit. p. 62.
34 Ibid. pp. 73–4.

Taiwan
1 R. Freedman, Ming-Cheng Chang and Te-Hsiung Sun, 'Taiwan's transition from high fertility to below-replacement levels', *Studies in Family Planning*, Vol. 25, No. 6, November–December 1994, pp. 318–20.
2 Ibid. p. 323.
3 Ibid. p. 324.
4 Ibid. pp. 324–5
5 Williamson, op. cit. pp. 129–48.
6 Ibid. p. 131.
7 Freedman, Chang and Sun, op. cit. p. 325.
8 Ibid. p. 324.
9 Gu and Roy op. cit. pp. 27–8; Freedman, Chang and Sun, op. cit. p. 324.
10 Gu and Roy, op. cit. p. 29.
11 Freedman, Chang and Sun, op. cit. p. 326.
12 Gu and Roy op. cit. p. 29.
13 Ibid. p. 20.
14 Ibid. p. 24.
15 Park and Cho, op. cit. p. 62.
16 Ibid. pp. 60–1.
17 Gu and Roy, op. cit. p. 24.
18 Ibid. p. 23.

Vietnam
1 UNICEF, *The State of the World's Children*, op. cit. p. 127.
2 Daniel Goodkind, 'Vietnam's one-or-two child policy in action', Population and Development Review, Vol. 21, No. 1, March 1995, p. 92.

3 Ibid. p. 85; Kua Wongboonsin and Vipan Prachuabmoh Ruffolo, 'Sex preference for children in Thailand and some other subcontinent Asian countries',
in *Asia Pacific Population Journal*, Vol. 10, No. 3, September 1995, p. 49.
4 Goodkind, op. cit. p. 90.
5 James Allman, Wu Qui Njam, Nguyen Minh Thang, Pham Bieh Sen and Wu
Duy Man, 'Fertility and family planning in Vietnam', *Studies in Family Planning*,
Vol. 22, No. 5, 1991, pp. 311–13.
6 Ibid. p. 312; Daniel Goodkind, 'Abortion in Vietnam', *Studies in Family
Planning*, Vol. 25, 1994, pp. 342–52.
7 Allman et al., op. cit. p. 311.
8 Ibid.
9 Goodkind 1995, op. cit. p. 107.
10 Dominique and Jonathon Haughton, 'Son preference' in the Vietnamese
household', unpublished manuscript.
11 Wongboonsin and Ruffolo, op. cit. p. 50.

India
1 M. Murthi, A. Guio and J, Dreze, 'Mortality, fertility and gender bias in India: a
district-level analysis', *Population and Development Review*, Vol. 21, No. 4, December 1995, p. 745.
2 Ibid.
3 UNICEF, *The State of the World's Children*, op. cit. p. 125.
4 Murthi et al., op. cit. p. 745.
5 Ibid.
6 N. Das, 'Sex preference and fertility behaviour: a study of recent Indian data',
Demography, Vol. 24, No. 4, 1987; D. C. Nath and K. C. Land, 'Sex preference
and third birth intervals in a traditional Indian society', *Journal of Biological Sciences*, Vol. 26, No. 3, 1994; T. Rajaetnam and R. V. Deshparde, 'The effects of
sex preference on contraceptive use and fertility in rural South India', *International Family Planning Perspectives*, Vol. 20, No. 3, 1994; all cited in A. M. Basu,
Culture, the Status of Women and Demographic Behaviour, Clarendon Press,
Oxford, 1992, pp. 104–5.
7 Ibid. p. 109.
8 Ibid.; D. A. May and D. M. Heer, 'Son survivorship, motivation and family size
in India', *Population Studies*, Vol. 22, No. 2, 1968, cited in Basu, op. cit. p. 109.
9 Miller, op. cit. pp. 168–9.
10 S. B. Agnihotri, op. cit. p. 2074; Murthi et al., op. cit. p. 772.
11 Agnihotri, op. cit. p. 2075.
12 Basu, op. cit. pp. 186–7.
13 Agnihotri, op. cit. p. 2076.
14 P. M. Visaria, *The Sex Ratio of the Population of India, the 1961 Census of India*,
Vol. 1. Monograph 10 of the Office of the Registrar General, New Delhi, 1961,
cited in Miller, op. cit. pp. 68–9.
15 Miller, op. cit.
16 Ibid.
17 S. Kishor, 'May God grant sons to all': gender and child mortality in India',
American Sociological Review, Vol. 58, April 1993, p. 247.
18 R. Saith and B. Harriss-White, 'The gender sensitivity of well-being indicators',
Development and Change, July 1999, p. 471.
19 Jean Sargent, Barbara Harriss-White and S. Janakarajan, 'Development, property and deteriorating life chances for girls in India: a preliminary discussion
with special reference to Tamil Nadu', Paper presented at Conference on
Adjustment and Development: Agrarian Change, Markets and Social Welfare

in South India 1973–1993, Madras Institute of Development Studies, 27–29 March 1996.

20 Murthi et al., op. cit. p. 774.

21 A. Malhotra, R. Vanneman and S. Kishor, 'Fertility, dimensions of patriarchy and development in India', *Population and Development Review*, Vol. 21, No. 2, June 1995, p. 290; S. R. Chunkrath and V. B. Athreya, 'Female infanticide in Tamil Nadu', *Economic and Political Weekly*, 26 April 1997, p. WS21.

22 Miller, op. cit. pp. 49–53.

23 Ibid. pp. 61–2.

24 Ibid. pp. 63–4.

25 S. Sudha and S. I. Rajan, 'Female demographic disadvantage in India 1981–1991', *Development and Change*, Vol. 30, No. 3, July 1999, p. 594.

26 Miller, op. cit. p. 55.

27 Ibid. pp. 49–53.

28 Vibhuti Patel, Sex determination and sex-preselection tests in India: modern techniques of femicide', *Bulletin of Concerned Asian Scholars*, Vol. 21, No. 5, 1989, pp. 2–10.

29 Ibid. p. 5.

30 Sargent et al., op. cit. p. 12.

31 George Sabu, R. Abel and B. D. Miller, 'Female infanticide in rural South India', *Economic and Political Weekly*, New Delhi, 30 May 1992, pp. 1153–6.

32 Swaminathan, M. S. 'Structural adjustment policy and the child in India', quoted in J. Sargent et al., op. cit. p. 12.

33 Sargent et al., op. cit. pp. 13–14.

34 Chunkath and Athreya, op. cit. pp. WS21–35.

35 Sudha and Rajan, op. cit. p. 595.

36 Miller, op. cit. pp. 13–5.

37 Alica W. Clark, 'Social demography of excess female mortality in India', Economic and Political Weekly, 25 April 1987.

38 N. Kelly, 'Some socio-cultural correlates of Indian sex ratios: case studies of the Punjab and Kerala', unpublished Ph.D. thesis, University of Pennsyvania 1975, cited in Miller, op. cit. pp. 68–9.

39 Miller, op. cit. pp. 81–2.

40 Kelly, op. cit. pp. 179–81, cited in Miller, op. cit. p. 167.

41 T. Dyson and M. Moore, 'On kinship structure, female autonomy and demographic behaviour in India', *Population and Development Review*, Vol. 9. No. 1, 1983; Basu op. cit. p. 8.

42 Kishor, op. cit. p. 247.

43 Murthi et al., op. cit. p. 774.

44 Monica Das Gupta, 'Selective discrimination against female children in rural Punjab, India', *Population and Development Review*, Vol. 13, No. 1, March 1987, p. 81.

45 Agnihotri, op. cit. p. 2075.

46 Malhotra et al., op. cit. p. 290.

47 Ibid. p. 295.

48 Sargent et al., op. cit. pp. 2–3, 10–11.

49 A. R. Beals, 'Strategies of resort to curers in South India', in C. Leslie (ed) Asian Medical Systems: A Comparative Study, University of California Press, 1976, p. 184–200, cited in Das Gupta, op. cit. p. 97.

50 G.B. Simmons, C. Smucker and E. Jensen, 'Postneonatal mortality in rural India: implications of an economic model', *Demography*, Vol. 19, No. 3, August 1982, pp. 371–89, cited in Das Gupta, op. cit. p. 97.

51 Das Gupta, op. cit. pp. 77–100.

52 Ibid. pp. 82–3.
53 Ibid. p. 95.
54 Agnihotri, op. cit. p. 2076.
55 Sudha and Rajan, op. cit. pp. 605–7.
56 Miller, op. cit. pp. 168–9.
57 Patel, op. cit. p. 4.
58 Ibid.
59 Ibid. p. 3.
60 Ibid.
61 R. K. Sacher et al., 'Sex selective fertility control — an outrage', *Journal of Family Welfare*, Vol. 36, No. 2, 1990 pp. 30–5, cited in Park and Cho, op cit. pp. 79–80.
62 A. Ramanamma and U. Bambawale, 'The mania for sons: an analysis of social values in Asia', *Social Science and Medicine*, 14B, 1980, pp. 107–10, cited in Park and Cho, op. cit. p. 81.
63 R. Jeffery, P. Jeffery and A Lyon, 'Female infanticide and amniocentosis', *Social Science Medicine (UK)*, Vol. 19, No. 11, 1984, pp. 1207–12.
64 Patel, op. cit. p. 4.
65 Achin Vanaik, 'Female foeticide in India, Times of India, 20 June 1986, cited in Patel, op. cit. p. 5.
66 D. Arora, 'The victimising discourses: sex technologies and policy', *Economic and Political Weekly*, 17 February 1996.
67 Patel, pp. 2–10.
68 Basu, op. cit. pp. 188–9.
69 Sudha and Rajan, op. cit. pp. 604.
70 Monica Das Gupta and P. N. Mari Bhut, 'Intensified gender bias in India: a consequence of fertility decline', Working Paper No. 95.02, Harvard Centre for Population and Development Studies, 1995, cited in Murthi et al. op. cit. p. 756.
71 Sudha and Rajan, op. cit. pp. 609–10.

Bangladesh
1 UNICEF, *State of the World's Children*, op. cit. p. 124; Iqbal Shah and J. G. Cleland, 'High fertility in Bangladesh, Nepal and Pakistan: motives vs means', in Leete and Alam op. cit. pp. 175–207; A. Ahmad, *Women and Fertility in Bangladesh*, Sage Publications, New Delhi, 1991, p. 13.
2 Ibid. p. 17.
3 N. R. Ahmed, 'Family size and sex preferences among women in rural Bangladesh', *Studies in Family Planning*, 1981, Vol. 12, p. 100, cited in A. I. Chowdury, B. Radheshyam and M. A. Koenig, 'Effects of family sex composition on fertility preference and behaviour in rural Bangladesh', *Journal of Biosocial Science*, Vol. 25, 1993, p. 455.
4 R. Bairagi and R. L. Langsten, 'Sex preference in children and its implication for fertility in rural Bangladesh', *Studies in Family Planning*, Vol. 17, No. 6, 1986, cited in A. T. P. L. Abeykoon, 'Sex preference in South Asia: Sri Lanka an outlier', in *Asia-Pacific Population Journal*, Vol. 10, No. 3, September 1995, p. 8.
5 M. Rahman, J. Akbar, J. Phillips and S. Becker, 'Contraceptive use in Matlab, Bangladesh: the role of gender preference', Studies in Family Planning, July–August 1992, Vol. 23, No. 4, pp. 233–4.
6 K. M. A. Aziz and C. Maloney, 'Life-stages, gender and fertility in Bangladesh', International Centre for Diarrhoeal Research, Dhakka, Bangladesh, 1985, p. 132.
7 Shah and Cleland, op. cit. p. 175.

8   Aziz and Maloney, op. cit. pp. 43–4.
9   Abeykoon, op. cit. p. 9.
10 Aziz and Maloney, op. cit. p. 43, 148; P. K. Muhuri and S. H. Preston, 'Effects of family composition on mortality differentials by sex among children' in Matlab, Bangladesh', *Population and Development Review*, September 1991, Vol. 17, No. 3, p. 416.
11 Muhuri and Preston, op. cit. p. 420.
12 Ibid. pp. 424, 431.

Pakistan
1   Shah and Cleland, op. cit. p. 176; Abeykoon, op. cit. p. 6.
2   UNICEF, State of the World's Children, op. cit. p. 126.
3   Shah and Cleland, op. cit. p. 189.
4   Ibid. p. 206; M. A. Khan and Ismail Sirageldin, 'Son preference and the demand for additional children in Pakistan', *Demography*, Vol. 14, No. 4, Nov. 1977, pp. 481–95.
5   Williamson, op. cit. p. 81.
6   Khan and Sirageldin, op. cit. pp. 481, 493.
7   Z. Sathar, 'Female mortality and health in Pakistan', Paper presented at the Workshop on Differential Female Mortality and Health Care in South Asia, Dhaka, January 1987, cited in Das Gupta, 1987, op. cit. p. 97.
8   Abeykoon, op. cit. p. 7.

3 Ethnographic Voices

China
1   Much of this chapter on China is based on my own fieldwork over the past 20 years and not referenced; the fieldwork of others is referenced as usual.
2   Hok-Bun Ku, 'Defining Zeren: Cultural Politics in a Chinese Village', unpublished Ph.D. thesis, School of Oriental and African Studies, University of London, 1998, p. 257.
3   Ibid. pp. 258–9.
4   Ibid. pp. 263–4.
5   Ibid. pp. 261–2.
6   Margery Wolf, *Revolution Postponed*, Stanford University Press, Stanford, California, 1985; pp. 196–7.
7   Biang Ji and Zhan Lin, 'Having children late or not having children is beyond reproach', Qingnian Yidai, No. 25, 1984, cited in Emily Honig and Gail Hershatter, *Personal Voices: Chinese Women in the 1980s*, Stanford University Press, Stanford, California, 1988, p. 188.
8   Wu Jinbo, 'I mistakenly blamed her', *Zhongguo Funu* (Women in China), 10 October 1982, p. 43, cited in Honig and Hershatter, op. cit. p. 204.
9   Gu Baochang, Xie Zhenming and Karen Hardee, *The Effect of Family Planning on Women's Lives: The Case of the People's Republic of China*, Family Health International, Durham, North Carolina, March 1998, p. 80.
10 Ibid.
11 Jiaotong Report, op. cit. pp. 3, 10–11, 42, 77.
12 Xie Zhening, 'Demand for childbearing of Chinese farmers and its changes in Zhejiang Province, China, in Symposium on Demography of China, Proceedings of the 23rd IUSSP General Population Conference, China Population, Beijing, October 1997, p. 159.
13 Gu Baochang et al. op. cit. 1998, p. 80.
14 A. Waley, *Translations from the Chinese*, New York, 1941, p. 72; 'Book of Poetry' quoted in *North China Herald*, Shanghai, 10 February 1931.

15 Wang Fuhua, 'Si Wen' (Four Questions), *Renmin Ribao Manhua Zengkan*, 5 March 1983, cited in Honig and Hershatter, op. cit. p. 327.
16 Margery Wolf. op. cit. p. 1.
17 *Women of China*, July 1997, p. 44.
18 *Renmin Ribao* (People's Daily), 7 April 1983.
19 Elisabeth Croll, 'The single-child family in Beijing: a first hand report', in E. Croll, D. Davin and P. Kane, op. cit. pp. 190–232.
20 Ibid. p. 228.
21 Beijing Women's Federation *It's as Good to have a Girl as a Boy*, Beijing, January 1983.
22 Honig and Hershatter, op. cit. p. 278.
23 Wu Jinbo op. cit. p. 43.
24 *Zhongguo Qingnian Bao* (China Youth), 24 April 1982, cited in Honig and Hershatter, op. cit. pp. 189–90.
25 Mei Hongjuan, 'Does killing one's own baby girl signify?' in D. Chu (ed.) *Sociology and Society in Contemporary China*, 1979–83, M. E. Sharpe Armunk, New York, 1984, pp. 28–35.
26 Deng Xiaoming in *Zhongguo Funu*, December 1983, pp. 37–8, cited in Honig and Hershatter, p. 305.
27 Elisabeth Croll, 'The State and the single-child policy', in Gordon White (ed.), *The Chinese State in the Era of Economic Reform*' Macmillan, London, 1991, pp. 295–317; Elisabeth Croll, *From Heaven to Earth*, Routledge, London, 1994, pp. 187–97.
28 Sulamith Heins Potter and Jack M. Potter, *China's Peasants: The Anthropology of a Revolution*, Cambridge University Press, Cambridge, 1990, pp. 246–50.
29 Liu Xin, 'Zhao villagers — everyday practices in a post-reform Chinese village', unpublished Ph.D. thesis, School of Oriental and African Studies, University of London, 1995, p. 243.
30 Gu Baochang et al., 1998, p. 79.
31 Ku, op. cit.
32 Ibid. p. 265–85.
33 Ibid.
34 Ibid. p. 267.
35 Ibid. p. 276.
36 Elisabeth Croll, 1985, op. cit. pp. 190–232.
37 'Worker sentenced for deserting wife and daughter', Survey of World Broadcasts, BBC, Caversham, England, 12 April 1983.
38 Cecilia N. Milwertz, *Accepting Population Control: Urban Chinese Women and the One-Child Family Policy*, Curzon Press, London, 1997, pp. 145, 196.
39 Ibid. p. 71.
40 Ibid. p. 138.
41 Ibid. p. 146.
42 Ibid. p. 140.
43 Ibid.
44 Ibid. p. 143.
45 Wang Shaoxian and Li Ninghai, op. cit. pp. 483–5.
46 Li Shuzhuo and Zhu Chuzhu, 'Gender differences in child survival in rural China: a county study', Paper pesented at the Annual Meeting of the Population Association of America, New York, 25–7 March 1999.

198   *Endangered Daughters*

India

1 Patricia Jeffery and Roger Jeffery, *Don't Marry Me to a Plowman!: Women's Everyday Lives in Rural North India*, Westview Press, Boulder, Colorado, 1996, pp. 39, 69.
2 Elisabeth Bulmiller, *May You be the Mother of a Hundred Sons: A Journey among Women in India*, Penguin Books, New York, 1990, p. 10.
3 S. Good (ed.), *Violence Against Women*, Arihant Publications, Jaipur, India, 1990, p. 72.
4 Leela Visaria, 'Unmet need for family planning in Gujarat: a qualitative exploration', *Economic and Political Weekly*, 26 April 1997, pp. 31–3.
5 D. Jacobson and S. Wadley, *Women in India: Two Perspectives*, Manchar Press, New Delhi, 1977, p. 76.
6 Ibid. p. 26.
7 Good, op. cit. 72.
8 Leela Visaria, op. cit.
9 Patricia and Roger Jeffery, 1996, op. cit. p. 96.
10 Patricia Jeffery, Roger Jeffery and A. Lyon, *Labour Pains and Labour Power: Women and Childbearing in India*, Zed Books, London, 1989, p. 192.
11 Ibid. p. 193.
12 M. Kishwar and R. Vanita (eds), *In Search of Answers: Indian Women's Voices from Manushi*, Zed Press, London, 1984, p. 84.
13 Bulmiller, op. cit. p. 113–14.
14 Sudha and Rajan, op. cit. p. 598.
15 Ibid.
16 Good, op. cit. p. 115.
17 Bulmiller, op. cit. p. 115–16.
18 Ibid. p. 117.
19 Ibid. p. 118.
20 Ibid. p. 122.
21 S. Kaur, *Wastage of Children*, Sterling Publications, New Delhi, 1978, p. 140.
22 Kishwar and Vanita, op. cit. pp. 87, 99–100.
23 Patricia Jeffery et al. 1989, pp. 4–5.
24 Jacobson and Wadley, op. cit. pp. 29–31.
25 Bulmiller, op. cit. pp. 103–4.
26 Patricia Jeffery et al., 1989, p. 141.
27 Ibid. p. 140–1.
28 Ibid. p. 145.
29 Ibid. p. 186.
30 Patricia and Roger Jeffery, 1996, op. cit. pp. 45–6.
31 Ibid. pp. 95–6.
32 Ibid. p. 96.
33 Ibid.
34 Patricia Jeffery, *Frogs in a Well: Indian Women in Purdah*, Vikas, New Delhi, 1979, p. 140.
35 Leela Visaria, op. cit. p. 32.
36 Patricia and Roger Jeffery, 1996, op. cit. p. 96.
37 Patricia Jeffery et al., 1989, op. cit. p. 145.
38 Bulmiller, op. cit. pp. 102–12.
39 Patricia Jeffery et al., 1989, op. cit. p. 145.
40 Ibid. p. 140.
41 Ibid. p. 143.
42 Ibid. p. 140.
43 Ibid. p. 141.

44 Patricia and Roger Jeffery, 1996, op. cit. p. 95.
45 Patricia Jeffery et al., 1989, op. cit. p. 193.
46 Ibid. p. 274.
47 Ibid.
48 Ibid.
49 Miller, op. cit. p. 93.
50 Ibid. p. 101.
51 Good, op. cit. p. 74.
52 Ibid.
53 Ibid.
54 Saith and Harriss-White, op. cit. p. 474.
55 Bulmiller, op. cit. p. 105.
56 Good, op. cit. p. 73.
57 Ibid. p. 94.

4 The generations

 1 Goldscheider, op. cit. p. 472
 2 I. M. Netting, R. Wilk and E. J. Arnould (eds), *Comparative and Historical Studies of the Domestic Group*, University of California Press, Berkeley, 1984.
 3 R. Rapp, 'Examining family history', *Feminist Studies*, Vol. 5, 1981.
 4 M. Krishnaraj and K. Chanana (eds), *Gender and the Household Domain: Social and Cultural Dimensions*, Sage Publications, New Delhi, 1989.
 5 R. A. Butatao and J. T. Fawcett, 'Influences on childbearing intentions across the fertility career: demographic and socio-economic factors and the value of children', *Papers of the East–West Population Institute*, Hawaii, Paper 60F, June 1983.
 6 Moni Nag, 'Economic value and costs of children in relation to human fertility', in N. Eberstadt (ed.), *Fertility Decline in Less Developed Countries*, Praeger Publishers, 1981, p. 275.
 7 E. Mueller, 'Economic costs and value of children: conceptualisation and management', in J. Fawcett (ed.), *The Satisfactions and Costs of Children: Theories, Concepts and Methods*, Honolulu: East–West Centre, 1972, p. 182, cited in Nag, op. cit. p. 275.
 8 H. Lebenstein, 'Relation of economic development and fertility', in L. Tabah, *Population Growth and Economic Development in the Third World*, Vol. 2, Ordina Editions, Belgium, 1976, quoted in Nag, op. cit. p. 275; see also G. S. Becker, 'An economic analysis of fertility in demographic and economic change in developed countries', Conference of the Universities National Bureau Committee for Economic Research, Princeton University Press, Princeton, 1960.
 9 J. C. Caldwell, 'Toward a restatement of demographic transition theory', *Population and Development Review*, Vol. 2, (3 and 4) 1976, pp. 321–66.
10 D. Friedman, M. Hechter and S. Kanawaza, 'A theory of the value of children', *Demography*, Vol. 31, No. 3, August 1994, pp. 375–40; Comment and Reply, ibid. Vol. 33, No. 1, February 1996, pp. 133–9.
11 Potter and Potter, op. cit. pp. 228–9; Charlotte Ikels, 'Settling accounts: the intergenerational contract in an age of reform', in Deborah Davis and Stevan Harrell, *Chinese Families in the Post-Mao Era*, University of California Press, Berkeley, 1993, pp. 307–33.
12 Patricia Jeffery et al., op. cit. p. 181.
13 Xie Zhenming, op. cit. p. 158.
14 Ibid.; Mu Aiping, 'To have a son: the one child family policy and economic change in rural China', in J. West, Zhao Minghua, Chang Xiangqun and

Cheng Yuan, *Women of China: Economic and Social Transformation*, Macmillan, London, 1999, pp. 137–55.
15 Gu Baochang et al., op. cit. March 1998, p. 54.
16 Patricia Jeffery et al., op. cit. p. 181.
17 Ku, op. cit. p. 260–1.
18 Ibid. p. 257.
19 Margery Wolf, *Women and the Family in Rural Taiwan*, California Stanford University Press, 1972.
20 Li Shuzhuo and Zhu Chuzhu, op. cit. Figure 2.
21 Ku, op. cit. p. 259.
22 Ibid.
23 Gu Baochang et al., op. cit. March 1998, p. 112.
24 Margery Wolf, *The Revolution Postponed: Women in Contemporary China*, Stanford University Press 1985, pp. 223–4.
25 Elisabeth Croll, 'Social welfare: trends and tensions', *China Quarterly*, No. 159, June 1999.
26 Mu Aiping, op. cit.
27 Patricia Jeffery et al., op. cit. p. 83.
28 Ibid. p. 182.
29 Ibid. p. 182; Patricia and Roger Jeffery, op. cit. p. 10.
30 Leela Visaria, op. cit. p. 32.
31 Patricia Jeffery et al., op. cit. p. 182.
32 Ibid. p. 183.
33 Patricia and Roger Jeffery, op. cit. pp. 269–70.
34 Patricia Jeffery et al., op. cit. p. 187.
35 Ibid. p. 185.
36 Xie Zhenming, op. cit. p. 158.
37 Patricia Jeffery et al., op. cit. p. 141.
38 Miller, op. cit. p. 105.
39 Bulmiller, op. cit. pp. 111–12.
40 Miller, op. cit. p. 157.
41 Ibid. pp. 133–59.
42 Ibid. p. 154.
43 Ibid. p. 158.
44 Patricia Jeffery et al., op. cit. p. 27; Patricia and Roger Jeffery, op. cit. p. 8.
45 Patricia Jeffery et al., op. cit. p. 27.
46 Patricia Jeffery et al., op. cit. p. 27; Patricia and Roger Jeffery, op. cit. p. 69.
47 Ibid. pp. 259, 261.
48 Ibid.
49 Karen Karpardia, *Siva and her Sisters: Gender, Caste and Class in Rural South India*, Westview Press, Boulder, Colorado, 1995, pp. 46–7.
50 Ibid. p. 59.
51 Ibid. pp. 42–3, 59, 67.
52 Judith Heyer, 'The role of dowries and daughters' marriages in the accumulation and distribution of capital in a South Indian community', *Journal of International Development*, Vol. 4, No. 4, 1992.
53 Kishwar and Vanita, op. cit. p. 89.
54 Ibid. pp. 30–5, 203–7, 209–10, 228–9.
55 Sudha and Rajan, op. cit. p. 593; Patricia Jeffery et al., op. cit. p. 182; Patricia and Roger Jeffery, op. cit. p. 10.
56 A. Sen, *Gender and Co-operative Conflicts*, World Institute of Development Economics Research, Helsinki, 1987.
57 Milwertz, op. cit. pp. 138, 147.

58 Ibid. pp. 136–7.
59 Karpardia, op. cit. pp. 66–7, 252–3.

5 Interpreting gender

1 S. Watkins, 'If all we know about women was what we read in demography, what would we know?', *Demography*, Vol. 30, 1993, pp. 351–77.
2 Chen Yu-kao (trans.), *Manual of Chinese Quotations*, Hong Kong, 1902, p. 173.
3 *Book of Changes XXXVII*, translated by J. Legge and cited in M. E. Burton, The *Education of Women in China*, New York, 1911, p. 19.
4 Ibid.
5 *Book of Rites IX:24*, cited in *Xin Qingnian* (New Youth), Beijing, Vol. 2, No. 4, December 1916.
6 See F. M. Smith, 'India's Curse, Varuna's Noose and the suppression of women in the Vedic Srauta Ritual', in Julia Leslie (ed.), *Roles and Rituals for Hindu Women*, Pinter Publications, London, 1991, pp. 17–83; J. Leslie, 'Essence and existence: women in religion in ancient Indian texts', in Pat Holden, *Women's Religious Experiences*, Croom Helm, London, 1983, pp. 89–112; C. Thompson, 'Women, fertility and the worship of gods in a Hindu village' in ibid. pp. 113–31.
7 Julia Leslie, 1983, op. cit.
8 W. F. Menski, 'Marital exceptions as dramatised in Hindu marriage rituals', in Leslie, 1991, op. cit. pp. 47–68.
9 Committee for Asian Women (ed.), *Silk and Steel: Asian Women Workers Confront the Challenges of Industrial Restructuring*, Publishing Committee for Asian Women, Hong Kong, 1995, p. 12.
10 Sulamith and Jack Potter, op. cit. p. 319.
11 C. Campbell, *The Romantic Ethic and the Spirit of Modern Consumerism*, Basil Blackwell, Oxford, 1987.
12 *The Economist*, London, 18 April 1998.
13 Elisabeth Croll, *Desires and Destinies: Consumption and the Spirit of Confucianism*, Inaugural Lecture, SOAS, 1987, pp. 1–21.
14 Mary Douglas and B. Isherwood, *The World of Goods*, Allen Lane, London, 1979; A. Appadurai (ed.), *The Social Life of Things: Commodities and the Politics of Value*, Cambridge University Press, 1986.
15 Daniel Miller, *Material Culture and Mass Consumption*, Basil Blackwell, Oxford, 1987 and 1994; Daniel Miller (ed.), *Modernity: An Ethnographic Approach*, Berg, Oxford, 1994; Daniel Miller, *Acknowledging Consumption*, Routledge, London, 1995.
16 Elisabeth Croll, *Changing Identities of Chinese Women*, Zed Press, 1995, pp. 69–108.
17 Li Xiaojiang, 'Gaige Zhongguo nuxing qunti yishi de juexing' (Economic reform and the awakening of women's consciousness), *Shehui Kexue Zhunxian* (Social Science Battlefront), No. 4, 1988, pp. 300–10, translated in C. Gilmartin, G. Hershatter, L. Rofel and T. White, *Engendering China: Women's Culture and the State*, Harvard University Press, 1994, pp. 360–82.
18 James Carrier (ed.), *Occidentalism*, Clarendon Press, Oxford, 1995.
19 Li Zezou, 'Women are the natural masters of the perceptual world', *Women of China*, 1 January 1993, pp. 35–7; Shu Ting, 'Different views', ibid. 1 March 1993, pp. 43, 49.
20 Lin Chun, Liu Bohang and Jin Yihong, 'Women's Studies in China', in A. M. Jaggar and I. M. Young (eds), *A Companion to Feminist Philosophy*, Blackwell, Oxford 1998.

21 L. Fruzetti, 'Conch shells, bangles, iron bangles: an analysis of ritual in Bengali society', unpublished Ph.D. thesis, University of Minnesota, 1975, p. 56, cited in Thompson, op. cit. p. 128.
22 Menski, op. cit. p. 47.
23 Jacobson and Wadley, op. cit. p. 60.
24 Liu Xin, op. cit. p. 142.
25 Leela Visaria, op. cit. p. 32.
26 Patricia and Roger Jeffery, op. cit. p. 88.
27 Patricia Jeffery et al., op. cit. p. 187.
28 Ibid. p. 88.
29 See Tamara Jacka, *Women's Work in Rural China*, Cambridge University Press, Cambridge, 1997; Karpardia, op. cit. p. 252.
30 Deepa Grover, 'Tomorrow's Woman, Today's Child', Paper presented for Regional Review of the Beijing Implementation of Platform of Action, UNICEF, Bangkok, 26–29 October 1999, p. 29.
31 Ibid.
32 Pun Ngai, 'Becoming Dagongmei: body, identity and transgression in reform China', Ph.D. thesis, School of Oriental and African Studies, University of London, 1997.
33 Wong Su-ling, *Daughter of Confucius: A Personal History*, London, 1953, pp. 86–7.
34 Ibid. p. 119.
35 Chow Chung-cheng, *The Lotus-Pool of Memory*, London, 1961, p. 13.
36 K. Wei and T. Quit, *Second Daughter: Growing Up in China*, Boston, 1984, pp. 17–19.
37 Ibid. p. 104.
38 Chow Chung-cheng, op. cit. p. 133.
39 Wong Su-ling, op. cit. p. 90.
40 Nie Fangfang, 'My being a girl caused Mother's death', in *Mommy, Daddy and Me*, ed. New World Press, Beijing, 1986, pp. 72–5.
41 Wu Shuang, 'Mom doesn't think men are superior to women anymore', ibid. pp. 31–3.
42 Diane Wolf, 'Daughters, decisions and domination: an empirical and conceptual critique of household strategies', in N. Visvanathan, L. Duggan, L. Nisonoff and N. Wiegersma, *The Women, Gender and Development Reader*, Zed Press, London, 1997, p. 126.
43 Sulamith and Jack Potter, op. cit. p. 193.
44 Ibid.
45 Frances Goldscheider, op. cit. p. 473.
46 Cecilia Milwertz, op. cit. p. 181.
47 Ibid. p. 140.
48 Kishor and Vanita, op. cit. p. 84.
49 Ibid. p. 87.
50 E. M. Rathgeber, 'WID, WAD, GAD: trends in research and practice', *The Journal of Developing Areas*, Vol. 24, July 1990, pp. 489–502.
51 Dyson and Moore, op. cit. pp. 35–60.
52 Das Gupta, 1987, op. cit. pp. 80, 82, 92.
53 Muhuri and Preston, op. cit. p. 417.
54 Basu, op. cit. pp. 157–224.
55 Murthi et al., op. cit. pp. 752–5.
56 Gu Baochang and Xu Yi, 'A general view of China's sex ratio at birth', in *Zhongguo Renkou Kexue* (China Population Science), Vol. 3, 1994; Peng Xizhe & Huang Juan, op. cit. p. 4.
57 Ibid.

58 Zhao Jinhui, Ma Yana and Hao Yanhua, 'Present fertility desire of employed and married population: a case of Harbin', in IUSSP Volume op. cit. p. 171.
59 Monica Das Gupta, Jiang Zhenghua, Xie Zhenming and Li Bohua, 'The status of girls in China', op. cit. pp. 455, 459–60.
60 Sudha and Rajan, op. cit. p. 591.
61 Wang Fuhua, 'Si wen' (Four questions), *Renmin ribao*, 5 March 1983, cited in Honig and Hershatter, op. cit. p. 327.

6 The girl child

1 In many countries including India and China there were some attempts to draw attention to discrimination against girls, but these were spasmodic rather than concerted and sustained.
2 *Girls' Rights*, Information Sheet, UNICEF/UNIFEM, January 1995.
3 *Women's Rights and Children's Rights*, ibid.
4 *Women and Girls: The Key to Development*, UNICEF, London, p. 4.
5 *Women's Rights and Children's Rights*, op. cit.
6 *Women's and Girls: The Key to Development*, op. cit. p. 4.
7 UNICEF, *The State of the World's Children*, UNICEF, Oxford University Press, Oxford, annual publication.
8 *To be born female . . .*, UNICEF, New York, 1994.
9 Ibid.
10 Ibid.
11 Ibid.
12 UNICEF, *Girls and Women: A UNICEF Development Priority*, UNICEF, New York 1993, p. 8; *Children First*, UNICEF, New York, Issue 38, Autumn 1998, p. 12.
13 *Education for Girls: Lifeline to Development*, UNICEF, New York, p. 3.
14 *Women and Girls: The Key to Development*, op. cit. p. 4.
15 Grover, op. cit. p. 25.
16 *Children First* op. cit.
17 *To be born female . . .*, op. cit.
18 Grover, op. cit. p. 1.
19 Most of the public action of rural women usually belonging to the marginalised tribal groups, the so-called low castes and the landless poor, have centred around survival issues, such as scarcity and restrictions of use of food, water, forest rights and demands for minimum wages.
20 Good, op. cit. p. xiv; A. Ramanamma, 'Female foeticide and infanticide — a silent violence', ibid. pp. 71–91.
21 M. M. Masarchras, 'Feminism hijacked down the slippery slope; foeticide to infanticide', ibid. p. 94.
22 J. Bagachi, J. Guha and P. Sengupta, *Loved and Unloved: The Girl Child in the Family*, Stree, Calcutta, 1997, p. 27.
23 Ibid. pp. vii–xii.
24 Ibid. p. vii.
25 Ibid.
26 Ibid. p. 206.
27 Ibid. p. 199.
28 Ibid.
29 Veen Poonacha (ed.) *The Childhood that Never Was: An Anthology of Short Stories on the Girl-Child*, Research Centre for Women's Studies, SNDT Women's University, Bombay, 1993.
30 Ibid. pp. 1–2.
31 Patel, p. 10.

32 Ibid.
33 Sudha and Rajan, op. cit. p. 597.
34 Ibid. p. 610.
35 Ibid. p. 595.
36 Ibid. p. 610.
37 UNICEF, *MEENA: The Girl Child in Asia*, UNICEF, Bangladesh, 1993; Grover op. cit. pp. 10–11.
38 'Why female infanticide still exists in Socialist China', *Women of China*, 1 May 1983, p. 1.
39 Beijing Women's Federation, *It's as Good to have a Girl as a Boy*, Beijing, January 1983.
40 Ibid.
41 Wu Shuang, op. cit. pp. 31—3.
42 Beijing Women's Federation, op. cit.
43 'Report on the Fifteenth National Congress of the Women's Federation', *Survey of the World Broadcasts*, BBC, op. cit. 23 September 1983.
44 Law of the People's Republic of China on Protection of Rights and Interests of Women, Adopted 5th Session of the National People's Congress on 3 April 1992. See Croll, 1995, op. cit. pp. 184–92.
45 *Women of China*, 1 January 1984.
46 'Female self-confidence must be fostered from childhood', *Zhongguo Funu*, April 1985, p. 34, translated in Honig and Hershatter, op. cit. pp. 38–9.
47 *China Population Today*, Beijing, April 1993.
48 Ibid. June 1993.
49 Ibid August 1994.
50 Law of the People's Republic of China on Maternal and Child Health, adopted 27 October 1994, see *Xinhua News Agency*, Beijing, 27 October 1994.
51 China Population Today, June 1993.
52 Ibid. April 1993; ibid. August 1994.
53 *Nongmin Ribao* (Peasants' Daily), 5 December 1991.
54 *Xinhua* (New China News Agency), Beijing, 7 March 1992.
55 Li Wei, 'China's fewer births and greater prosperity co-operatives', *Women of China*, 1 November 1993.
56 Ibid.
57 China Population Today, June 1996, pp. 16–19.
58 Ibid. p. 18.
59 Ibid. p. 19.
60 ibid. p. 17.
61 *The Programme for the Development of Chinese Women (1995–2000)*, 27 July 1995, All China Women's Federation, Beijing.
62 *National Programme for Child Development in China in the 1990s*, All China Women's Federation (ACWF), Beijing.
63 Zhan Yuan, Closing speech, in Collected Papers from the Symposium on the 'Girl Child Development Strategy in Poverty–Stricken areas of China', Kunming, Yunnan, China, February 1997, unpublished.
64 Ibid.
65 Ibid.
66 'The girl child in China: a public education campaign', document prepared for ACWF/UNICEF, Beijing 1998, unpublished.

Index